BESTSELLING
BOOK SERIES

D1192758

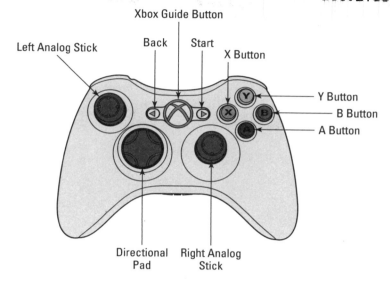

Xbox Guide Button

Back   Start

Left Analog Stick   X Button

Y Button

B Button

A Button

Directional   Right Analog
Pad   Stick

Right Shoulder Button   Left Shoulder Button

Right Trigger   Left Trigger

Connect Button

Playing music from your iPod through the Xbox 360

1. Plug your USB iPod cable into the iPod.

2. Plug the USB cable into one of the ports on the Xbox 360.

3. From the Media Blade, choose Music and press A.

4. From the Music page, choose your iPod from the device list and press A.

5. In the Music Player, choose the music you want to listen to and press A.

For Dummies: Bestselling Book Series for Beginners

Xbox 360 For Dummies®

Cheat Sheet

Connect your Xbox 360 to a Windows Media Center PC

1. On your Windows Media Center 2005 (or later) PC, go to Windows Update at `http://windows update.microsoft.com`.
2. Download all of the latest updates and rollups for the Windows Media Center PC.
3. On the Xbox 360, go to the Media Blade, select Media Center and press A.
4. On the Windows Media Center PC open the Media Center Extender Manager by clicking All Programs⇨Accessories⇨Media Center⇨Media Center Extender Manager.
5. Click File⇨Add New Extender and follow the wizard that appears.
6. On the Xbox 360, press A

    You'll be given an 8 digit key.
7. Copy this key to the wizard in Media Center PC and finish the wizard.

At this point the machines should join and you'll be able to open the Windows Media Center user interface from the Xbox 360.

Add a Wireless Controller to your Xbox 360

1. Turn on the controller by pressing the Guide button.
2. Press and hold the small white Connect button on the front of the Xbox 360.
3. Press the Connect button on the Xbox 360 Wireless Controller. (This button is located on the front of the controller between the shoulder buttons.)

    The ring of light on the console and the controller will spin and flash. A quarter of the ring will be left glowing after this operation. This quarter indicates the number of the controller on the system.

Controller Numbers Indicated by the Controller Ring of Light

Upper Left - Controller 1

Upper Right - Controller 2

Lower Left - Controller 3

Lower Right - Controller 4

For Dummies: Bestselling Book Series for Beginners

Xbox 360™
FOR
DUMMIES®

Xbox 360™ FOR DUMMIES®

by Brian "Brize" Johnson and
Duncan "Festive Turkey" Mackenzie

WILEY
Wiley Publishing, Inc.

Xbox 360™ For Dummies®

Published by
Wiley Publishing, Inc.
111 River Street
Hoboken, NJ 07030-5774
www.wiley.com

Copyright © 2006 by Wiley Publishing, Inc., Indianapolis, Indiana

Published by Wiley Publishing, Inc., Indianapolis, Indiana

Published simultaneously in Canada

For general information on our other products and services, please contact our Customer Care Department within the U.S. at 800-762-2974, outside the U.S. at 317-572-3993, or fax 317-572-4002.

For technical support, please visit www.wiley.com/techsupport.

Wiley also publishes its books in a variety of electronic formats. Some content that appears in print may not be available in electronic books.

Library of Congress Control Number: 2005935156

ISBN-13: 978-0-471-77180-7

ISBN-10: 0-471-77180-5

Manufactured in the United States of America

10 9 8 7 6 5 4 3 2 1

1B/RQ/QR/QW/IN

WILEY

About the Authors

Brian "Brize" Johnson is a Program Manager at Microsoft. He's an avid gamer who spends much of his free time getting pummeled by his kids in Halo 2. Brian lives in Redmond, Washington, with his wife Kathy and their three kids, Will, Hunter, and Buffy. You can contact Brian through his blog at http://bufferoverrun.net.

Duncan "Festive Turkey" Mackenzie is a software developer at Microsoft working on their Web publishing systems. When he isn't working or writing, he spends most of his time with his wife and two kids, and when they are asleep he fires up the Xbox. If he isn't online playing Halo 2, then he is probably staying up way too late playing an RPG like *Knights of the Old Republic,* or *Jade Empire* or (most likely by the time you read this) *Elder Scrolls.* You can contact Duncan through his Web site, www.duncanmackenzie.net.

Dedication

Brian: To my mom and dad, who bought me my first game console in the mid 1970s, before I even knew what a game console was. (How cool is that?!)

Duncan: To my wife, who puts up with the game controllers on the coffee table and the long nights I spend "researching" various Xbox games.

Authors' Acknowledgments

First we would like to thank our agent, Claudette Moore, who spent a lot of time doing the hard work around getting this book off the ground. We're sure that it wouldn't have happened without her expertise and diligence.

Putting books together is really, really hard work. With that in mind we would like to thank the very professional staff at Wiley. First, we would like to thank our Acquisitions Editor, Melody Layne, who put up with a couple of gamers putting together a book. We would like to thank the Project Editor, Pat O'Brien, who made sense of the words we wrote and turned our text into a real book. Thanks to Tonya Cupp, and to Andy Hollandbeck and the rest of the Dummies Technology staff. Many thanks to our production and layout experts, Adrienne Martinez, Shelley Lea, and Barb Moore. A big thanks goes out to our reviewer, Bill Moorehead.

At Microsoft, we would like to thank everybody from the Xbox and Windows Media Center teams who helped us, especially Larry "Major Nelson" Hryb. Larry's passion for this console and his dedication to customers comes through in everything that he does.

Finally, we would like to thank our families for putting up with us during the process. For Duncan that was his wife, Laura, and his kids, Connor and Jada. For Brian, that was his wife, Kathy, and his kids, Will, Hunter, and Buffy.

—Brian and Duncan

Publisher's Acknowledgments

We're proud of this book; please send us your comments through our online registration form located at www.dummies.com/register/.

Some of the people who helped bring this book to market include the following:

Acquisitions, Editorial, and Media Development

Project Editor: Pat O'Brien

Acquisitions Editor: Melody Layne

Copy Editor: Tonya Cupp

Technical Editor: Bill Moorehead

Editorial Manager: Kevin Kirschner

Media Development Specialists: Angela Denny, Kate Jenkins, Steven Kudirka, Kit Malone, Travis Silvers

Media Development Coordinator: Laura Atkinson

Media Project Supervisor: Laura Moss

Media Development Manager: Laura VanWinkle

Media Development Associate Producer: Richard Graves

Editorial Assistant: Amanda Foxworth

Cartoons: Rich Tennant (www.the5thwave.com)

Composition Services

Project Coordinator: Adrienne Martinez

Layout and Graphics: Carl Byers, Andrea Dahl, Mary J. Gillot, Stephanie D. Jumper, Barbara Moore, Lynsey Osborn, Heather Ryan

Proofreaders: Leeann Harney, Jessica Kramer

Indexer: TECHBOOKS Production Services

Special Help
"Secret Squirrel"

Publishing and Editorial for Technology Dummies

Richard Swadley, Vice President and Executive Group Publisher

Andy Cummings, Vice President and Publisher

Mary Bednarek, Executive Acquisitions Director

Mary C. Corder, Editorial Director

Publishing for Consumer Dummies

Diane Graves Steele, Vice President and Publisher

Joyce Pepple, Acquisitions Director

Composition Services

Gerry Fahey, Vice President of Production Services

Debbie Stailey, Director of Composition Services

Contents at a Glance

Table of Contents

Introduction

Welcome, gamers! Before you get started, let us tell you a little bit about this book. *Xbox 360 For Dummies* started life as a little book that I (Brian) started writing in order to help my nephews and other family members get their original Xbox consoles online. We wanted to spend a little family time playing games cross-country. When the Xbox 360 was announced, we decided to write the book with the new console in mind.

For that to work out, I needed to bring in a couple of big guns to help. I contacted Larry "Major Nelson" Hryb, who was immediately interested in helping users get up and running with the Xbox 360. We added Duncan "Festive Turkey" Mackenzie, because he's an expert in audio, digital media, HDTV, and the Windows Media Center PC.

We've come up with a book we hope helps gamers get up and running quickly with the Xbox 360. We also wrote this to help parents understand the console and get a firm idea what gaming is all about.

As you can probably tell, the Xbox 360 holds much, much more than meets the eye. There hasn't been a game console quite like the Xbox 360, and never has a home entertainment system been anywhere near this powerful. This book's ultimate goal is to help you get the most you possibly can from your Xbox 360.

What's in This Book

This book is designed to get new users up and running quickly with the Xbox 360. In the course of working on the book, we discovered something pretty interesting: The Xbox 360 works really well out of the box. Much of what we needed to do as advanced gamers is right there and pretty easy to figure out.

This book isn't for the advanced gamer. It's for the man who's hooking up his Xbox 360 to a TV for the first time. It's for the mother who wants an to make informed decisions about the games her children play. With that in mind, we wanted to make *Xbox 360 For Dummies* a really good reference for users. We add interesting, useful tips where appropriate, we offer cursory advice on equipment, and we talk a lot about the connectedness of the Xbox 360. That is, we make it easy to understand how to hook up your console to the Internet, to other computers, and to your home entertainment system. Finally, we want to help new gamers discover the possibilities for community around the Xbox 360. Xbox Live presents a unique communication opportunity.

Because things change so frequently in gaming, we set up a site to support the book. At `http://xbox4dummies.com`, you find additional information about the Xbox 360, updates, and a chance to e-mail us with your ideas and thoughts about the book.

How to Use This Book

You can read this book from cover to cover, or you can pick and choose pieces of information.

- If you bought this book before you got the Xbox 360, you can prepare for your console's arrival. Review the first couple of chapters to find out about hooking up your Xbox 360 to your TV and how you're going to connect to Xbox Live through your high-speed Internet connection.

- If you're looking for a TV or home theater system to go with your new Xbox, read Chapters 8 and 9.

- If you're looking for a quick read, head on to the Part of Tens for Web sites worth visiting, Xbox 360 accessories worth owning, and games worth checking out.

- If you're getting an Xbox 360 for your family, be sure to check out Chapter 11 and Chapter 16. These chapters show you how to set up the Xbox 360 with a password.

How This Book Is Organized

Xbox 360 For Dummies is divided into five parts, each of which explains a different aspect of Xbox 360 gaming and media play.

Part 1: Xbox 360 Out of the Box

The first part of the book explains what the Xbox 360 is and how it can fit into your digital lifestyle. We tell you about the console, we introduce you to online gaming, and we help you get a new Xbox 360 hooked to your TV and to the Internet.

Part II: The Xbox 360 Blades

The Xbox 360 is a unique gaming console because of its rich user experience outside of gaming. The Xbox 360 isn't a PC, but it's a lot like a computer; the blades let you do things you probably haven't done through your TV before. This part tours each blade and makes it easy to use some of the powerful functionality built into the console.

Part III: Xbox 360 in Your Entertainment System

We help you pick a new HDTV and sound system, explain the parental controls, describe console customization, and reveal ways your console can entertain guests.

Part IV: Pushing the Outer Limits

Your Xbox 360 does lots of cool stuff. Here's the maximum chill.

Part V: The Part of Tens

The Part of Tens lists information we thought you might find interesting. What are some Web sites that detail your console? How can you make friends online? How does the system fit into your family's schedule? What cool accessories are available for the system?

Icons Used in This Book

If you're a *For Dummies* fan, then you'll quickly recognize these icons. If you're new to *For Dummies* books, welcome!

This icon indicates a little piece of knowledge that's going to make your life easier. Take a look and save it for later. Tips are fun, and they can make you seem oh-so-smart.

You need this information almost all the time while you're gaming.

Be very careful or something bad might happen. You don't want to lose all your game saves, do you?

This little guy indicates a piece of geek data that you can either read or ignore. If it were important, it would be a Tip, and if it were dangerous, it would be a Warning, so feel free to skip over it.

Where to Go from Here

Read the book. Play some games. Visit the sites. Make some friends. Gaming with this powerful console can be casual or it can consume your life. The choice is yours. This book makes it easy to get into gaming, to get onto Xbox Live, and to get out there and have some fun.

Part I
Xbox 360 out of the Box

The 5th Wave
By Rich Tennant

@RICHTENNANT

Alex asked for Xbox 360, but instead he received the Life's—Not—A—Game—Cube.

Y'know, the whole world wasn't created for your entertainment, and money doesn't just grow on trees. What about your future? You think it's going to be all fun and games...huh?

In this part . . .

*J*ump right in here to get up and running with your Xbox 360. We introduce you to the Xbox 360 — especially that all-important little matter of hooking up your Xbox 360 to your television.

Chapter 1 discusses the Xbox 360 and what you'll find in the box. Two versions of the Xbox 360 are available to customers outside of Japan, and this chapter tells you about the differences between these versions.

Then, plow into Chapter 2 to see how to hook up your Xbox 360 and get playing. Discover how to plug your Xbox 360 into your TV either through the composite video cable — or if you have a television that supports it, the component cables used to hook the Xbox 360 to an HDTV. You'll also see how to connect your Xbox 360 to a computer network.

Chapter 1

Meet the Xbox 360

*T*he Xbox 360 is a gaming console. The definition of *gaming console* has evolved over the years, but its core remains the same: a platform from which to play great games. The Xbox 360 does that and much, much more: It rips and plays your favorite singer's CD, plays the DVD you just rented, keeps you in touch with your auntie, and grabs hold of your PC for a full-on TV experience.

It's an exciting time for digital entertainment. The Xbox 360 is a hugely powerful system that introduces crisp, clear, high-definition gaming for the first time ever and offers an incredible, fully-featured online service in Xbox Live.

This chapter is worth reading, even if you already have an Xbox 360. But if you can't wait another second, you can skip to Chapter 2 and connect your Xbox 360 console now. You can read this chapter later.

Parents, Start Here

If your children will play with the Xbox 360 (or any other system), you should know what the console can do. It's both

✔ A gaming system with games from tranquil to potentially disturbing

✔ A powerful communication device

Children can communicate with strangers on Xbox Live and in the game forums on the Internet. People of all ages and intents frequent the forums. But the Family Settings in Xbox 360 allow you to set a pass code before anyone can use the Xbox Live functions, which means you get to control access and can monitor online use (see Chapter 11 for further instructions on the Family Settings).

There's a lot to know about Xbox 360 if you're a parent:

- ✔ Keep children safe while playing in Xbox Live (see Chapter 4).
- ✔ Use the tips in Chapter 16.
- ✔ Check the game ratings (see Chapter 11).

Playing with an Xbox 360

The Xbox 360 is more than just a game console. It offers a ton of extra functionality.

Games

Xbox 360 signals the arrival of the next generation of video games. It's the first console system to support high definition, meaning that video games have simply never looked as good as they do on Xbox 360. Better yet, with the combination of incredible graphics, surround-sound support for every game, and online options, you get the trifecta of gaming features that every gamer wants to try.

Visual clarity, incredible sounds, and online functionality are only part of the story; this next generation of gaming means game developers can craft experiences that video gamers have never witnessed before. Realistic worlds, where locations look virtually like their real-life counterparts; beautiful fantasy settings that you can lose yourself in; and inventive situations that you've never played before usher in a true step forward in interactive entertainment, and it's all delivered on Xbox 360.

DVDs

You have to take a break from gaming every once in a while, right? The Xbox 360 is high-end video hardware that fits into a home entertainment system. The Xbox 360 makes a great DVD player.

Chapter 5 describes how to use your Xbox 360 to play your DVD movies.

Music

The Xbox 360 provides high-fidelity audio output that makes your home entertainment system sing:

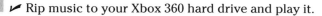

- ✔ Play music directly from

    - • CDs

    - • Your portable MP3 player

    - • Standard PCs

    Chapter 9 shows how you use your Xbox 360 to play your music.

- ✔ Play music from your Windows Media Center PC.

    Chapter 13 shows you how to connect your Xbox 360 to your Windows Media Center PC.

- ✔ Rip music to your Xbox 360 hard drive and play it.

Xbox Live

In olden times (that's before 2001), nearly everything that you played on your game console required a disc or cartridge.

Times have changed:

- ✔ All Xbox 360 games have online features, such as

    - • The ability for the game publisher to provide more content (such as additional game levels, equipment, and characters)

    - • Public scoreboards on both your own Xbox 360 console and on the Web so that you can compare your game scores with the scores of your friends and others

    - • Online play with other Xbox Live gamers (Xbox Live Gold membership required)

- ✔ You can download games, demos, trailers, and gamer pictures from the online Xbox 360 Marketplace.

- ✔ You can update your console by plugging into the Internet.

✔ You can download emulator software that lets you play original Xbox games on your Xbox 360. (And you get to enjoy them with graphics upgrades that boost the resolution of your old games to 720p — which means high-definition; if you thought Halo 2 looked good on the original Xbox, just imagine how great it looks now in glorious high definition . . . you'll drool!)

Communications

The Xbox 360 provides a number of communications tools:

✔ Communicate by both text and voice.

✔ Talk to your friends who come online while you're playing.

✔ Leave messages for friends who aren't online.

And how much more fun is it to talk to your brother while you're racing each other or playing a football game?

Chapter 4 shows how to use the communications features.

What the Xbox 360 can't do

The Xbox 360 does a lot, but it can't do everything. You need other equipment for these jobs:

✔ **Recording video.** The Xbox 360 isn't a video recording device. You can't pause live TV with the Xbox 360 without a Windows Media Center PC.

✔ **Playing high-definition DVDs.** The Xbox 360 isn't a high-definition (HD) DVD player.

HD DVDs require a special reader, and the Xbox 360 doesn't have one. (At the time of the Xbox 360's release, there weren't any high-definition DVD discs or players on the market, except for some expensive experimental equipment for video professionals.)

✔ **Surfing the Web.** The Xbox 360 can connect to the Internet, but only through Xbox Live. You can access the whole Internet through a Windows Media Center PC, but you need to do some work to get a scenario like that working. Chapter 13 shows you how.

✔ **Replacing your cable box.** You need to connect to a Windows Media Center PC to play TV though your Xbox 360. This is described in Chapter 13.

✔ **Replacing your PC.** The Xbox 360 is a powerful console, but you can't do your homework on it — unless your homework includes reviewing video games!

Extending your Windows Media Center PC

The Windows Media Center PC can be extended to the Xbox 360 through your home network.

The Windows Media Center PC lets you record and play TV and provides a user interface that works great from the couch. When networked with an Xbox 360, the Media Center functionality of the Windows Media Center PC is available to you from your couch. This lets you keep the Windows Media Center PC in your office or den while you access your PC's video features from the Xbox 360 in the living room.

We guide you from the Windows Media Center PC to the Xbox 360 in Chapter 13.

Xbox 360 Packages

In the United States, Canada, and the United Kingdom, the Xbox 360 comes in two versions, as described in Table 1-1:

✔ The loaded Xbox 360 package is simply labeled the Xbox 360 System. (It comes in a white box.)

Many retailers call this the "Premium Xbox 360 System," but the box just says "Xbox 360 System."

This package includes the console and several desirable accessories, including the Xbox 360 wireless controller, Xbox Live headset, and (for a limited time at launch) a remote control.

✔ The Xbox 360 Core System includes the Xbox 360 console and the minimum accessories you need to play Xbox 360 games with most TV sets.

Table 1-1	Xbox 360 Retail Packages	
Component	*Xbox 360 Core System*	*Xbox 360 System ("Premium")*
Xbox 360 Console	Yes	Yes
Wireless Controller	Optional	Yes
Wired Controller	Yes	Optional

(continued)

Table 1-1 *(continued)*

Component	Xbox 360 Core System	Xbox 360 System ("Premium")
Hard Drive	Optional	Yes
Headset	Optional	Yes
Component HDAV Cable (for TV)	Optional	Yes
Composite A/V Cable (for TV)	Yes	Included in Component HDAV Cable
Power Cable	Yes	Yes
Xbox Live	Free Silver membership	Free Silver membership

Look for promotional deals on Xbox 360 systems from both Microsoft and individual retailers. You might find packages and bundles with extra goodies, such as

- ✔ Media remote control (see Chapter 10)
- ✔ Xbox Live Gold subscription (see Chapter 4)
- ✔ Xbox 360 games

You won't get any *game discs* in the Xbox 360 console packages from Microsoft unless a retailer adds games in a "bundle." If the Xbox 360 System will be a gift, make sure someone's giving a game, too.

Shopping Smart

Which Xbox 360 package should you buy? It depends on

- ✔ What you want to do with the console
- ✔ How much money you have in your pocket today

"Premium" Xbox 360 System buyers

The best reason to start with the loaded Xbox 360 System in the white box (some stores call it the "Premium" system) is that it's usually the cheapest, most convenient way to get all these Xbox 360 accessories and capabilities.

If you need only a few of the extra accessories in the loaded Xbox 360 System, the total price may be like getting the rest of the accessories for free. Free is good.

The loaded Xbox 360 System in the white box probably is a wise buy if you want at least two or three of the following capabilities.

Save and pause games

The basic Xbox 360 console can't save games while you play or when you want to stop a gaming session. If you want to save games, you must have either

- **Xbox 360 Hard Drive:** Included with the loaded Xbox 360 System in the white box and optional for other systems.

  Chapter 2 shows how to install the hard drive.
- **Xbox 360 Memory Unit:** Optional for any Xbox 360 System.

Cordless control

The loaded Xbox 360 System package includes a wireless game controller, so you don't have a cord on the floor between your Xbox 360 console and your seat. (You wouldn't want a cord on your TV remote, would you?)

The wireless controller has all the same functions as the wired controller, but without that pesky cord getting in the way. Even with the addition of the batteries (included in the box), it's weighted and balanced perfectly. The batteries will last for around 25 hours of play time and can be recharged with the Play and Charge cable (an optional accessory).

Chapter 10 covers the Xbox 360 wireless game controller (including optional rechargeable batteries).

Chat while playing online games

The loaded Xbox 360 System package includes a headset that plugs right into your controller. (The headset is optional for the Xbox 360 Core System.) The headset includes a headphone speaker and a microphone. If you want to chat with opponents while you play online games with Xbox Live, you need a headset.

The Xbox Live headset uses a special connection. You can't plug any other headphones into the unit to get the same voice communication. You have to use the specific Xbox Live headset.

Chapter 9 gives you an earful about the Xbox 360 headset.

Play original Xbox games

You need an Xbox 360 hard drive to play most original Xbox games (because the original Xbox has a built-in hard drive).

The Xbox 360 hard drive is included with the loaded Xbox 360 System, and you can add a hard drive to the Xbox 360 Core System.

Connect fancy TV sets

If you have a high-performance TV that uses component video inputs, you'll probably get the best Xbox 360 picture with the component HDAV cable that's included in the loaded Xbox 360 System package.

Chapter 8 covers the ins and outs of connecting any Xbox 360 console to your TV. However, there are a couple of quick ways to check whether your TV is compatible with Xbox 360 component video:

✔ Look on the TV set for one of these TV-industry buzz words:

  • HDTV

  • HDTV-ready

  • EDTV

✔ Look for red, green, and blue component video plugs on the back of the TV. The component video plugs may be labeled either

  • Y, Pb, and Pr

  • Y, B-Y, and R-Y

The Xbox 360 component HDAV cable has a yellow video plug that works with many TVs that don't use component video. (The cable in the Xbox 360 Core System has only the yellow video plug. You can add the Component HDAV Cable if you want component video with the Core system.)

Xbox 360 Core System buyers

The Xbox 360 Core System is the starting point for gamers who want to

✔ Play Xbox 360 games on most TVs

✔ Keep the accessories (and cost) to an absolute minimum

It includes the least you need for Xbox 360: a console, a wired controller, and thou.

If you're sure that the Core System is right for you, we think you should add either a *hard drive* or a *memory unit* so you can store your games. Get one when you buy the Xbox 360 Core System or as soon as you can. You won't regret it.

You can add all the Xbox 360 accessories to the Core System, including all the accessories that are included in the loaded Xbox 360 System. The only difference is that the loaded Xbox 360 System costs less than a Core System and separate accessories.

Making Your Way around the Xbox 360

In this section, we take you on a little tour of the Xbox 360 console. When you're familiar with all the plugs and inputs, including the USB connections, you can plug in all your accessories in a jiffy.

The Xbox 360 console can be placed either upright *(wide)* or on its side *(tall)* when you connect it. Either way, it works just fine.

Down in front

Figure 1-1 shows the front of the Xbox 360.

Figure 1-1: The front of the Xbox 360 console with the ports labeled.

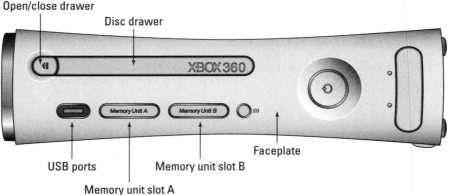

Open/close drawer

Disc drawer

XBOX 360

Memory Unit A   Memory Unit B

Faceplate

USB ports

Memory unit slot B

Memory unit slot A

The front contains the console gadgets you'll use or change most often:

✔ **Power button**

Back when Grandpa walked five miles uphill both ways in the snow to rent anime videos, folks called this the *on/off switch*.

✔ **Two memory unit slots**

✔ **Two USB ports**

The front USB ports are for connecting

- Wired controller
- MP3 music player or digital camera
- Glowing snowman — hey, it can brighten up the whole room from your Xbox 360 USB port!

✔ **Disc tray** (for games, DVDs, and music CDs)

✔ **Bonding button** (so you can tell your Xbox 360 console which wireless game controller is yours)

Chapter 2 shows how to bond an Xbox 360 wireless game controller to your console.

The front of the Xbox 360 console also has an infrared port that works with Xbox media remote controls. (Chapter 10 covers the media remotes.)

Chapter 10 shows how to personalize the front of your Xbox 360 console with a custom faceplate.

Hiding in back

Figure 1-2 shows the back of the Xbox 360.

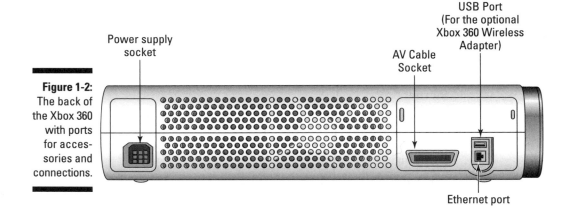

Figure 1-2: The back of the Xbox 360 with ports for accessories and connections.

Power supply socket

USB Port (For the optional Xbox 360 Wireless Adapter)

AV Cable Socket

Ethernet port

Designing the Xbox 360

Jonathan Hayes and his team at Microsoft (in conjunction with Astro Studios of San Francisco and Hers Experimental Design Laboratory in Osaka, Japan) designed the Xbox 360.

The Xbox 360 system and controller have a distinctive shape that's both functional and attractive. The prominent button on the front of the console opens the door to your Xbox 360 experience.

While they worked out the aesthetics, the designers used words like

✔ Open

✔ Clear

✔ Consistent

✔ Athletic

✔ *mirai* (a Japanese word meaning "forward looking")

The back of the Xbox 360 console is less populated than the front, but the ports are important:

✔ **Power supply socket**

This big rectangular port is where you connect the Xbox 360 power supply.

✔ **AV cable socket**

Here's where you plug in the console end of your AV cable.

Depending on your equipment and cable, the other end can connect to

- TV sets (see Chapter 2 and Chapter 8)
- Computer monitors (see Chapter 8)
- Audio systems (see Chapter 2 and Chapter 9)

✔ **USB port**

This rear USB port is intended for use with the optional Xbox 360 Wireless Networking Adapter (see Chapter 12), but it can also be used for

- A third wired controller
- Any of the USB devices suggested in the preceding section

✔ **Ethernet port**

This is where you can plug in

- Your home network (see Chapter 12)
- A high-speed Internet connection (see Chapter 4)
- A system link connection to another Xbox 360 console (see Chapter 12)

You can find out all about the accessories for the Xbox 360 in Chapter 18.

Connecting to Your Home or the World

Xbox 360 is a platform that can make use of many of your existing entertainment and communications systems.

Tuning into the TV

The Xbox 360 is designed for both

- ✔ Maximum performance on modern HDTVs

   Xbox 360 also works with most computer monitors. Chapter 8 shows you how.

- ✔ Compatibility with any standard TV set

High definition describes many technologies, but for the Xbox 360, the most important difference between HDTV and standard TV is the number of lines of resolution on the screen:

- ✔ In the United States and Canada, standard NTSC broadcast signals have 480 lines of resolution.

- ✔ In PAL system countries (such as the United Kingdom, Australia, and Singapore), standard broadcast signals have 576 lines of resolution.

Xbox 360 games are designed for 720 lines, and these lines are scanned differently than standard TV, making for a much denser picture. Higher resolution screens make for better pictures.

Introducing the Xbox 360 to your PC

The Xbox 360 is a great device for connecting and playing the digital content, such as pictures and music, from your Windows PC.

How much better is HDTV?

If you're into geeky math stuff, you can figure it out easily. A standard-definition TV draws a picture using 480 lines. A standard NTSC TV (in the US and Canada) uses 480 *interlaced* lines (480i), meaning that the lines are alternated in a fast flickering way that the naked eye can't pick up. *Progressive* format (480p) means that the 480 lines are all beamed at the same time, giving greater visual clarity. By comparison, one form of HDTV (called 720p) draws a picture 720 lines all at the same time, hence the vastly increased visual clarity. The highest resolution of HDTV draws 1080 lines in interlaced (or alternating) mode (1080i).

If you want to know what that means in terms of the number of pixels on the screen:

- 480i = 640 × 480 = 307,200 pixels
- 720p = 1280 × 720 = 921,600 pixels
- 1080i = 1920 × 1080 = 2,073,600 pixels

There are three times as many pixels on the screen at 720p (which every Xbox 360 game supports) than there are on a standard TV. No wonder things look so much clearer on HDTV.

Windows Media Center PC

Many of the latest PCs are Windows Media Center PCs, which are designed for viewing from a TV and for

- Recording and watching TV
- Viewing home videos
- Listening to music
- Viewing photos

People who purchase Windows Media Center PCs often use them primarily as a desktop computer in an office or bedroom, so they can't take advantage of all the benefits that come with the Windows Media Center side of the PC. That's where the Xbox 360 comes in.

Using your home network, you can connect to a Windows Media Center PC and make the output from that connection your primary TV portal. This lets you pause live TV, record shows, and access all the digital content that you store on the PC. As you can see in Chapter 13, combining Xbox 360 with your Windows Media Center PC gives you instant access to your vacation videos, family photos, and your full music collection. Figure 1-3 shows the movies screen on the Windows Media Center PC.

Kill Bill: Vol. 2
★★★★ 2004 ENCOREP Oct 30 10:10 AM

On Now
On Next
Genres
Top Rated
Actors/Directors
Title Search

Girl, Interrupte
Parenthood
Rapid Fire
The Fighting T
Northfork
Northfork
Village of the
Cold Mountain
Kill Bill: Vol. 2

36 of 52

Figure 1-3:
Find a movie
to watch
on the
Windows
Media
Center PC
through the
Xbox 360.

Other Windows PCs

If your Windows PC isn't a Media Center PC, you can still access your
Windows PC digital library through Windows Media Connect.

Chapter 6 shows you how to use Windows Media Connect with Xbox 360 and
your Windows PC.

Windows Media Connect turns your PC into a media server that can host
music and photos for your Xbox 360. This capability is available in Xbox 360
through the Media blade shown in Figure 1-4.

Blades are the pages of the Xbox 360 dashboard. They're described in detail
in Chapter 3.

Congregating with the community

If you have an Xbox 360, you may get . . . attached to it. No worries — others
have felt this so strongly that they've formed huge communities on the
Internet where they can talk about their systems and the games they play on
them. Join other attached people at www.xbox.com and share your passion.

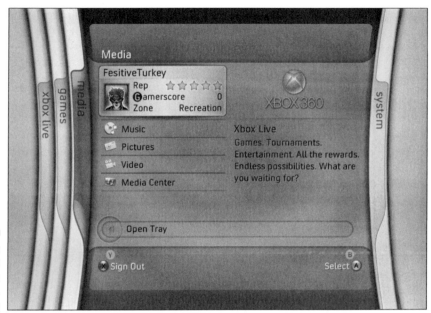

Through Xbox.com you can

✔ Get online support.

✔ Visit the forums for information from other users.

✔ Get the scoop on upcoming games.

This community is big, and it's great. When you ask questions on the forums at `http://forums.xbox.com`, community members quickly answer them.

Got a question about how to get through a level in a new game? Need to know how to rise in the rankings? Someone has probably answered it on Xbox.com. Save yourself some time:

✔ Look in the FAQ (Frequently Asked Questions) at the top of some of the forums you visit.

✔ Search for your question in the forums. You'll find the Search link at the upper right of the Forum page. To perform a search, follow these steps:

    1. Click the Search link on the page.

    2. Enter the text you're looking for and press Enter.

       For example, if you're looking for tips for getting through Kameo, try entering phrases like `Stuck Kameo` or `Kameo Level 1`.

Enter only important words to find what you need. For example, `Stuck Kameo` probably is better than `Stuck in Kameo` because `Stuck in Kameo` automatically skips answers that don't have the unimportant word `in`.

These searches can lead you straight to the answer you're looking for.

Whew! Ready to connect your Xbox 360 now? Chapter 2 is your guide!

Chapter 2

Setting Up Your Xbox 360

- -

In This Chapter

▶ Finding out what's in the box

▶ Planning an installation

▶ Connecting your Xbox 360 to a TV

▶ Connecting your Xbox 360 to your audio system

▶ Linking to your home network

▶ Testing your system

- -

*A*lthough setting up your Xbox 360 is pretty easy, it takes a little planning to get the most out of the 360 when paired with your home entertainment system. With the advent of high-definition television (HDTV), digital audio, and a number of other wonderful new technologies comes a complexity that might require a bit of reference. Don't worry — this chapter makes all these technologies clear and gives some good ideas for putting your home entertainment system together.

This chapter shows how to make easy TV connections with the cables that come with the Xbox 360 console so you can get started. But this book also shows how to make all kinds of special connections with TVs, audio systems, computers, home networks, in-car video systems, and multiple Xbox 360 consoles. Look in the Index or the Table of Contents for the connections you need.

Opening the Box

The Xbox 360 comes in two distinct versions. The Xbox 360 System (sometimes called the "Premium" version) is fully loaded, while the Xbox 360 Core System has fewer accessories but everything you need to get your game on.

Xbox Live requires an Xbox 360 Hard Drive (included with the loaded Xbox 360 System) and a high-speed Internet connection.

TV cables

Wondering whether you need to purchase a specific type of cable to connect your Xbox 360 to your TV? The answer is, "Probably not, but maybe." The cable you need depends on what connections your TV has.

If you're using a *computer monitor,* you probably need a VGA cable. It's covered in Chapter 8.

HDAV component cables

If you have an HDTV or an EDTV with component video inputs, you probably want the HDAV cable that's included with the loaded Xbox 360 System. (If you have the Xbox 360 Core System, you can buy the HDAV cable separately.)

The HDAV cable has both composite and component plugs. It works with HDTV, EDTV, and standard *(SDTV)* TVs.

The HDAV video cable connects to

- ✔ **Video input jacks.** Depending on your TV, you can connect

  - **Component video** (three jacks, usually labeled Y, Pb, and Pr).

    Component video is the best video quality for Xbox.

  - **Composite video** (one jack, usually just labeled Video In).

- ✔ **Audio input jacks.** Depending on your audio system, you can connect

  - **Digital audio** (with an optional Toslink audio cable)

    Chapter 9 shows how to connect digital audio.

  - **Stereo audio input jacks** (white for left and red for right).

Some TVs have yellow front composite jacks. These are usually used to hook up a device, like a camcorder, temporarily. This is a great set of jacks to use when you visit a friend and you want to play without tearing wires out of the back of the TV.

Figure 2-1 shows the HDAV component cable and its connectors.

There is a small switch at the base of the HDAV cable that lets you switch between

- ✔ **TV**

  If you set the switch to TV, the signal will go through the yellow composite plug.

✔ **HDTV**

If you set the switch to component, then the video signal will go through the three component plugs.

Always use the HDTV switch position if you're using the three component video plugs (even if the TV isn't an "HDTV").

Figure 2-1:
The Xbox 360 HDAV cable has both standard and component jacks.

Composite video cable

The Xbox 360 Core System comes with a composite cable that carries only a composite video signal.

The HDAV cable includes a yellow composite video jack, so you can use it with either composite or component video inputs.

Because the composite cable has only one video connection, it doesn't have a video switch.

You can't use *digital* audio with the standard composite video cable.

SCART (United Kingdom)

If you need a SCART connector for your TV, you probably received a SCART *adapter* with your Xbox 360 console. You can connect this adapter to your TV, then use the yellow *composite video* connector on the cable that came with your Xbox 360 console.

The SCART adapter isn't an *HDTV* video connection. If you have an HDTV with a SCART connector, connect with either

✔ Component video (the red, green, and blue video jacks on the HDAV cable)

✔ Advanced SCART cable (optional for Xbox 360 consoles; see Chapter 8)

Xbox 360 controller

The controller is the main input device for your Xbox 360. You use the controller to configure the system after it's connected to the TV. You can see the controller in Figure 2-2.

Figure 2-2:
The Xbox 360 controller is used to navigate all aspects of the Xbox 360.

The Xbox 360 controller comes in two varieties:

✔ **The wireless controller:** Connects with the same technology used for cordless phones

✔ **The wired controller:** Includes a 9-foot cable

The cable has a breakaway point where it connects with the console, so a running child or dog doesn't bring the console smashing to the floor.

You find the following options on the controller:

✔ Nine buttons (ten on the wireless controller)

• A button

• B button

- • X button
- • Y button
- • Start button
- • Back button
- • Left Shoulder button
- • Right Shoulder button
- • Bonding button (wireless only)
- • Guide button
- ✔ Two analog sticks
- ✔ One directional pad
- ✔ Two triggers
- ✔ One headset port

Xbox 360 console

The Xbox 360 *console* is that attractive metal box in the Xbox 360 packaging.

Chapter 1 shows the connections on the front and back of the console.

Documentation package

The Xbox 360 comes with a short booklet that explains how to connect your Xbox 360 to a TV and may have more information.

Save the booklet, along with the warranty information, somewhere safe. Although every Xbox 360 console is tested extensively, problems could occur with your display (not seeing an image on screen), power supply, or even the wireless connections. Though problems are unlikely, keeping the booklet handy ensures that you have all the information you need to contact Microsoft and have the problem resolved.

One of the options you might find in the box is an extended warranty. *The Xbox 360 is not user serviceable.*

The Xbox 360 Guide button

You use all the buttons on the controller for one thing or another, but pay special attention to one of them: The big Xbox 360 Guide button, in the middle of the controller, opens the Xbox 360 Guide. The Xbox 360 Guide is your home base for whatever game or entertainment experience you're in. When you press it, you have instant access to the Guide, which is essentially your control panel for the Xbox 360. Chapter 3 introduces the Xbox 360 Guide.

Planning Your Xbox 360 Installation

You probably want to put your Xbox 360 where all your friends can see it. After all, it's quite attractive! But you should consider practical issues when planning your installation.

Controllers

A game console can string extra wires across the room. When you're placing your console (and yourself), think about

- ✔ How long controller wires need to be
- ✔ Whether to buy wireless controllers

In general, the Xbox 360 wireless controllers are probably the best controllers ever made for a game system. They run on batteries, or you can get a rechargeable kit for them. Every Xbox 360 supports wireless controllers, and the chance of interference is very low. If you can get wireless controllers, you should.

Connections

If you have an HDTV or a home theater system, take advantage of all the high-end Xbox 360 features on the HDAV cable.

For maximum performance, use these connections:

- **Component video outputs.** These are the red, green, and blue plugs on the HDAV cable.
- **Toslink digital audio output.** This is an optical cable you can buy separately that plugs into your home entertainment system.

Toslink is the optical version of SPDIF (Sony/Philips Digital Interconnect Format) digital audio. If you have a component with a SPDIF *coaxial digital* input, you can try using a Toslink-to-coaxial adapter to connect from your Xbox 360 console.

Orientation

The Xbox 360 can stand either horizontally or vertically in your system. How you place your console is purely a matter of taste and space; it works well in either position. Where you place your console is a matter of keeping things running. See Table 2-1 for rules and regulations.

Table 2-1	Do's and Don'ts for Placing Your Xbox 360
Do	*Don't*
Give it room to breathe.	Don't block the fan in the back of the console.
Keep it cool.	Don't put it where you can trip on the console or cords.
Make room for the DVD tray.	Don't put it where you can spill food or drink on it.
Keep it dust free.	Don't eat off of it.

Connecting the Xbox 360 to a TV

You have a number of ways that you can connect stuff to your TV. This section helps you determine how best to connect your Xbox 360.

Understanding the connections

Your Xbox 360 comes with a video cable that can connect to a standard composite video plug. If they're color coded, composite jacks are usually yellow. The Xbox 360 is also ready, out of the box, to connect to a component input. A component input takes plugs for each of the base colors that make up a TV signal. These colors are red, blue, and green. These receptacles should be color coded accordingly on your TV.

Newer TVs usually have at least one component input on the back, along with a number of standard video inputs. These inputs let you connect all sorts of devices to your TV, including DVD players, cable boxes, VCRs, digital video recorders, and (of course) game consoles. You usually assign each device to a different video input and then change the selected input on the TV when you want to use a different device.

You have a choice to make when you add the Xbox 360 to your system. You can use your component input for the Xbox 360 or use that input for another device (like the input from your HDTV cable box). Which one should you use for this special set of inputs? It really depends on whether your other devices deliver high-definition output:

- ✔ If gaming is what you love most, connect the Xbox 360 to your component input. You'll be glad you did.

- ✔ If you pay for HDTV from your cable or satellite provider, you may want to keep the cable box connected to the component input.

- ✔ If you're using a standard TiVo, save the component input for the Xbox 360. The TiVo doesn't use HDTV, so that would be a waste.

- ✔ The Xbox 360 can play DVDs, so connect the Xbox 360 to the component input unless you have a specialized DVD player.

This chapter covers only the video connectors that are included with most Xbox 360 consoles. Check Chapter 8 if you need to connect an Xbox 360 console to

- ✔ VGA (standard computer monitor)

- ✔ S-Video (the socket that looks like a computer keyboard connector)

  Deciding whether to use S-Video? Here's the story:

    - • *Component video* (the red, blue, and green connectors) usually outperforms S-Video.

    - • S-Video is a little better than the yellow *composite connector.*

- ✔ Advanced SCART HDTV (mostly in the United Kingdom)

If you received a SCART *adapter* with your Xbox 360, it *isn't* HDTV.

✔ Vport (a special connector on some TVs for the original Xbox)

If your TV has a Vport connector, connect your Xbox 360 with *component video* (the red, blue, and green connectors), if you can.

✔ RF (standard antenna or cable connector)

Hard Drive

If you bought an Xbox 360 System, the Hard Drive came attached in the box. If you purchased an Xbox 360 Core System and you bought a Hard Drive separately, you'll need to attach the Hard Drive to the Xbox 360 yourself. To attach a Hard Drive to the Xbox 360, follow these steps:

1. **Turn off your Xbox 360.**

2. **Take the cover off the hard drive bay on the end of the console to reveal the bay.**

   The front of the Hard Drive is the skinny end. The fatter end should be turned toward the back.

3. **Put the Hard Drive into the drive bay, back first.**

   The back of the drive should fit under a lip at the back of the bay.

4. **Push down the front of the Hard Drive and you should hear a click indicating that the drive is seated properly.**

Headset

The Xbox 360 Headset plugs right into the base of the Xbox 360 controller. (The Xbox 360 Headset isn't included with the Xbox 360 Core System, but it can be purchased separately.)

The headset works on both the wired and the wireless controllers. To attach the headset to the controller, follow these steps:

1. **Hold the controller facing forward, as you would while playing a game.**

2. **Find the plug on the end of the Xbox 360 Headset and turn it so that the mute switch is facing up.**

3. **Push the Xbox 360 Headset plug into the base of the Xbox 360 controller.**

   You can adjust the volume on the headset using the wheel at the base of the plug.

   You can mute your microphone by using the switch on base of the plug.

Multiple component inputs

Some newer TVs have multiple component inputs, so it's easier to display more than one device at high resolution. If you just can't live without more than one component input, you can buy a component video switch. A *component video switch* is a box that connects to your TV and exposes two or more component input panels on the back. To switch between video sources, you use a remote control or press a button on the front of the box. These boxes can be somewhat expensive (there's a lot of wire in there!), but it's worth it if you want to get everything you can out of your video sources.

Plugging it in

To get started putting all of this together, gather your Xbox 360, the video cable, the power cable, and your controller.

Don't plug the Xbox 360 into the wall socket until the other connections are in place.

Follow these steps:

1. **Plug the rectangular end of the audio/video cable into the audio/video cable port on the back of the Xbox 360.**

2. **Plug the audio/video cable into your TV.**

   If you have the composite cable (as shown in Figure 2-3), plug the cable into the yellow composite jack.

Figure 2-3:
The composite video cable.

If you have the HDAV cable, the connection depends on your TV connection:

- If you're using component inputs, then use the red, green, and blue plugs and set the cable switch to HDTV (even if your TV isn't called an HDTV).

  Figure 2-4 shows the component jacks.

- If you don't have component inputs, use the yellow composite plug and set the cable switch to TV.

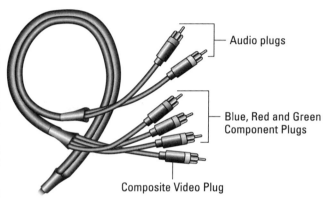

Figure 2-4: The red, blue, and green video plugs used with the component output setting.

Audio plugs

Blue, Red and Green Component Plugs

Composite Video Plug

Power supply location

One of the unique characteristics of the Xbox 360 is its rather large power supply. The reason the power supply is so large has to do with heat. By putting the power components outside of the Xbox 360, the Xbox 360 engineers were able to reduce the heat inside of the Xbox 360 and they were able to reduce the size of the console overall.

The power supply is an extremely important component of the system, so you place it where you can avoid problems:

✔ Place the power supply where it can get air.

✔ Don't put it in an enclosed cabinet.

✔ Don't place the power supply on a rug.

That will keep air from flowing around the power supply and may cause power problems later.

✔ Place the power supply with its feet on the ground. (Don't lay it on its side.)

✔ Don't place the power supply near other sources of heat.

✔ Try to keep the power supply free of dust.

If you have the HDAV cable, you must toggle the video switch to the appropriate video source, or you won't see any picture when you turn on your Xbox. Figure 2-5 shows this switch.

3. Plug the square end of power cord into your Xbox 360.

Some TVs and receivers have both component and composite inputs for a single video source. For example, "Input 1" may be either component or composite video. Check your TV's instructions for details.

Figure 2-5: This switch toggles the video between the composite and the component plugs.

Connecting Your Sound System

The audio/video cable on the Xbox 360 has standard stereo audio plugs (white for left and red for right). You can also use an optional Toslink optical connector.

If you connect Xbox 360 video to your TV with a standard RF cable, you don't need a separate audio connection to the TV. The audio plug will be connected to the RF converter, and the cable will carry both signals.

Left and right audio cables

Connecting the left and right audio plugs to the appropriate jacks on your TV or receiver is simple:

1. Plug the red audio cable into the red audio jack.

2. Plug the white audio cable into the white audio jack.

Many TV sets have several pairs of audio jacks. Make sure you're using the correct audio jacks for the video jack that you connect to your Xbox 360.

Don't cross the wires! There's no danger, but the two plugs are meant for the left (white) and right (red) sides of your TV's sound system. If you switch the audio cables, sounds that should be on your right when you play are on your left. When turning to meet an opponent who you hear sneaking up, you turn your back on him instead.

Toslink audio cable

If you connect your Xbox 360 with Toslink, you may need to specify that you want to use Toslink digital input for audio for that device. (Some TVs and receivers assume that the audio is standard left and right audio unless you select another input.) Find out more about connecting this type of audio cable in Chapter 9.

Most TVs and receivers have their own internal software, so choosing audio and video inputs looks different on each one. You may need the TV or receiver manual to select the audio inputs for your Xbox 360 connection.

Connecting to the Internet

If you have a broadband Internet connection, complete your Xbox 360 installation by connecting your home computer network to your console.

You can't use a dialup Internet connection with the Xbox 360.

Your Internet connection opens the door to a huge opportunity for fun and extra content called *Xbox Live*. (Xbox Live requires a hard drive.)

Setting up Xbox Live is described in detail in Chapter 4.

Connect your Xbox 360 to your home computer network one of two ways:

✔ **Ethernet:** Connect the Xbox 360 directly to your network through the Ethernet port in the back of the console.

The Xbox 360 is usually connected either

 • Through a router.

 • Directly to a modem.

Silver and gold

One of the great things about the Xbox 360 is that it connects to the Internet so you can do things like play with other people online, get software updates, and download games and other content from Xbox Live. With the Xbox 360, Microsoft introduces two levels of membership for Xbox Live: Silver and Gold.

The Silver membership on Xbox Live is free — yes, *free* — and you can use that membership

to do all sorts of interesting things on Xbox Live (which we discuss in detail in Chapter 4). The Gold membership level costs $49.99 (US) per year and lets you play games head to head with others online.

The bottom line is this: Connect your Xbox 360 to the Internet if you have a broadband connection. You get tons of benefits.

✔ **Wireless:** Requires either

- The Xbox 360 wireless adapter.
- A wireless Ethernet adapter from a hardware vendor.

Network configuration is automatic on the Xbox 360. When you plug into the wired network, the Xbox 360 determines the proper connections automatically. For a wireless connection, you may need to enter a key code when you connect to the network. Chapter 3 talks more about the different ways of connecting your Xbox 360 to the Internet.

Flipping the Switch and Testing

After you have your Xbox 360 in place with the audio/video and network cables plugged in, test whether it's working properly:

1. **Plug the power cable into the wall.**

2. **Turn on your Xbox 360 by pressing the power button on the console.**

3. **If you have a wireless controller, press and hold the bonding button on the controller and the console at the same time.**

   When the light runs around the ring on the controller, the controller and console are bonded.

4. **Select the appropriate input on your TV or receiver and check whether you get video and audio from your Xbox 360.**

   If you don't see the Xbox 360 on your TV, check the settings in the "Troubleshooting" sidebar in this chapter.

5. **Test whether sound works correctly by pressing the shoulder buttons on the Xbox 360 controller.**

   This switches from blade to blade, which is described in detail in Chapter 3.

   You should hear a sound effect go from left to right or right to left, depending on which blade you switch to.

6. **If it's all working, take a minute to**

   • Straighten the cables.

   • Place the Xbox 360 just the way you want it.

     Give the box room to breathe!

Kick back and relax! You've connected your Xbox 360.

Chapter 3 introduces you to the software setup.

Troubleshooting Error Messages

The Ring of Light around the power button on the Xbox 360 is a beautiful thing. It normally glows green and makes you feel really good about being and Xbox 360 gamer. Sometimes though, the Ring of Light is an indicator of a potential problem. If the ring is showing red, you might have a problem with your console. The following sections list error messages associated with red on the Ring of Light.

If you're getting the following errors and none of the suggested steps are helping make them go away, call Xbox 360 support. The phone numbers for Xbox 360 support in the U.S. are:

USA: 1-800-4MY-XBOX

International (direct dial to U.S.): 425-635-7180

Hearing Impaired (TDD device): 1-866-740-9269 or 425-635-7102

The hours for Xbox support are

9:00 a.m. to 1:00 a.m. Eastern Time

12:00 p.m. to 10:00 p.m. Pacific Time

One red light flashes

This usually indicates that the Xbox 360 has experienced a hardware failure of some sort. To troubleshoot this, try turning off your console, reseating all

Troubleshooting

If you don't see the picture, check these items and settings:

✔ The switch on the Xbox 360's HDAV cable. (You don't need to worry about this if you are using the composite cable.)

✔ The video source selection on your TV — cycle through the video sources on your TV and see if you can find your signal there.

✔ The video input where the cable plugs into your TV.

the connected cables, and restarting your Xbox 360. One of the problems associated with this can be a hot power supply. Make sure that your power supply is on a flat, even surface with plenty of ventilation. Don't place your power supply on a carpet.

Two red lights flash

This usually indicates that the console has become too hot. To troubleshoot this issue, make sure that your Xbox 360 has plenty of room to breathe. Turn off the console for 30 minutes to cool it off and start it again.

Three red lights flash

This is usually an indication of some sort of hardware failure. Try shutting off the console and then disconnecting and reconnecting the different cables on the machine.

Four red lights flash

Four red flashing lights on the Xbox 360 usually indicate a problem with the video connection. Try turning off the Xbox 360 and disconnecting and then reconnecting the video adapter on the back of the Xbox 360 and check the connection you've made to the back of your television or monitor. If everything seems okay and you still see a message, try using a different video cable or connection type if you can to make sure that the problem isn't with the cable.

Part II
The Xbox 360 Blades

The 5th Wave   By Rich Tennant

"Wait a minute... This is a movie, not a game?! I thought I was the one making Keanu Reeves jump kick in slow motion."

In this part . . .

Get the scoopage on Xbox 360 *blades,* which are pages in your Xbox 360 dashboard, containing most of the functionality in the Xbox 360 outside the games themselves. Here's the place to see what blades are, how to walk through the initial setup, how to create an Xbox Live account, and much more.

Chapter 3 introduces the four main blades found in the Xbox 360. We walk you through the initial setup screens on the Xbox 360 and show you how to create a profile.

Chapter 4 describes the Live Blade. This is the blade you use to interact with your Xbox Live account if you have a high speed connection to the Internet. Chapter 5 tells you all about the Media Blade, which you use to rip and play music from your Xbox 360 hard drive, play music from PCs around your house, and even play music directly from your iPod.

Chapter 6 shows you how to use the System Blade. This blade is essentially the control center for your Xbox 360. From this blade, you can set the parental controls on the Xbox 360 and set your preferences for video and sound output. Chapter 7 reveals the Games Blade, which you use to track your progress on games you've played. You can also view your achievements and access the Xbox Live Arcade games you've purchased on Xbox Live Marketplace.

Chapter 3

Dealing with the Dashboard

In This Chapter

▶ Getting set up

▶ Adding profiles

▶ Navigating the Dashboard

*T*he Xbox 360 Dashboard is where you control your Xbox 360's software features, including your profiles, access to your game saves, music and video, and content that you download from Xbox Live. This chapter introduces you to the Dashboard.

Part II explains in detail all the ways the Dashboard gives you control over your Xbox 360 experience.

Initial Setup

When you turn on your Xbox 360, you first need to perform the initial setup. This process lets you

✔ Select your language

✔ Create your gamer profile

✔ Create an Xbox Live account

If you followed the setup steps in Chapter 2, you're ready to get started. Press the Start button on your Xbox 360. Now!

Choosing your language

The first choice you need to make is the language you want the Dashboard to use. This page lets you choose what language you see when navigating the Dashboard.

Follow these steps to set your preferred language:

1. **Select the language you prefer to use in the Dashboard.**

   Press forward and back on the left analog stick to highlight your pre-ferred language.

2. **Press the A button on your controller to set the language.**

Creating a gamer profile

After selecting your language, you automatically switch to the Gamer Profile menu. Your gamer profile is an identity that

✔ Stores your data on the Xbox 360 console (either on the hard drive or on a memory unit)

✔ Connects you to Xbox Live

The gamer profile setup process is when you choose a cool *gamertag* that

✔ Identifies you on Xbox Live

✔ Identifies the gamer profile where you store your personal game data

   Each person in your household can have his or her own gamer profile stored on one Xbox 360 hard drive or memory unit.

A personal gamer profile requires a *memory device* (either a hard drive or a memory unit). The Xbox 360 Core System doesn't include *any* memory; you have to add an optional device. Skip straight to the "Finalizing Setup Details" section in this chapter if your Xbox 360 console doesn't have a memory device.

The following sections show how to use the right gamer profile option for your Xbox 360. There's a special instruction section in this chapter for each of your three choices:

✔ **Create an offline profile**

   The offline profile doesn't connect to Xbox Live by default. Use the offline profile if

   • You aren't hooking up your Xbox 360 to the Internet.

   • You prefer to play games without Xbox Live.

You can set up an offline profile and *add* an Xbox Live account later.

✔ **I am a member of Xbox Live**

✔ **I want to join Xbox Live**

Xbox Live requires a high-speed Internet connection. (The Silver level of Xbox Live membership is free! Read more about the levels in Chapter 4.)

Create an offline profile

An *offline profile* is an Xbox 360 identity you don't use with Xbox Live.

If your Xbox 360 has a high-speed Internet connection, you can create an Xbox Live profile. You can skip to one of the following sections:

✔ **I am a member of Xbox Live**

✔ **I want to join Xbox Live**

Your offline profile's scores and other data (such as your preferred controller settings) are stored on a memory unit or hard drive and are available only on the Xbox 360 that you are playing on.

Creating a new offline profile is easy. Follow these steps:

1. **Press A to use the default option, "Create an offline profile."**

   A blade slides in from the left side of the screen to let you select a device on which to save your gamer profile.

2. **Select a storage device and press A.**

   You can save your profile to either

   • Your hard drive (included with the loaded Xbox 360 System)

   • A memory unit (optional for any Xbox 360 system)

   After you press A, a keyboard screen appears (Figure 3-1) and prompts you to enter your gamer profile name.

3. **Create your gamer profile name and press the Start button.**

   For each letter of the name, use the left analog stick (or direction pad) to move the cursor around the keyboard; press A to select a letter.

   Navigating around that blade keyboard isn't difficult, but it's quicker if you know the shortcuts we present in the "Swiss army controller" sidebar in this chapter.

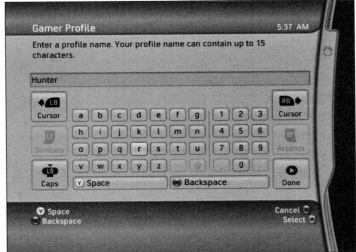

Figure 3-1:
Create a
new gamer
profile.

4. After you've typed your name in, you can either

- Press the Guide button on your controller.

- Highlight the Done button on-screen and press A on the controller.

After you press the Done button (or just press the Start button on the controller — the result is the same), the Gamer Picture screen opens.

After you create your profile, you can choose a *gamer picture*. The sidebar, "Putting on your game face," shows you how.

After creating an offline profile, you're ready to set the Family Settings or High Definition Settings or to go to the Xbox Dashboard. You can skip to the section, "Finalizing Setup Details," later in this chapter.

If you want to use *Xbox Live,* the following sections show you how.

Create an Xbox Live profile

If your Xbox 360 console is connected to a high-speed Internet service, you can create a profile that uses *Xbox Live.*

Before you connect to Xbox Live, make sure your Xbox 360 console is connected to your home network or high-speed Internet modem to ensure a smooth connection. Chapter 2 shows how to set up your Internet connection for Xbox 360.

The Xbox Live setup steps depend on whether you're already an Xbox Live member.

Swiss army controller

The following buttons help you enter and change text the fast and easy way:

✔ **Switch between *uppercase* and *lowercase* letters.**

Press straight down on the left analog stick.

✔ **Show *extra characters* (such as accents in Spanish or French).**

Pull the left and right triggers.

✔ **Move the cursor *between* letters.**

Press the left shoulder button to move the cursor left; press the right shoulder button to move it right.

✔ **Delete text to the *left* of the cursor.**

Press the X button.

✔ **Delete text to the *right* of the cursor.**

Press the right shoulder button to move the cursor to the right of the text; then press the X button to backspace over the text you've entered.

✔ **Create a *space* between words.**

Press the Y button.

I am a member of Xbox Live

If you're an Xbox Live member already, you can add your Xbox Live account to your gamer profile after you select the Xbox 360 console's language.

Follow these steps to use Xbox 360 with your existing Xbox Live account:

1. **On the Gamer Profile screen, use the left analog stick (or the direction pad) to scroll down to "I am a member of Xbox Live" and then press A.**

   Your Xbox 360 automatically connects to the Xbox Live service. Your system may tell you that it's downloading updates.

   When the system downloads are complete, you're prompted for your current Xbox Live gamertag.

2. **Press A to open the Keyboard screen and then enter your current gamertag.**

   Enter your gamertag *exactly* the way you're currently using it. (Your gamertag is *case-sensitive*. If you create your gamertag with capital letters, you must use the same capital letters to retrieve your gamertag.)

Putting on your game face

When you have a profile, you can choose a gamer picture for yourself:

- A set of gamer pictures comes with a new Xbox 360.
- You can get additional pictures either by playing — and winning! — Xbox 360 games or by getting on Xbox Live.

The accompanying figure shows the Gamer Picture blade. From this blade you can choose a picture for your Xbox 360 profile. Follow these steps to change your picture:

1. Use the left analog stick to highlight the picture you want.
2. Press A to select the picture.

   The selected picture is chosen and you go right to the completion screen.

You can change your gamer picture at any time from the Xbox Dashboard. Follow these steps:

1. Click your Gamer Card from the Live blade.
2. Choose Edit Gamer Profile from the Gamer Profile blade.

The little triangle at the bottom of the pictures list indicates that more pictures are available. Use the left analog stick to move down and see those pictures.

3. **If you want to use a Microsoft .NET Passport account with Xbox Live, follow the on-screen instructions.**

Microsoft recommends using a Passport account with Xbox Live. The sidebar "Linking your gamertag" has the lowdown.

After migrating an existing Xbox Live profile, you can use your Xbox 360 on Xbox Live, and you're ready to set the Family Settings or High Definition Settings or to go to the Xbox Dashboard. You can skip to the section, "Finalizing Setup Details," later in this chapter.

I want to join Xbox Live

If this is your first Xbox, or if you have never had an Xbox Live account, you can create a new Xbox Live account after you select your console's language.

Follow these steps to create an Xbox Live account with your Xbox 360:

1. **On the Gamer Profile screen, select "I want to join Xbox Live" and then press A.**

Your Xbox 360 automatically connects to the Xbox Live service.

The default starting place is the Xbox Live menu.

2. **Scroll to the Join Xbox Live option and press A.**

You are prompted that you are leaving the current session.

3. **Select Yes and press A to continue.**

Your system may tell you that it's downloading updates. When the download of any available updates is completed, you're prompted for a gamertag to use on Xbox Live. The Keyboard blade automatically opens.

Linking your gamertag

Linking your gamertag to your Microsoft .NET Passport account is easy. If you don't have an account (your *Hotmail* e-mail address is your Passport account login), go to `www.passport.net` and follow the instructions to create your free account.

To link your gamertag, go to `www.xbox.com/en-US/support/howto/gamertaglinking.htm` and follow the instructions. With your gamertag linked to your Passport account, you'll have tremendous flexibility to access your Xbox Live account information online, including seeing such information as your own achievements and your friends list.

Associating a Microsoft .NET Passport account with your gamertag lets you

✔ Easily convert your original Xbox Live account to your Xbox 360.

✔ Track such game details as your achievements and friends list at `www.xbox.com`.

B is for backward

The B button is your friend. If you make a mistake while you're entering information on one page and don't realize it until you go to the next page, pressing B usually takes you back a page.

Be prepared with at least *three* gamertags that you will be comfortable using. (Xbox Live usually charges Microsoft Points if you want to change your gamertag later.)

4. **Enter your gamertag and press Start.**

   The "Swiss army controller" sidebar has tips for using the Keyboard blade.

   Xbox Live checks the availability of your selected gamertag.

   - If the name isn't available, you're prompted to try another name.
   - If the gamertag is accepted, you are automatically prompted to link to your Passport account.

5. **Select your current Passport account status:**

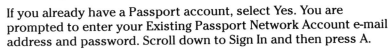

   - *Yes, I do* (you have a Passport account)

     If you already have a Passport account, select Yes. You are prompted to enter your Existing Passport Network Account e-mail address and password. Scroll down to Sign In and then press A.

     After you sign in to an existing Passport account, you can skip to Step 16.

   - *No, create one* (you don't have a Passport account)

6. **If you select *No, create one,* you can now choose your Locale.**

   The Account Information screen appears.

   Set your region properly to avoid billing problems.

7. **Set your preferred language.**

8. **Set your birthdate:**

   a. Choose Birthdate and then press A to bring up the Birthdate page.

   b. Use the left analog stick to set the date.

     Change the numbers by moving the stick up and down. Pressing left and right moves you between fields.

c. When the date is correct, press the B button.

You return to the Account Information page.

d. Select Next and then press A.

You're prompted for your e-mail address.

9. **Enter your e-mail address:**

a. Press A to open the Keyboard blade.

b. Enter your e-mail address.

c. Select Done and press A.

d. Select Next and press A.

10. **Select a password, a secret question, and a secret answer.**

Navigate through these items, using the Keyboard blade to fill them.

11. **Select Next and then press A.**

The next Account Information screen appears.

12. **Enter your first name, last name, phone number, and contact e-mail address.**

The Terms of Use appear.

13. **Read the Terms of Use.**

14. **To accept the terms, choose Accept and press A.**

If you don't accept the Terms of Use, you can't create an Xbox Live account.

The next screen offers you a choice of account types.

15. **Pick your Xbox Live membership type.**

When creating a new Xbox Live account, you have two basic choices:

- The *Gold* (paid) account lets you in on multiplayer games on Xbox Live.

- The *Silver* (free) account lets you download game updates and purchase new content through Xbox Live.

I've got a secret

The secret question and secret answer help identify you if you forget your password. The secret question category lets you choose from some questions about your history and tastes. Don't use information that's easily available to others. For example, if you run a Web site dedicated to chicken wings, don't use the favorite food question for your secret word. A few celebrities with have been caught using a pet's name as a security question. (Their pets' names aren't really a secret.)

Table 3-1 shows the choices from the Xbox Live Membership Type screen.

Table 3-1	Xbox Live Membership Choices
Choice	*Description*
Redeem Prepaid Code	Use this option if you have an Xbox Live prepaid card. (You can buy these in stores.)
Xbox Live Monthly Gold Membership	Pay for Xbox Live by the month.
Xbox Live 3-Month Gold Membership	Pay for 3 months of service.
Xbox Live 12-month Gold Membership	Pay for 1 year of Xbox Live.
Xbox 360 Silver Live Membership	This account is free. (You may be offered a free Gold trial membership when you sign up for a Silver account.)

16. **Confirm your account type choice (and enter payment details if you chose Xbox Gold).**

17. **Choose a gamer picture.**

18. **Choose your level.**

    If you choose Silver, you may be offered a Gold trial membership.

    You can change your level at any time. Your choices are

    - *Recreation:* This is for players who want to play mostly for fun.

    - *Pro:* This is your level if you want to be super-competitive on Xbox Live. This is the choice of most really good players.

    - *Family:* This level is for kids and for people who might be concerned about hyper-competitive gamers and bad language.

    - *Underground:* This level is for players who like to play by their own rules. *Trash-talking* (which might be considered "spirited banter" with other players) won't get you in trouble here.

19. **Decide whether you want to subscribe to e-mail information about Xbox Live.**

After you've created a new profile, you're ready to proceed to the final setup details.

The end of this chapter shows how to use a different gamer profile for each member of your household.

Finalizing Setup Details

If you've built a new profile for your Xbox 360, you see the Initial Setup Complete screen. From here, you have just a few more details to set on your Xbox 360.

The Initial Setup Complete screen lets you choose the console's parental controls. If you want to set those controls, Chapter 11 shows how to use the Xbox 360 features that let you control which games, movies, and materials are available to your family.

High definition settings

The High Definition Settings option is part of the Initial Setup. You can use these options with your Xbox 360 if

✔ **You're connected with** *component video.*

Chapter 2 tells you how to connect a component video cable. You can't use the High Definition Settings options without component video.

✔ **You have a TV that uses at least one of these resolution levels:** *480p, 576p, 720p,* **or** *1080i.*

The TV may be called "EDTV," "HDTV", or "HDTV-ready."

Chapter 8 provides the technical TV details.

TV settings

Before trying a high-resolution Xbox 360 setting, see if you need to manually select your TV's resolution:

✔ If your TV's owner's manual says it *automatically* selects the input resolution, you don't need to change the TV's resolution settings before choosing the Xbox 360 setting.

✔ If your TV's owner's manual says you must *manually* select the input resolution, follow the TV's instructions to select one of these resolutions for the component video input:

• **1080i**

1080i component video is technically the highest resolution for most HDTVs, but it's not always the best option for the Xbox 360. Try it if your TV isn't classed as an EDTV and you have problems when your TV is set to the 720p option.

• **720p**

720p is the best resolution for your Xbox 360 if your television has it. (An "EDTV" may not work with 720p video.)

- **576p**

  If you connect an Xbox 360 with component video cables in a *PAL* system country (such as the United Kingdom, Australia, or Singapore), you can probably use 576p with your TV.

- **480p**

  If you have an *EDTV (Enhanced Definition Television)* in the United States or Canada, 480p may be the only resolution option that works for you.

If you don't know how to view the component video input on your TV screen, check your TV's owner's manual. Your TV may require you to *assign* the component video connection a name (like *Input 1*) so you can use that name to change channels to the component video connection.

Xbox settings

You can set the video resolution higher than 480i (in the United States and Canada) or 576i (in PAL countries, like the United Kingdom) if the component cable is attached to your Xbox 360 console.

A component cable uses *red, green,* and *blue* plugs.

You set Xbox 360 for your TV's resolution from the Display Settings page.

If your Xbox 360 is connected with a component video cable, try all of the console's resolution settings with the following steps until you find the best picture setting for your TV.

To set your Xbox 360 for best picture performance, follow these steps:

1. **On the Display settings in the System blade, highlight the HDTV Settings tab and press A.**

2. **Choose the screen resolution setting with the left analog stick and press A.**

   The screen resolution options you see may depend on your country's TV standards:

   - 480p
   - 576p (in PAL system countries, such as the United Kingdom)
   - 720p (the best setting for Xbox 360)
   - 1080i

   If your TV works with the selected setting, a blade asks whether you want to keep the settings.

3. **If a blade asks whether to keep the settings, follow these steps to keep the settings:**

   a. Select Yes, Keep These Settings.

   b. Press A to confirm the change.

If you don't see this blade, your display can't use the selected resolution. Xbox 360 automatically switches back to the previous resolution after about ten seconds. You can go back to Step 2 and try a different resolution.

Widescreen video

If you aren't using 720p or 1080i high-definition component video, the second setting on the Display Settings page lets you choose between normal and widescreen video. (Widescreen video is *automatic* for 720p and 1080i.)

Chapter 8 explains widescreen video.

After completing the video setup, you can either change any other console settings or select Xbox Dashboard. You're finished with the initial setup on your Xbox 360!

You can run initial setup again at any time from the System blade.

Introducing Blades

Dashboard blades are the user interface for your Xbox 360. The blades are the Dashboard's heart, letting you track users, check Xbox Live status, tweak settings, play media, and use parental controls.

Navigating between blades

To move between the blades in the Xbox Dashboard, you can either

✔ **Press the left analog stick left and right.**

   The blades switch instantly with the sound of a very satisfying swoosh!

✔ **Press the shoulder buttons.**

✔ **Press left and right on the direction pad.**

✔ **Pressing A activates the item highlighted on-screen.**

To sign out of your profile, press X. After signing out, you can still access the blades, but you can't do anything specific with your account. Sign in again by highlighting the Sign In item at the top of the Xbox Live blade and pressing A.

Xbox 360 Dashboard

Every function of your Xbox 360 is managed through the Dashboard, which is a series of four "blades" (menu screens) that you access to control your Xbox Live options, your Games, your Media, and the System settings.

Xbox Live blade

The Xbox Live blade opens by default when you start the system. You can see the blade in Figure 3-2.

The Xbox Live blade is the place for

- ✔ Staying in touch with your friends on Xbox Live
- ✔ Purchasing items through the Xbox Live Marketplace
- ✔ Your gamer card
- ✔ Xbox Live events for anyone in the community to attend

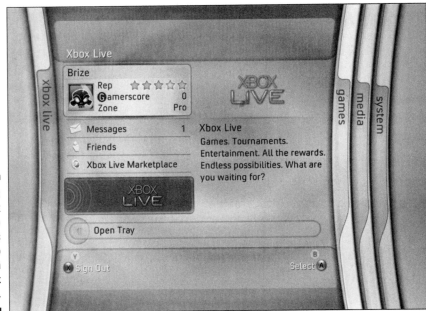

Figure 3-2:
The Xbox Live blade connects you to friends on the Xbox Live service.

We tell you all about the Xbox Live blade in Chapter 4.

Xbox Live Silver memberships are *free!* Be sure to get one of these if you have a high-speed Internet connection.

Games blade

The Games blade is where you track your games and achievements on your Xbox 360.

Think of the Games blade as your trophy room!

You can also use this blade to access your Xbox Live Arcade games. Figure 3-3 shows the blade in the Dashboard.

We tell you all you need to know about the Games blade in Chapter 7.

Figure 3-3: View your Xbox 360 gaming history on the Games blade.

Media blade

The Media blade provides access to all sorts of entertainment media, right through your Xbox 360 console:

✔ Connect to a PC on your network to listen to music and look at pictures.

✔ Plug an iPod into your Xbox 360 and listen to music through your sound system.

✔ Watch video downloaded from Xbox Live.

✔ Connect to a Windows Media Center PC on your network and get a full-on TV experience, as described in Chapter 13.

Figure 3-4 shows the Media blade, which we tell you about in Chapter 5.

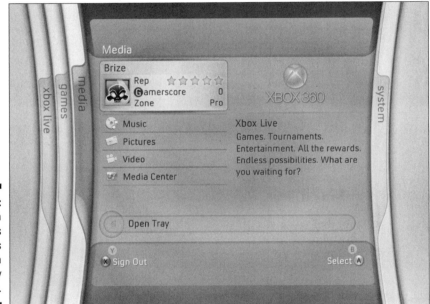

Figure 3-4:
The Media blade gives you access to media from many sources.

System blade

Control your Xbox 360 settings on the System blade. You can

✔ Change the video and audio settings.

✔ Set a content password.

✔ Access memory cards and drives.

✔ Rerun the Initial Setup program.

We cover the Initial Setup program earlier in this chapter.

Chapter 6 details the System blade, which is shown in Figure 3-5.

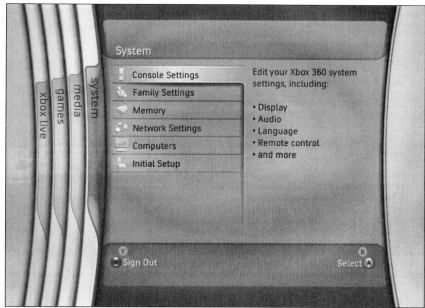

Figure 3-5:
The System blade puts you in control of your Xbox 360 settings.

Multiple Gamers

Each member of your family can have his or her own profile on the Xbox 360. This way, players can keep their own scores, game saves, and Xbox Live information separate.

Players can't share an Xbox Live Gold account at the same time. If you want to play on Xbox Live at the same time, you probably need more Gold accounts (unless you're playing a game that allows multiple players on the same home console).

Adding profiles

To create a new profile, press the Guide button in the middle of the controller to bring up a Navigation blade that contains

✔ Your gamer score

✔ Your message center

✔ A music interface that lets you play background music

You can get to this system navigation blade at any time — whether you're playing a game, watching a DVD, or listening to music — by pressing the Xbox 360 Guide button in the middle of the controller.

To create a new Xbox 360 profile, follow these steps:

1. **Press X.**

    You're prompted to confirm your decision to sign out at the Sign Out blade.

2. **At the confirmation screen, you can select either**

    • *Yes, sign out* (this completes the sign out process)

    • *No, don't sign out* (this returns you to the Xbox 360 Dashboard)

    After confirming that you want to sign out, return to the Guide navigation page (Figure 3-6), where you can

    • Sign in again with any of the profiles that will automatically be found on the hard drive

    • Create New Profile

    • Recover a gamertag from Xbox Live

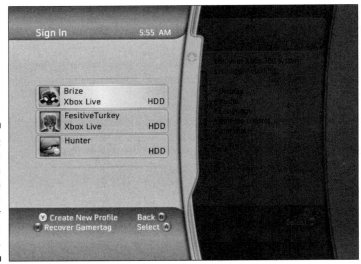

Figure 3-6:
Use the
Xbox Live
blade to
choose a
profile or
create a
new one.

If you've created a profile with an associated Xbox Live account and you lose that profile, you might need to recover it. You might lose a profile if you're carrying it on a memory unit, for example.

3. **Use the left analog stick (or direction pad) to scroll down to the Create Gamer Profile option and then press A.**

   The Select a Device blade appears, where you can

   - Select your hard drive (if you have one attached)
   - Select your memory unit (if you have one attached)

   This is where the gamer profile is saved.

4. **Scroll to your chosen storage device and press A.**

   The gamer profile blade appears.

5. **Type a name for the new profile and then select Done.**

6. **Press A to get to the Save Gamer Profile screen.**

   On the Save Gamer Profile screen, you can also

   - Join Xbox Live.
   - Customize the profile.

7. **Choose Done and press A.**

   The new Gamer Profile is saved.

Switching profiles

You can switch your offline and Xbox Live profiles on your Xbox 360 at any time. Follow these steps:

1. **Press the Guide button in the middle of the controller.**

   This opens your profile blade, where you can view your current profile gamer score, see which friends are online, and set personal settings.

2. **Press X to switch your profile.**

   You will be asked if you want to sign out; signing out will lose any unsaved progress in the game you are playing. You have two options:

   - *Yes, sign out*
   - *No, don't sign out*

3. **Use the left analog stick or direction pad to scroll up to "Yes, sign out" and then press A.**

4. **Select Sign In at the top of the blade and press A.**

   The Sign In screen lists the gamer profiles saved on your Xbox 360.

You can also use the Guide screen to

- Create New Profile
- Recover Gamertag from Xbox Live
- Select Personal Settings

5. **Use the left analog stick or direction pad to scroll to the profile you want to use and then press A.**

At this screen you can also

- Press Y to create a new profile
- Press X to recover a gamertag

You will be signed in with that profile's settings.

Chapter 4

The Live Blade

*Y*our Xbox 360 console is a powerful game system, but it can also connect to a virtual online world: Xbox Live. If you think Xbox Live is all about playing (and winning) online games, think again! Xbox Live, the Microsoft game service for Xbox 360 owners, can extend the fun you get out of your Xbox 360 console in new and exciting ways.

What's Xbox Live?

Xbox Live isn't required, but it enhances your entertainment experience. When your console's set up and connected to your home network (as described in Chapter 2), you're ready to get online.

Xbox Live is a free service *and* a subscription service. How can it be both? Simple. For each profile on your Xbox 360, you can create one of two different types of membership levels:

✔ **Silver account**

The free Silver account lets you access a wide variety of features on Xbox Live.

✔ **Gold account**

The paid Gold account offers all of Silver's features, plus the ability to participate in online multiplayer fun.

Blocking Xbox Live access

If you want to *stop* Xbox Live access on your Xbox 360 console, follow these steps:

1. **Navigate to the System blade by using the left analog stick on the controller.**

   The System blade opens and lists the display items.

2. **Highlight Family Settings and press A.**

3. **Choose Console Controls and press A.**

   If you already have a pass code set, you will need to enter it again to access the Console Controls menu.

   The Console Controls menu appears.

4. **On the Console Controls menu, select Access to Xbox Live.**

5. **Press the A button to select one of the following Xbox Live access options: *Allowed* or *Blocked***

6. **When you've selected the Xbox Live access you want, press B to exit the setup menu.**

   The Set Pass Code menu option appears automatically.

If you don't want to set a new pass code, you can stop here.

7. **If you want to set or change the pass code, Scroll down to the Set Pass Code menu option and press A; then Press a sequence of *four controller buttons* to be your pass code.**

This code is a four-button combination that you select by using the direction pad, left and right triggers, left and right shoulder buttons, the X button, and the Y button.

For example, you could set the code to be X,X,Y,Y or left Directional pad, right Directional pad, up Directional pad, down Directional pad.

You will be asked to *repeat* your pass code to make sure it's what you want.

Make sure you write down and save your pass code. If you forget the code, you have to contact technical support to reset the console. You can find contact information for support at `www.xbox.com/support`.

Table 4-1 shows the difference between the Silver and Gold accounts.

You can see a person's subscription level by looking at the color behind their Gamertag. Silver for Silver and gold for — you guessed it — Gold.

Table 4-1	Xbox Live Silver and Gold Memberships	
Feature	*Silver*	*Gold*
Multiplayer games		X
Exclusive Marketplace downloads		X

Feature	Silver	Gold
Supports *every* Xbox 360 game		X
Receive auto updates	X	X
Friends list	X	X
Family settings	X	X
Message Center	X	X
Xbox Live Marketplace	X	X
Gamer profiles	X	X

Let's go online

When your console is networked and you've created a profile (which Chapter 3 shows how to do), it's time to get online! Use your controller to navigate to the Xbox Live blade.

You can navigate the blades with

- ✔ Shoulder button
- ✔ Directional pad
- ✔ Left analog stick

Navigation in the Xbox 360 dashboard is simple:

- ✔ **Change the blade, page, or tab that you're on** by either
  - • Pressing left or right your stick or Directional pad
  - • Pressing the left or right shoulder buttons
- ✔ **Select a different item** by pressing forward or back on the stick or the Directional pad.

The Xbox Live blade is the blade that opens when you turn on your Xbox 360. You can see the Live blade in Figure 4-1.

Think of the Xbox Live blade as Xbox 360's equivalent to the home page in your Web browser.

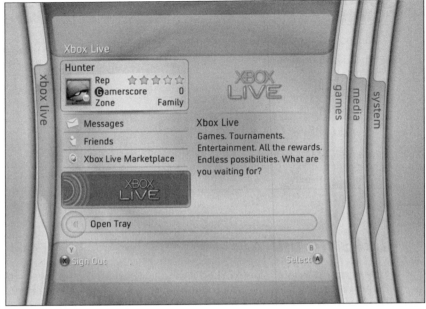

Figure 4-1:
The Xbox
Live blade is
where you
start
playing.

Your *Gamercard* is in the upper-left corner of the Live blade, as shown in Figure 4-2.

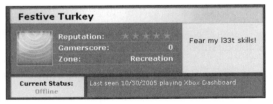

Figure 4-2:
Your
Gamercard.

Your Gamercard tells other players about you. It has your

- ✔ **Gamertag**
- ✔ **Gamer picture** (which you choose when you set up your profile as described in Chapter 3)
- ✔ **Reputation** (Rep) score
- ✔ **Gamerscore**
- ✔ **Gamer Zone**

    This is the Xbox Live zone where you're registered to play. The Gamer Zone tells others what type of player you are and how you like to play on Xbox Live.

Gamercards

Xbox Live lets you can build your own online identity. On Xbox Live, you have one name that spans all areas of the service, including games.

In Xbox Live, Major Nelson in *Halo 2* is the same Major Nelson who beat you in *Perfect Dark Zero*. On some other gaming services, players can

- ✔ Use a different name in every game.
- ✔ Change their names without any penalty.

Gamertag

A *Gamertag* is a player's online name.

You choose your own Gamertag when you're setting up your profile (as shown in Chapter 3). Your profile name is your Gamertag. If you don't like your Gamertag, you can use points to make a change.

The color behind a Gamertag indicates the player's Xbox Live membership level: Silver or Gold. Only Gold members can play games with you on Xbox Live (and you must be a Gold member, too).

Gamer Picture

You can personalize your Gamercard by choosing a Gamer Picture:

- ✔ All players can choose from a basic set of pictures.
- ✔ Some games offer other gamer pictures when a player completes the game.

You can change your Gamer Picture as often as you like. Chapter 3 shows you how.

Gamer Pictures are limited to items available on Xbox Live or through games or other special promotions:

- ✔ You can't use your own images.
- ✔ You can't modify the existing images.

Rep

Your *Rep* is your Xbox Live reputation score, a sort of snapshot of how other players see you. Your Rep is an average of other players' reviews of you. You can't change or vote on your own Rep score.

Xbox Live uses the star system for ratings.

✔ **5 stars is the top Rep score.**

A high Rep score means other players like playing with you.

New Xbox Live players automatically start with 3 Rep stars.

✔ **1 star is the lowest Rep score.**

Many players avoid playing with people who have a low Rep score.

You can submit player reviews only if you play someone. You can submit your own player feedback through the player's profile (discussed later in this chapter).

Gamerscore

Xbox 360 games can have up to 100 Gamerscore points that you can unlock by completing tasks in the game.

For instance, you might get

✔ 5 Gamerscore points for finishing the first level

✔ 50 Gamerscore points for defeating the *Big Boss* on the highest level. (A *boss* is a game character that you usually face at the end of a level.)

Points add up. The more tasks you complete, the higher your Gamerscore on Xbox Live.

Gamerscore points aren't the same as *Microsoft Points,* which are covered later in this chapter.

Gamer Zone

Xbox Live Gamer Zones are used for player matchmaking. Gamer Zones are one method that Xbox Live uses to match you with people of similar playing style. Which Gamer Zone you choose determines which game sessions you're most likely to join.

Figure 4-3 shows the Xbox Live Gamer Zones:

✔ **Recreation:** For gamers that just want to have fun.

✔ **Pro:** For gamers that want to compete and win!

✔ **Family:** For kids and adults who want to have very clean fun.

✔ **Underground:** For those who don't like to play by society's rules.

Gamer Zones indicate a player's *attitude,* not a player's *skill.* For instance, if you really don't care what a game's final outcome is, Recreation is a great Gamer Zone for you.

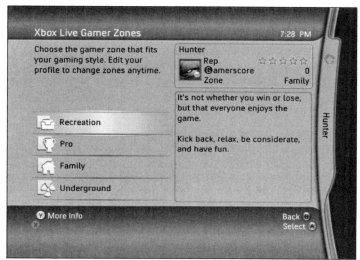

Figure 4-3:
The Xbox
Live Gamer
Zones.

You can change your Gamer Zone any time from *either* your Xbox 360 *or* your PC:

✔ In Xbox 360, you can just open your Gamer Profile and choose Edit Gamer Profile.

✔ On your PC, you can follow these steps:

1. **In your browser, go to** www.xbox.com.

2. **Log in with your Passport account.**

3. **Click your Gamer Card in the upper left of the Xbox.com home page.**

4. **On your My Gamer Card page, click Edit Gamer Profile.**

5. **In the Gamer Zone section, choose the Gamer Zone you want to be in.**

   You can also change your Gamer Picture from this page.

The Gamer Profile Screen

The Gamer Profile screen comes up when you select your Gamer Card in the Xbox Live blade and press A. From here, you can

- ✐ View games you've played.
- ✐ Edit your profile.
- ✐ View your Rep.
- ✐ Set game defaults.
- ✐ Manage your account.

Figure 4-4 shows the Gamer Profile screen.

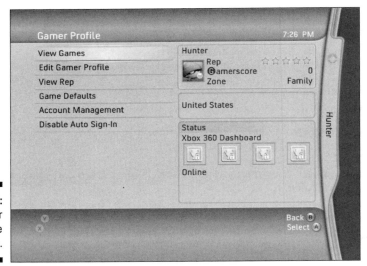

Figure 4-4: The Gamer Profile screen.

If you choose View Games by pressing forward or back on the left analog stick and then pressing A, a list of all the games you've played on your Xbox 360 console appears; it looks like the one in Figure 4-5. From this list, select an individual game title to see the date and achievements you've unlocked.

In Figure 4-5, you can see that I have yet to open any achievements in any of the games I've played. (Been a little busy with the book!)

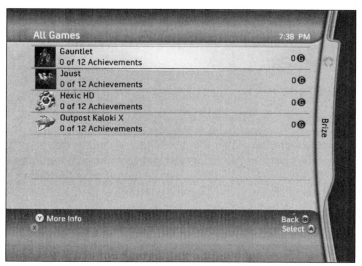

Figure 4-5:
The Games
screen.

If you select Edit Gamer Profile, you can change your

- ✔ Gamer picture
- ✔ Motto
- ✔ Gamer Zone
- ✔ Gamertag
- ✔ Account settings

Take a look at each of these in more detail.

Gamer picture

Other players see this picture when they look at your Gamercard. In this screen you can choose your gamer picture or download more pictures from Xbox Live. You can change this as many times as you'd like.

Motto

Set up your motto and make a statement to other gamers. You have 21 characters to use for this purpose. Be creative!

Gamer Zone

Choose what Gamer Zone you'd like to be associated with: Recreation, Pro, Family, or Underground. While you can change this at any time, it's good to choose one nearest to your playing style.

The Gamer Zone you choose loosely defines your playing style, not your skill! If you choose Pro and you're really a Recreation-style player, then your reputation may not be as good as if you were in the Recreation section.

Gamertag

Changing your Gamertag costs some Microsoft Points, so select carefully the first time.

Account management

The Account Management section contains your personal membership information for Xbox Live. Figure 4-6 shows the Account Management screen. Take a look at its parts and what you need to enter.

- ✓ **Memberships:** Get information about your current Xbox Live membership (Silver or Gold).

- ✓ **Contact Information:** Update your mailing address here.

- ✓ **Passport Network Information:** Enter or change your Passport password.

  If you use your Passport anywhere else (a Hotmail address, for example) and you change your password, you'll need to enter your new password here as well!

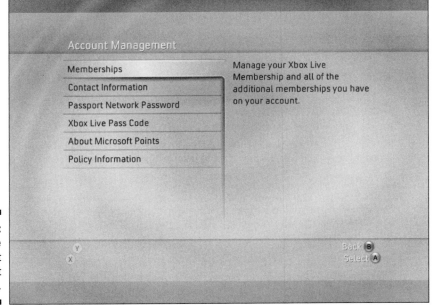

Account Management

Memberships

Contact Information

Passport Network Password

Xbox Live Pass Code

About Microsoft Points

Policy Information

Manage your Xbox Live Membership and all of the additional memberships you have on your account.

Y

X

Back (B)

Select (A)

Figure 4-6:
The Account Management screen.

✔ **Xbox Live Pass Code:** You can set a simple pass code to protect others from using your account. Instead of a password made up of words and numbers, use a combination of four of the following controller buttons:

- Y
- X
- LT
- RT
- LB
- RB
- DIRECTIONAL PAD

After you enter your pass code, enter it again to ensure it's what you want. For example, you might enter a pass code like: X Y LT RT

Write down your pass code and don't lose it. If you forget your pass code, you can't access your profile or account!

✔ **About Microsoft Points:** Microsoft Points is what Microsoft calls a *stored value system*. This system lets you use points to purchase content for your Xbox 360, including

- Games
- Levels
- Gamer pictures
- Themes

Purchased points never expire, but points gained through game promotions have an expiration date. Game promotion points might come with a game or might be added to your account because you played in a special event. Points with the earliest expiration date are used automatically when you purchase something new.

✔ **Policy Information:** Here you can read the legal stuff — Xbox Live Terms of Use, Privacy Statement, and Code of Conduct. Of these three documents, the Code of Conduct is probably the most practical for Live Gamers.

To get back to the Gamer Profile screen from Account Management, press B. On the Gamer Profile screen, you can disable auto sign-in. You guessed it: Auto sign-in automatically signs you in to Xbox Live when you turn on your Xbox 360. This very useful feature lets you connect to Xbox Live the moment you turn on your console.

The Xbox Live Code of Conduct

Normally, we would skip over something as potentially boring as policy, but Xbox Live has got a pretty compelling set of rules to play by. These rules are from the Code of Conduct:

- Don't use Xbox Live or Xbox.com to do anything illegal. Microsoft is not responsible for anything you say on the service/website or for anything that happens because of what you say; you alone are responsible.

- Don't harass, abuse, or spam other players.

- Don't scream, yell, threaten, or stalk other players.

- Don't distribute, post, publish, upload, disseminate or discuss defamatory, infringing, obscene, sexual or other unlawful materials like child pornography or illegal drugs including images, audio, video, or text.

- Don't post links to websites that violate the Code of Conduct.

- Don't give out information that personally identifies you (such as your real name, address, phone number, credit card number, etc.) while you're playing. This includes voice chat and the names you create for your gamertag or mottos. This information could be used by other players for illegal or harmful purposes. Also, don't give out the personal information of other players.

- Don't create a gamertag or motto that other users may be offended by, this includes comments that look, sound like, stand for, hint at, abbreviate, or insinuate any of the following: profane words/phrases, sexually explicit language, sexual innuendo, hate speech (including but not limited to racial, ethnic, or religious slurs), illegal drugs/controlled substances, or illegal activities.

- Don't create a gamertag or motto that references controversial religious topics, notorious people, organizations, or sensitive current or historical events that may also be considered inappropriate.

- Don't cheat in a game unless cheats have been deliberately enabled.

- Don't modify or hack game content to create cheats.

- Don't intentionally play with someone else who is using mods in order to help inflate your rank, also known as 'boosting'.

- Don't post links to materials that could harm other users' computers or would allow others to inappropriately access software or Web sites.

- Don't impersonate or harass Microsoft employees, moderators, or staff members.

- Any non-game-related conversation that takes up a substantial amount of the forum or chat space and prevents users from finding game-related information may be considered a violation of the Code of Conduct.

- Don't use the forums or chats for any commercial purpose without the express consent of Xbox.com. You may only create an account for yourself as an individual. You may not create an account for your corporation or other business entity.

The whole Xbox Live Code of Conduct is posted at www.xbox.com.

Send and Receive Messages

Communication is one of the fun and useful features of Xbox Live. You can communicate with others on Xbox Live through the Community blade.

To bring up the Community blade, follow these steps:

1. **Select the Messages item on the Xbox Live blade.**

2. **Press A.**

   This brings up the Community screen shown in Figure 4-7.

Here you can

✔ Send a new message, a chat invite, a game invitation, or a friend request.

✔ Retrieve messages that others have left for you.

✔ Add friends to your list.

✔ See a list of people you've played with.

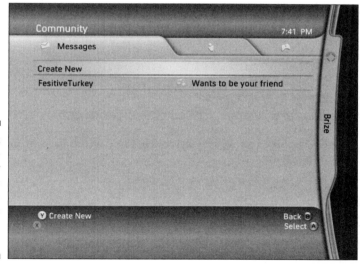

Figure 4-7: The Community screen lets you create messages and add friends.

Gamer Profiles

Moving the left analog stick to the right while you're on the Community screen opens the Friends tab. Selecting a player in the Friends tab and pressing A brings up a player's profile. You can see a typical profile in Figure 4-8. From their profile screen, you can start a conversation with your friend or challenge your friend to a game.

The Gamer Profile screen is also available for gamers you've played with on Xbox Live. Selecting someone from the Players screen lets you send a friend a request or provide feedback.

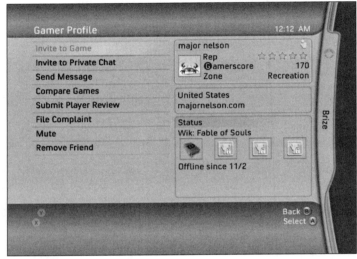

Figure 4-8:
The Gamer
Profile
screen is
available
from
Community.

Sending a message to another player

To send a message to another player, follow these steps:

1. **Open their player profile by selecting their name in your Friends tab or the Players tab.**

2. **Press A.**

   The player's Gamer Profile opens.

3. **Choose Send Message.**

   The Message screen appears, as shown in Figure 4-9.

4. **Add the message:**

   • To send a text message, highlight Add Text, press A, and key in your message.

   • To send a voice message, highlight Add Voice and use the recorder to create your message.

5. **Send the message.**

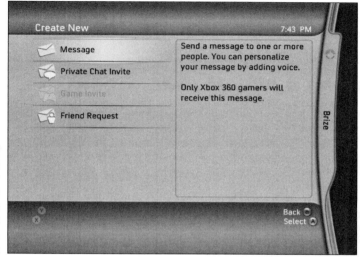

Figure 4-9:
Create your message on the Message screen.

Got a group of friends you like to play with? Let every member know that you're going to be online at a certain time. To add multiple message recipients to a message, highlight Edit Recipients on the message screen and choose the players you want to add, as shown in Figure 4-10.

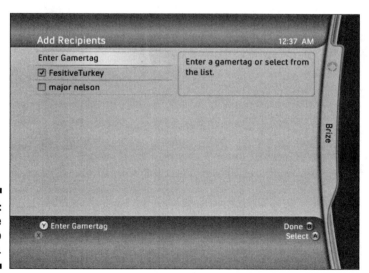

Figure 4-10:
Add multiple recipients to a message.

To add a voice message, you need to have a headset plugged into your controller — and make sure it's on your head!

You can add text and voice to the same message. This option is useful if you want to specify a playing time. The recipient can quickly see the time in a text message without having to listen to the voice message more than once.

Starting a private chat

A private chat lets you talk with another person on Xbox Live directly.

To use private chat, you and your recipient must be online at the same time. You can initiate a private chat by choosing Invite to Private Chat from their Gamer Profile.

You can have up to four private chats with different people at that same time. Figure 4-11 shows what the private chat window looks like. Choosing a different person in the Chat Channels section changes the input to that person (sort of like call waiting). So for example, if I'm chatting with Major Nelson and I get a chat request from Festive Turkey, I can say, "Just a second Major," and talk with Festive Turkey for a minute.

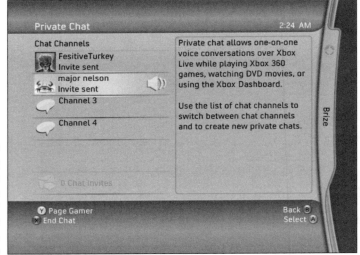

Figure 4-11:
You can participate in up to four chats at the same time.

Providing player feedback

Playing games with all sorts of interesting people makes Xbox Live fun. However, "interesting" can be a problem if players don't adhere to the guidelines mentioned in "The Xbox Live Code of Conduct" sidebar in this chapter.

To provide feedback on a player, follow these steps:

1. **Choose that player's name from the Friends or Players list.**
2. **Open the selected player's Gamer Profile screen.**
3. **Highlight Submit Player Review, then press A.**

   The Submit Player Review screen appears, as shown in Figure 4-12.

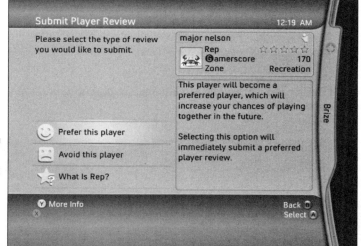

Figure 4-12: Submit feedback on a player, either good or bad.

4. **Highlight the type of feedback you want to provide, then press A.**

   Read more about feedback and playing well with others in Chapter 12.

Muting somebody

Sometimes the problem with a player is simply that he talks too much, or worse, she sings while playing. Use the Mute option on a players profile to take care of that. It's much less aggravating than scolding someone. They're most likely making noise to get attention, anyway.

Using the Xbox Live Marketplace

Xbox Live Marketplace is where you can buy content, such as

- ✔ Games through Xbox Live Arcade.
- ✔ Themes, which are custom skins for your Xbox 360 Dashboard.
- ✔ Xbox Live memberships.

You can see the Xbox Live Marketplace screen in Figure 4-13.

Xbox Live Marketplace is based on a system called Microsoft Points. Instead of using cash, you use *points* to buy the content you want to add to your Xbox 360.

Microsoft Points aren't the same as *Gamerscore points,* which are covered previously in this chapter.

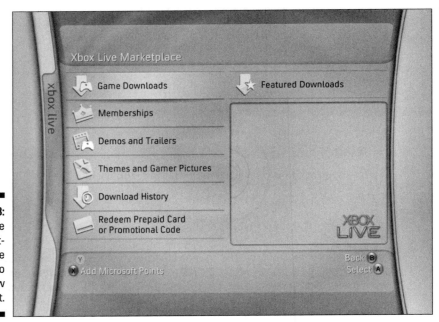

Figure 4-13:
Xbox Live Marketplace is the place to go for new content.

Acquiring points

You can get Microsoft Points for Xbox Live in two ways:

- ✔ Promotional codes
- ✔ Xbox Live Marketplace

Promotional codes

You can acquire free Microsoft Points by using promotional codes from products that you might buy or ads you might see in magazines.

Xbox Live Marketplace

You can buy Microsoft Points through Xbox Live Marketplace.

Xbox Live Marketplace purchases require that you either purchase Microsoft Points online (with a credit card) or purchase a card containing Microsoft Points from a retailer. Chapter 3 shows you how to set it up.

To purchase Microsoft Points from Xbox Live Marketplace, follow these steps:

1. **Open the Xbox Live Marketplace screen.**

2. **Press X.**

   The Add Microsoft Points screen appears, as shown in Figure 4-14.

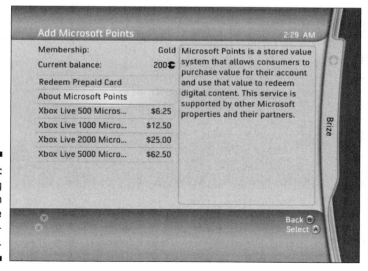

Figure 4-14: Purchasing points from Xbox Live Marketplace.

Microsoft Points prices can change, so the current cost may be different from what is shown in Figure 4-14.

Spending points

When you have enough points in your Xbox Live account, you can buy things like games on Xbox Live.

To purchase a new game, follow these steps:

1. **On the Xbox Live Marketplace screen, choose Game Downloads, then press A.**
2. **Switch to All Games by pressing right on the left analog stick.**
3. **Choose Xbox Live Arcade, then press A.**
4. **Choose the type of game you want to play, then press A.**
5. **Choose a game, then press A.**

   This brings up the screen shown in Figure 4-15.

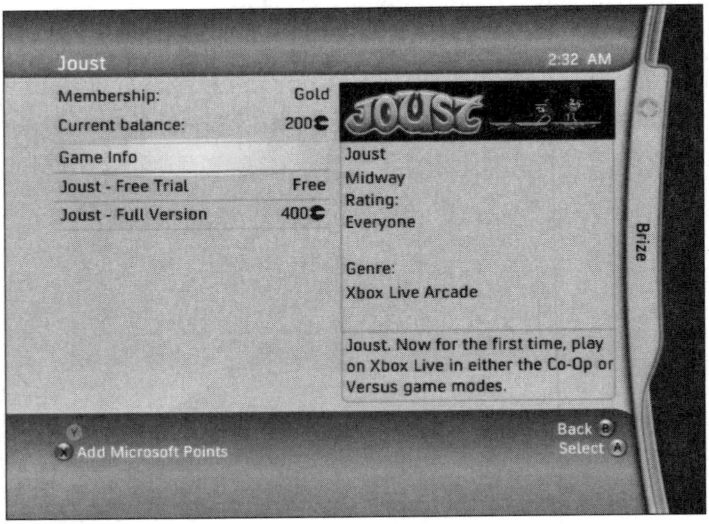

Figure 4-15:
Purchasing a new game on Xbox Live Marketplace.

If you have enough points, you can purchase the game. If you need more points, press X to add more points to your account.

Finding Out What's Happening Online

Part of the Xbox Live experience is available from your PC. Go to
www.xbox.
com and sign in with your Passport account. After you log in, your
Gamercard appears on the Xbox.com home page. Click your Gamercard to
access your Gamer Profile. This profile is available to other Xbox 360 gamers.
Figure 4-16 shows a Gamer Profile.

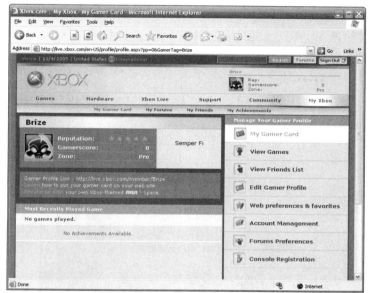

Figure 4-16:
Viewing
your Gamer
Profile on
Xbox.com.

Your gamer profile on Xbox.com lets you

> ✔ **View this information:**
>
>> • Gamercards (your own and others)
>>
>> • Your game history and achievements
>
> ✔ **Change these preferences:**
>
>> • Your personal preferences, such as Gamertag, Gamer Picture,
>> Motto, and Gamer Zone
>>
>> • Xbox.com Web preferences
>>
>> • Xbox.com Forums preferences
>
> ✔ **Register your console.**

Share your Gamercard

One of the ways that you can share the Xbox Live experience with your friends and family is by adding your Gamercard to your Web page or to your Web log (blog). Full details are on Xbox.com, but in a nutshell, just add a bit of code to your page to make your card show up. To add your Gamercard to a Web page, replace *mygamercard* in the following code with your own Gamertag:

```
<iframe src="http://gamercard.xbox.com/mygamercard.card"
    scrolling="no"frameBorder="0" height="140" width="204">
    mygamercard</iframe>
```

As your Rep changes, your card changes automatically. The accompanying figure shows how the card looks on a blog page.

You can also add your Gamertag to an MSN Spaces blog. You can see Brian's at `http://spaces.msn.com/members/brianjo`. Visit Xbox.com for details.

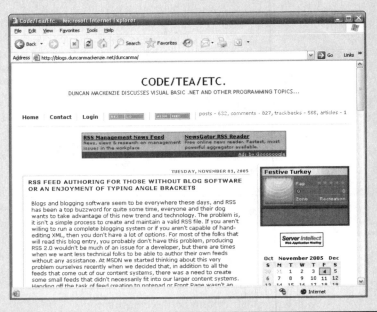

Chapter 5

The Media Blade

In This Chapter

▶ Watching DVDs on your Xbox 360

▶ Playing music from your iPod

▶ Viewing pictures from your PC

*Y*ou walk in the door, pull your MP3 player from your pocket, hook it up to your stereo, and fire up some tunes. After fixing a snack, you unwrap that great new CD you just bought and rip it onto a hard drive — but just when you start listening, your buddy shows up with photos from his trip. You hook up his camera so he can show you, on your TV, where he got that tan. Looking at pictures gets old, so you fire up *Project Gotham 3,* toss your friend a controller, and pick your new CD as the game soundtrack. When you finish kicking your friend's butt up and down the race course, you put in a DVD and watch a movie.

The Xbox supports many features that aren't directly related to games. Most of these features take advantage of the fact that the Xbox 360 is hooked up to a TV in your family room. This chapter shows you how to tap into music, photos, and movies on your Xbox 360. Your interface to these features is through the Xbox 360 Media blades, which expose all your options for music, photos, and video.

DVD Movies

Every Xbox 360 can play DVD movies right out of the box — no additional parts necessary.

If you have Xbox 360, you probably don't need a separate DVD player.

Watching a movie on the Xbox 360 is a straightforward process.

Console operation

It's easy to start a DVD movie with Xbox 360:

- ✔ The movie is loaded automatically if you either
  - Pop the DVD into the tray (like a game disc).
  - Switch the console power on with a DVD in the drive.
- ✔ If you have a movie in the drive when you're using the Dashboard, you can pick the "Play DVD" option from the bottom of any of the blades.

When the movie loads, the movie's menu screen usually appears automatically. You can use the arrow keys and OK button on your remote control (or the Directional pad and A button on a regular Xbox 360 controller) to start the movie.

Remote control

Although you can watch movies without any additional hardware, you will probably find it useful to have an Xbox 360 remote control.

If you're watching a DVD and press the Xbox Guide button (the orb with an X carved into it) on the remote, you're taken right into the dashboard. The rest of your Xbox's features are never far away.

There are two Xbox 360 remotes:

- ✔ A larger remote (called the "Universal Media Remote").

  Figure 5-1 shows the Universal Media Remote.

  This is sold separately for use with any Xbox 360 console. This remote has more features for your complete home entertainment system, such as

  - TV volume control
  - TV channel selection

  The Universal control even lights up when you press it. That makes watching scary movies in the dark even better!
- ✔ A small remote known as the "Media Remote."

  This remote is included with some of the first Xbox 360s sold (but it works with any Xbox 360 console).

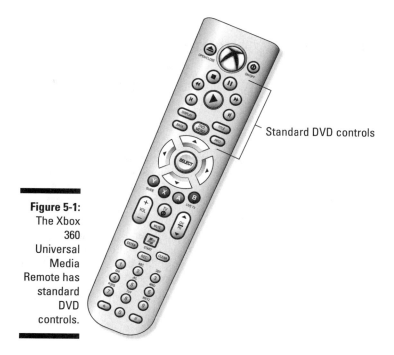

Standard DVD controls

Figure 5-1:
The Xbox
360
Universal
Media
Remote has
standard
DVD
controls.

Either of the Xbox 360 remotes can perform standard DVD activities, such as

- ✔ Using the DVD's menu
- ✔ Pausing the movie

Parental control

Any parental controls you've set up are in effect when you play a DVD. You need to enter a pass code before viewing content that exceeds the allowed rating.

Chapter 11 has full information on

- ✔ Parental controls
- ✔ Movie and game ratings

Setting DVD rating controls

Follow these steps to set DVD rating controls on your Xbox 360 console:

1. **Navigate to the System blade by using the left analog stick on the controller.**

   The System blade opens and lists the display items.

2. **Highlight Family Settings and press A.**

3. **Choose Console Controls and press A.**

   If you already have a pass code set, you need to enter it again to access the Console Controls menu.

   The Console Controls menu appears.

4. **On the Console Controls menu, select DVD Movie Ratings.**

   Now you can choose the movie ratings you will allow to be played on this Xbox 360. (Chapter 11 covers movie rating systems.)

5. **Select an option in the DVD Movie Ratings menu and press B.**

   If you select Allow All DVD Movies, any DVD put in the Xbox 360 will run.

When you press B to exit the Movie Ratings menu, the Set Pass Code menu option appears automatically.

If you don't want to set a new pass code, you can stop here.

6. **If you want to set or change the pass code, scroll down to the Set Pass Code menu option and press A, then press a sequence of *four controller buttons* to be your pass code.**

   This code is a four-button combination that you select by using the direction pad, left and right triggers, left and right shoulder buttons, the X button, and the Y button.

   For example, you could set the code to be X,X,Y,Y or left Directional pad, right Directional pad, up Directional pad, down Directional pad.

   You will be asked to *repeat* your pass code to make sure it's what you want.

Make sure you write down and save your pass code. If you forget the code, you have to contact technical support to reset the console. You can find contact information for support at www.xbox.com/support.

Progressive scan video

Progressive scan is a feature of the DVD output in the Xbox 360 (and is a standard feature of most recent DVD players), producing smoother output when playing movies on televisions that support high definition (see the sidebar "Progressive scan," in this chapter, for more information).

Progressive scan

HDTVs and the Xbox 360 output content using *progressive scan,* which means that all of the lines of the picture are drawn for every frame. Normal-definition TVs and non-progressive-scan DVD players display content as *interlaced,* outputting all the odd lines for one frame, then all the even lines for the next frame, and so on. By displaying full frames, progressive scan produces a smoother, better-looking picture. In specifications of video devices (such as DVD players and TVs), the letters *p* and *i* are often used to indicate progressive and interlaced output, respectively. 480p indicates output that has 480 lines of vertical resolution and uses progressive scan, while 1080i indicates 1,080 lines of resolution with interlaced output.

Progressive scan video only works when

✔ Your console is hooked up to a monitor that supports a resolution of 480p (such as any high-definition TV, or HDTV)

✔ Your cables and connectors can support high-definition display. These are either

  • Component video

  • VGA

Quiet mode

The Xbox 360 kicks itself into quiet mode when you watch a movie, so the console can slow down its cooling system. The result isn't silence, but it's a lot closer to it than the first Xbox (which was *loud*).

Accessing Your PC

One of the Xbox 360's more compelling media features is its support for a technology called Windows Media Connect. This feature lets you access music and photos stored on a computer — and you can get the media right from the Xbox 360's dashboard.

Your PC must meet only a few requirements to share its music and photo information with the Xbox 360:

✔ A valid network connection

✔ Windows XP Service Pack 2 (or a higher service pack)

✔ Windows Media Connect software

Stopping at 480p

If you have an HDTV, 480p (the *p* indicates progressive) is the second-lowest resolution you can display (regular TV is the lowest). But 480p is the output for a DVD. Why aren't movies viewed at 720p or 1080i (the i indicates interlaced)? You're limited by the quality of the source material. A DVD's video content is stored as 480p so no work is required to produce 480p output. In fact, the content normally has to be reduced in quality for viewing on normal-definition TVs.

To produce 720p or 1080i output, a DVD player would have to scale the content up and use fancy math to *interpolate* (make an educated guess about) the missing information. In the end, you might not see much of an improvement for the hassle and expense of an external DVD player. Having said that, I actually own a DVD player that outputs 720p/1080i (the Samsung DVD-HD931), and I find that movies really do look better on 720p. However, I bought this player over a year ago and doubt I would've if the Xbox 360 had been available at the time. If you get a DVD player that is capable of higher than 480p output, I recommend looking for one that uses DCDi (Faroudja) technology to perform the conversion.

In the future, a new form of DVD will natively support high definition, but two competing standards exist: HD DVD and Blu-ray. Saying which one will dominate is difficult. We recommend waiting until at least 2007 before you buy a high-definition DVD player.

If you have a *Windows Media Center PC*, skip to Chapter 13. Windows Media Center PCs usually are ready to connect directly to your Xbox 360.

Setting up your PC

Windows Media Connect requires the right PC setup. Here's how to make sure you're ready.

Windows PC systems

Windows Media Connect requires a recent version of Windows XP with the right upgrades.

Windows XP

The basic requirement for Windows Media Connect is a Windows XP computer. (If you have a Windows XP computer, you see the Windows XP logo whenever you start your computer.)

If you bought your PC before October 2001, it didn't come with Windows XP.

If your Windows PC isn't running Windows XP, you have a couple of options:

- ✔ **Upgrade your existing PC to Windows XP.** You can buy the full upgrade in a boxed package, like other retail software.

  Before you open the upgrade box, make sure your PC meets the minimum requirements printed on the upgrade package.

- ✔ **Buy a PC with Windows XP installed.**

  If your PC is so old that it didn't come with Windows XP, you'll be amazed how cheaply you can buy a new, better PC with Windows XP (especially if you plan on reusing your existing monitor, keyboard, and mouse).

Service Pack 2

Microsoft regularly releases Windows updates for the latest computer and entertainment technology. These releases are called *Service Packs.* Windows Media Connect requires a Windows XP PC with Service Pack 2.

If you bought your PC before August 2004, it didn't come with Service Pack 2.

To check whether your Windows XP computer has Service Pack 2, follow these steps:

1. **Right-click your "My Computer" icon on the desktop of your PC.**

2. **Select "Properties."**

   The current version of Windows will be listed there, along with "Service Pack 2," if it's installed.

If your Windows XP PC doesn't have Service Pack 2, you can download the service pack and install it from `http://update.microsoft.com`.

Windows Media Connect

Windows Media Connect is a piece of software that allows devices on your network, such as the Xbox 360, to browse and access photos and music stored on your Windows XP PC. It's a requirement if you want to access any PC-based media from your Xbox 360.

You may need to install or configure Windows Media Connect on your PC.

Installation

Windows Media Connect may already be installed on your PC. Here's how to check for it (and install it if necessary):

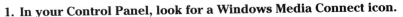
1. **In your Control Panel, look for a Windows Media Connect icon.**

   Look under the Sounds, Speech, and Audio devices category if you're using category view.

   If you see the Windows Media Connect icon, you can skip to the following section, "Configuration."

2. **If you don't see the Windows Media Connect icon, follow these steps to download and install the software onto your PC:**

   a. **Connect to** `www.xbox4dummies.com`.

   b. **Click the Downloads link.**

   c. **Click the Windows Media Connect link.**

   d. **If you're prompted to choose between saving and running the download, choose "Run."**

Configuration

When Windows Media Connect is installed, you need to configure it by specifying folders you want to make available to your Xbox 360.

Follow these steps to allow file sharing on your PC with Windows Media Connect:

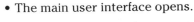

1. **In the PC's Control Panel, click the Windows Media Connect icon.**

   The icon's location depends on your Control Panel view:

   - In category view, the icon is under the Sounds, Speech, and Audio Devices category.

   - In classic view, the Windows Media Connect icon will appear in the full list along with all the other Control Panel icons.

   When you click the Windows Media Connect icon, either

   - The main user interface opens.

     If the main user interface opens, skip to Step 3.

   - The Windows Media Connect wizard starts.

     If the wizard opens, go to Step 2.

2. **If the Windows Media Connect wizard starts (see Figure 5-2), follow these steps to switch to the full interface:**

   a. **Don't select any of the listed devices on the "Select the devices . . ." page.**

   b. **Click Next.**

   c. **Select "Let Me Choose" from the listed options.**

   d. **Click Finish.**

This launches you into the full user interface (UI), shown in
Figure 5-3.

Figure 5-2:
The
Windows
Media
Connect
control
panel
launches
into a
wizard on
first use.

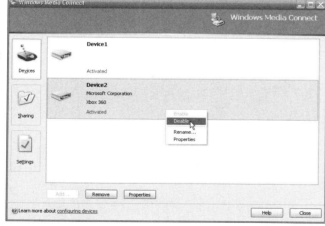

Figure 5-3:
The main
Windows
Media
Connect
UI can
configure
devices and
share
folders.

After you run the Windows Media Connect wizard once, the full user
interface appears whenever you select this control panel.

3. **In the Windows Media Connect window, select the Sharing button from the three options listed along the left side.**

4. **Select folders you want to share:**

   • By default, your My Pictures and My Music folders are shared.

   • If you want to share other folders, the sidebar "Sharing media
     folders," in this chapter, shows you how.

Sharing media folders

By default, the Windows Media Connect wizard shares My Pictures and My Music folders. If your media are stored in other folders, carefully pick other folders to share.

Follow these steps in the Windows Media Connect application's Sharing section for each folder:

1. **Click the Add button.**

   The Add dialog box (shown in this sidebar's accompanying figure) lets you name your folders for viewing on the Xbox 360 and specify access options.

2. **Identify a folder to share.**

3. **Select or deselect the Only Share This Content When I Am Logged In option.**

Make your decision based on the access you want other users to have. The Only Share . . . option restricts content sharing to when you're on the host PC. Normally, if you want to be able to access your music whenever you're using the Xbox 360, you leave this option unchecked.

4. **Choose "Make this content available to all devices" or "Make this content available only to the selected devices . . ."**

   Specify devices in the box below this option if you would like to restrict content sharing to only certain devices (such as your Xbox 360). If your Xbox 360 isn't listed, the "Connecting with Xbox 360" section in this chapter shows how to configure Windows Media Connect so it appears.

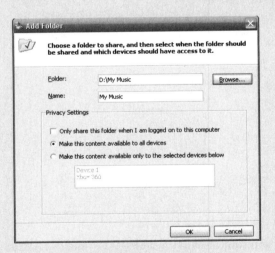

5. **If you want folder sharing to start automatically when the PC starts, check "Automatically start folder sharing . . ." in the Settings area of the Windows Media Connect application.**

   At this point, Windows Media Connect is ready to start sharing with any client devices, including your Xbox 360.

Connecting with Xbox 360

To use music and photos from your PC, your Xbox 360 needs to be connected and activated as a device for Windows Media Connect.

If Xbox 360 is listed in your PC's Devices tab and doesn't have red text below it, it's ready for Windows Media Connect. Skip to the section "Browsing and accessing media," later in this chapter.

Connecting the device

If the Xbox 360 isn't listed in the PC's Devices tab, follow these steps to connect:

1. **Connect your Xbox 360 on the same network as your PC.**

   Chapter 2 shows how to connect Xbox 360 to a home network.

   When you connect the Xbox 360 and it's powered up, a notification balloon on your PC tells you that a device is available.

   Don't click the balloon. If you click that balloon, you restart the Windows Media Connect wizard. You don't need to do that.

2. **Open the PC's Windows Media Connect control panel.**

   Your Xbox 360 should now be listed in the Devices tab.

   If your Xbox 360 doesn't appear in the Devices tab now, check www.xbox.com/pcsetup for support options.

Activating the device

If the Windows Media Connect device labeled Xbox 360 is marked *Activated,* you don't need to do anything else. You're ready to skip to the following section, "Browsing and accessing media," and start using music and photos from your PC with your Xbox 360.

If your Xbox 360 is marked *Deactivated* in the Devices tab, follow these steps to activate it:

1. **Right-click Xbox 360 in your devices list.**

2. **Select Enable to allow this device to connect to your PC.**

When Windows Media Connect is configured and your Xbox 360 is activated as a device, you're ready to start browsing music and photos with your Xbox 360.

Browsing and accessing media

After your Xbox 360 and your PC are all set up with Windows Media Connect, you can go to Xbox 360's Dashboard at any time to access your music and photos on your TV.

Playing music

To select from all of the music installed on your PC and play it through your Xbox 360, follow these steps:

1. **Open the Xbox 360 Dashboard.**

2. **Select the Media blade.**

3. **Select Music.**

   The Music page slides into view, as shown in Figure 5-4.

   The page's Computer option is the Windows Media Connect server — your PC — that the Xbox 360 detected and connected to.

4. **Select Computer.**

   If menu choices such as Artists and Albums appear at this point, then you're ready to go straight to Step 5.

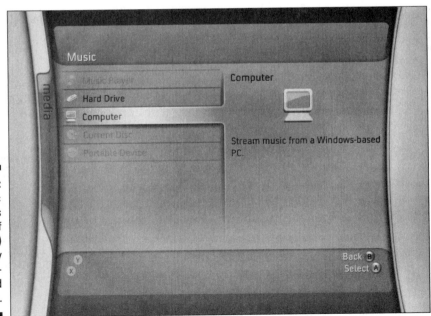

Figure 5-4:
The Music page lists a PC (if available) and any USB-connected devices.

The first time you choose Computer on the Music or Pictures blade, Xbox 360 guides you through the steps of setting up a connection with a PC running Windows Media Connect:

a. Confirm that you have Windows Media Connect installed on your computer.

b. Choose from the list of available PCs found on your local network.

There are two machines running Windows Media Connect in my house, so I see them both (see Figure 5-5).

After selecting a computer, if you are shown a "Can't connect" message, you need to enable the Xbox 360 device on your home PC. (The section "Connecting with Xbox 360," earlier in this chapter, shows you how.)

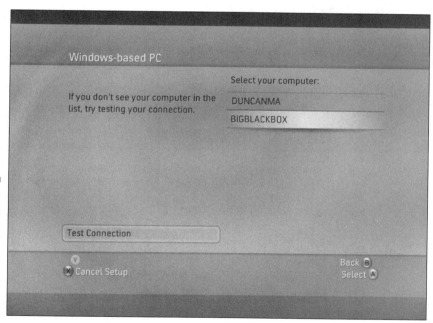

Figure 5-5:
More than
one
computer
can be
available
on your
network.

5. **Select an option (Albums, Artists, Genres, . . .) to browse your music collection.**

Xbox 360 arranges your content so you can browse music by such categories as album or artist. See Figure 5-6.

6. **Browse to an artist, album, or song.**

After you browse to an artist, album, or song (see Figure 5-7), you can start the music with one of the options listed on the bottom of the screen:

- **Y:** Plays an entire category.
- **A:** Shows a category's contents for choosing individual songs.

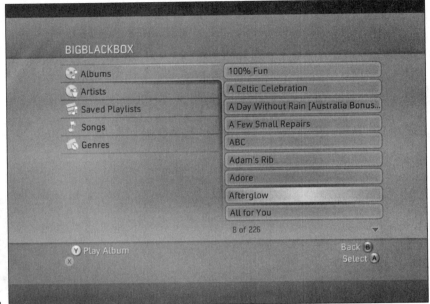

Figure 5-6:
Music files
are grouped
by artist,
album, and
genre.

When you're playing music, the "Music Player" view is shown (see Figure 5-8).

The music player view is pretty useful when you're just listening to music and even includes visualizations, but you don't have to stay on this view. You can use the rest of the Dashboard as you wish and the music will keep playing. Selecting Music and then Music Player from the menus on the Media blade can take you right back to this view whenever you wish.

Viewing pictures

If you shared at least one folder of images on your PC, you can use the Photos option on the Xbox 360's Media blade to view them right on your TV. Follow these steps:

1. **Open the Xbox 360 Dashboard.**

   To get to the Dashboard, you can either

   - Press the "Guide" button on any Xbox 360 controller or remote.
   - Remove the game disc or DVD from the Xbox 360.

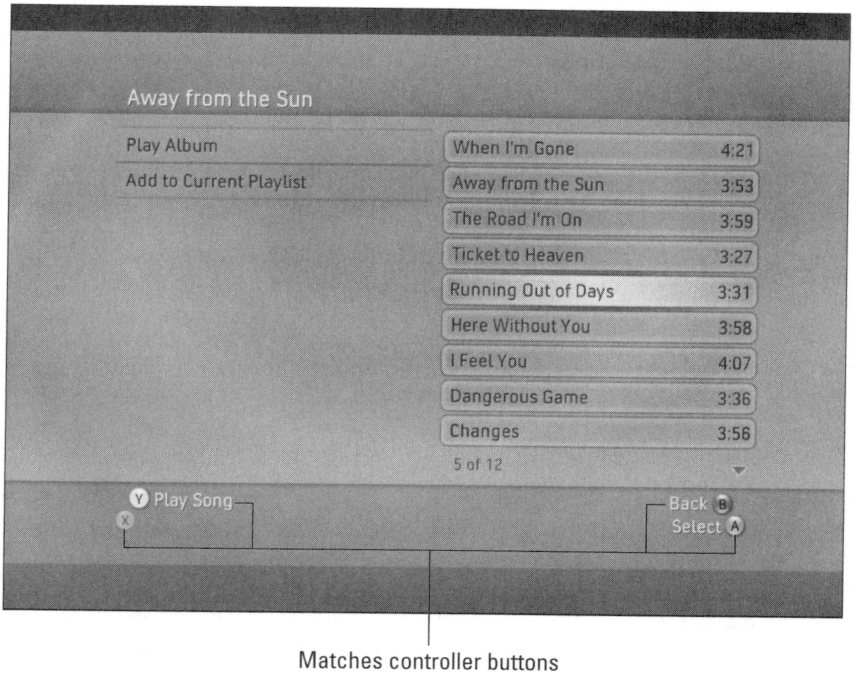

Figure 5-7: You can find and play your music by using the buttons on your controller or remote.

Matches controller buttons

Figure 5-8: The Music Player view shows you what is "Now Playing."

2. **Select the Media blade.**

3. **Select Pictures.**

   The first option on the page is Computer, representing your connected PC.

   Photos are displayed in a series of directories according to how they're stored on your PC. See Figure 5-9. All image directories end up being displayed in the top list of folders, regardless of how they were nested on your PC. For example, if you have two folders full of photos that are both named "Family" but one is under `C:\CurrentPics\Family` and the other is at `C:\OldPics\Family`, you end up with two folders listed on your Xbox 360: `Family` and `Family 1`. This can be confusing at first, depending on how your photos are set up on your PC, but it makes all your photos available within one click on the Xbox 360.

4. **Select a folder to view its images.**

Figure 5-9: Browse photos on a connected computer.

Troubleshooting

Can't get your PC and Xbox 360 connected? Check whether your Xbox 360 is listed in the Windows Media Connect control panel, under the Devices tab. The following problems are the most common.

Deactivated

Confirm that your Xbox shows up in the Windows Media Connect control panel under the Devices tab.

If your Xbox 360 is marked *Deactivated,* follow these steps in the Windows Media Connect control panel to make it active:

1. **Right-click the Xbox 360 item.**
2. **Select Enable to make your Xbox 360 active.**

Unlisted

If your Xbox doesn't appear in the Windows Media Connect control panel under the Devices tab, then you likely have a network issue.

Connection

Check your physical network connection between the two devices.

See Chapter 2 for more information on network configuration.

Firewall

A firewall can prevent connections between Xbox 360 and your PC. You have a couple of options to fix this problem:

- ✔ If you're using the Windows XP SP2 firewall, check `www.xbox4 dummies.com/windowsmediaconnect` for a link to directions about setting up your Windows XP SP2 firewall so it allows two devices to connect.

- ✔ If you're using other firewall software, check the documentation that comes with your firewall for the steps to allow traffic through a specific port.

 Table 5-1 lists network ports that Windows Media Connect uses to

  • Discover compatible devices.

  • Communicate over the network.

Table 5-1	Ports Used by Windows Media Connect
Protocol	*Port*
TCP	10243
UDP	10280
UPnP UDP	1900

If this information isn't enough to get you up and running, check out the Support options at www.xbox4dummies.com/windowsmediaconnect.

USB Media Devices

USB ports let you connect many devices and access content, such as photos and music files.

The Xbox 360 has three standard USB ports:

- ✔ Front (2)

  Use the front USB ports for connecting wired controllers, cameras, and music players so they are very accessible.

- ✔ Back (1)

  Use the rear USB port to connect the optional wireless network adapter, if you have one; otherwise you can use it just like one of the front ports.

USB devices that Windows XP recognizes as mass storage and removable storage should work with the Xbox 360. Most USB-connectable cameras and music players do provide this recognition. But you aren't limited to just cameras and music devices; anything that shows up as a drive in Windows XP without installing its own software should work. Some examples of devices that you can connect are

- ✔ Memory Card readers, such as
  - CompactFlash
  - Secure Digital (SD)
  - Memory Sticks
- ✔ Digital cameras
- ✔ USB keydrives (portable storage devices, often small enough to fit on a keychain)
- ✔ Music players, such as the Rio Carbon, Creative Zen, and Apple iPod
- ✔ A Sony PSP

After you've connected a device, follow these steps to access any media that it contains:

1. **Go to the Media blade.**

2. **Select Pictures or Music, depending on the content stored on the device.**

An entry for your connected device appears on the appropriate page, as shown in Figure 5-10.

Depending on your device, the corresponding menu item label might be either

- Generic (like "Digital Camera")
- Specific (like "Canon PowerShot SD400")
- Personalized (like "Duncan's iPod")

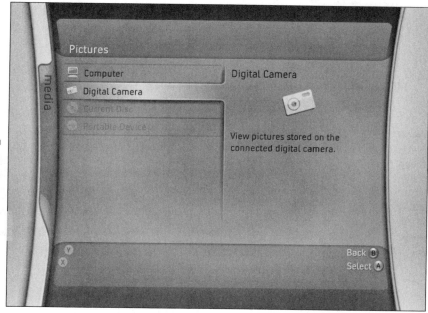

Figure 5-10: Devices show up under Pictures or Music based on the content they contain.

After you select the item, your browsing experience is essentially the same as

- ✔ Music/photos from a PC on your network
- ✔ Music/photos/videos on the Xbox 360's hard drive

Files with playback restrictions, including those purchased from an online site such as Napster, will show up as blocked (note the songs with the No icons next to them in Figure 5-11).

Your connection to these USB-connected devices is *read-only:*

- ✔ You can view or listen.
- ✔ You *can't* add, delete, or change content.

TIP

Turn off or disconnect your devices when you're done working with them. Some digital cameras and music players won't go into standby while they're connected to a USB port. That could lead to dead batteries if you leave them connected to your Xbox 360 overnight.

Figure 5-11:
Browsing the music available on a connected device.

Viewing photos

Regardless of the source (digital camera, your PC, or right off the Xbox 360's hard drive), the experience of browsing and using your photos has some common elements.

Slideshow

Whenever you view a folder of images, you have the option to start a slideshow, which play through all the images, fading from picture to picture.

When a slideshow is running, or when you're viewing a single picture, if you press the Directional pad on your controller or the remote, you get a small taskbar of options. These options, shown in Figure 5-12, include the ability to

✔ Move backward and forward through the current folder

✔ Turn shuffle on and off

✔ Rotate images (either counterclockwise or clockwise)

Figure 5-12:
The photo
taskbar lets
you move
through
your
images.

Toggle Repeat On

Set as background

When viewing the directory view of images, where they are all displayed as *thumbnails* (small preview images shown in a grid), you can select any photo to be the background of your Xbox 360's Dashboard by using the X button on your remote or controller. Your chosen image will appear behind all of the Dashboard blades, like the image shown in Figure 5-13.

To remove your custom image, either

- ✔ Select a different photo from the Photos option on the Media blade.
- ✔ Follow these steps to choose a different theme:

    1. Press the "Xbox Guide" button on your remote.

    2. Select Personal Settings.

    3. Select Themes.

    4. Choose the theme you want.

    If you don't know what theme you were using before, then you were probably using the Xbox 360 default settings (shown in the list with the word *Default* next to it).

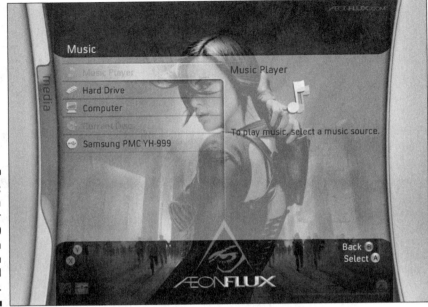

Figure 5-13:
You can
make your
Xbox 360
distinct with
a custom
background
image.

Ripping music from CDs

If you want to put some music right onto the hard drive of your Xbox 360, you can *rip* (copy the music from) one of your CDs:

1. **Insert a music CD.**

   The Music Player page appears.

2. **Select Rip CD.**

3. **Select the tracks you want to extract from the disc.**

   Ripping proceeds over the next few minutes; see Figure 5-14 for a look at the nice animated graphic that appears while your Xbox 360 rips the music. Good thing it's there because you can't really do much else with the Xbox until this process completes.

    Don't use any other Xbox 360 features while ripping is in progress. If you do, ripping is canceled.

If an Internet connection is available, the Xbox 360 uses it to gather artist, album, and song information, much like Windows Media Player does if you rip a CD onto your computer.

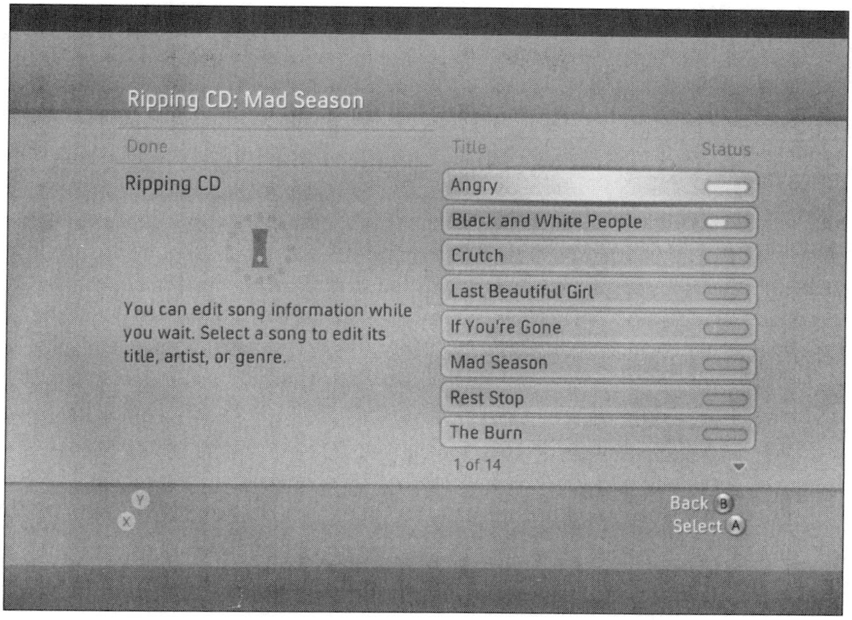

Ripping CD: Mad Season

Done	Title	Status
Ripping CD	Angry	
	Black and White People	
	Crutch	
You can edit song information while you wait. Select a song to edit its title, artist, or genre.	Last Beautiful Girl	
	If You're Gone	
	Mad Season	
	Rest Stop	
	The Burn	
	1 of 14	

Back **B**
Select **A**

Figure 5-14:
A nice animated graphic appears while your CD rips.

Media integration in the Guide

When you bring up the Guide by pressing the center Xbox button on your controller during a game, you can access a very limited form of the Music section of the Media blade by selecting "Select Music" below the small music control taskbar. Figure 5-15 shows the result.

This lets you pick a music source, even from an attached device like an iPod, and play it while you go back to your game. The UI is a limited form of the standard Media blade, but it does allow you to access music on

✔ The Xbox 360's hard drive

✔ Attached devices

✔ Your Windows XP PC

After you have your music selected and playing, you can use the music taskbar to

✔ Move to the next song.

✔ Pause the music.

✔ Toggle the shuffle setting.

✔ Adjust the music playback volume.

For more information

Check out our Web site at `www.xbox4` `dummies.com` for

✔ Additional information and links to even more information about Xbox 360 media features

✔ Links to portable devices that work well with the Xbox 360

✔ Links to the downloads necessary to get Windows Media Connect working on your network

---

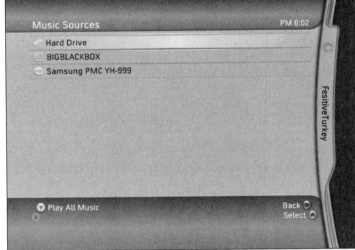

Figure 5-15:
From this blade, press A to pick and play music.

Videos

Xbox 360's Media blade exposes a Videos page. From here, you can browse through and select any of the videos currently stored on the Xbox 360's hard drive:

✔ Enjoy the preinstalled videos.

✔ View videos you get from Xbox Live's marketplace:

• Free trailers for games and movies

• Movies you buy with either online points (detailed in Chapter 4) or cold, hard cash

You can access any video on your console through the Media blade's Videos option.

Chapter 6

The System Blade

*T*he System blade tells Xbox 360 about your other equipment, such as your TV. In this chapter, we tell you about some of the blade's most important settings and how to set and change them properly.

Some of the settings in this chapter are discussed in more detail in other chapters in the book, and we point that out when it applies.

Setting Up with the System Blade

After your Xbox 360 is set up, you probably won't spend a lot of time on the System blade. You do spend some quality time there as you enter the console's video resolution, audio, networking, and family settings.

You can see the System blade in Figure 6-1.

The System blade provides links to six subpages:

✔ Console settings

✔ Family settings

✔ Memory

✔ Network settings

✔ Computers

✔ Initial setup

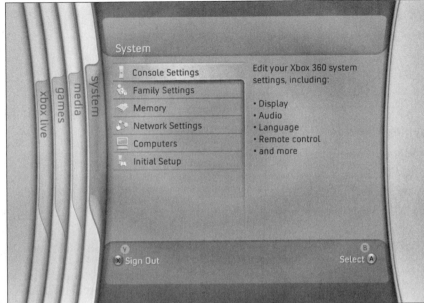

Figure 6-1:
The System
blade is
your control
center.

Console Settings

The System blade console settings are straightforward. Figure 6-2 shows the Console Settings page. All items open subpages, where you can change the settings.

Display

The Display page lets you choose your video settings.

The choices you have in setup for the display depend on your video cable:

- ✔ If you have the Component HDAV cable installed, and you have an HDTV, you can set the video resolution on the console.

- ✔ If you are using the composite cable, you should be able to plug in and go, but you won't be able to use any of the high definition features of your television.

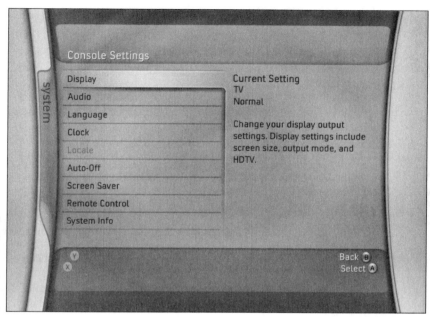

Figure 6-2:
The Console
Settings
page of your
Xbox 360.

Component HDAV cable

If you use the *Component HDAV* cable (which comes with the loaded Xbox 360 System), you have some choices to make.

If you have an HDTV, the highest possible setting is usually either 720p or 1080i. You can set the display to 480p or 576p (depending on your country) in high definition, but we recommend doing that only if either

- ✔ Your *HDTV* doesn't produce a good picture at higher resolutions.
- ✔ You have an *EDTV* that isn't compatible with 720p or 1080i component video.

The loaded Xbox 360 System comes with a video cable with both composite video output and component output plugs. A switch at the base of this cable lets you toggle the video output between

- ✔ **HDTV** (for component video)

  If you have an EDTV with component video inputs, connect the component video and use the "HDTV" switch position. This chapter shows how to set up your EDTV with component video.

TV (for composite output)

 If your TV doesn't have component video, the section, "Testing with composite video," later in this chapter, shows how to connect the yellow composite video plug.

Component video settings

If you're using the HDAV cable with component video, follow these steps to set or change the display:

1. **Bring up the Xbox 360 Dashboard.**

 Press the Guide button on the controller if you're playing a game. Then press the Y button.

2. **Use the direction pad to scroll to the System blade.**

 The top selection on the menu is Console settings, and is selected by default.

3. **Click A to access a page of submenus.**

 The top option in the list is the Display menu and is highlighted by default.

4. **Press the A button to access the Display settings option menu.**

 The Display menu appears with two options: *HDTV settings* and *Screen format.*

5. **If you're using component video, press A to see the HDTV settings.**

 Use HDTV settings for component video, even if your TV is an *EDTV.*

6. **Select the best component video resolution for your TV and then press A.**

 Depending on your country, you may have the option of choosing *480p, 576p, 720p,* or *1080i:*

 • If you have an HDTV or HDTV-ready TV, try the *720p* option first.

 The native resolution for games on the Xbox 360 is 720p. If your television supports 720p resolution, this setting gives you the best visuals and performance for Xbox 360 games.

 • If you have an EDTV, first try *480p* (in the United States and Canada) or *576p* (in PAL-system countries, such as the United Kingdom).

 When you press A, the resolution is set to your selection.

 When you change resolution settings (if you switch between 720p and 1080i, for example) you see a confirmation prompt asking whether you want to keep the setting or return to your previous setting.

7. **Respond according to whether you see a confirmation prompt:**

   • If you can read the prompt, follow the instructions on screen to confirm the resolution.

   If you don't press A within 10 seconds to accept the new setting, the Xbox 360 automatically reverts to the previous resolution.

   • If you can't see a prompt, your TV may not accept the resolution you chose. Just wait 10 seconds; the Xbox 360 automatically reverts to the previous resolution.

   If your TV doesn't accept the selected resolution, try Step 6 again at a different resolution.

8. **After the HDTV setting is set, press the B button.**

   Xbox 360 returns to the Display menu.

9. **Select the Screen format option:**

   • Select the Widescreen option if you have a widescreen TV (16:9).

   • Select the Normal TV option if you have a traditional TV screen shape (4:3).

If you can't get a picture with the composite/component cable, set the switch at the cable base to TV to turn on composite output and use the yellow composite video connection. (You might want to do this if you use your Xbox 360 away from your home system.)

For more information about changing TV displays, check Chapter 8.

Testing with composite video

If you can't get a picture with component video, follow these steps to get your Xbox 360 console up to speed with composite video and the HDAV cable:

1. **Switch your HDAV cable to TV (composite video).**

2. **Use the yellow composite plug to connect your Xbox 360.**

3. **Use the composite video picture to start testing other settings.**

Composite cable

You don't need to change any Xbox 360 console display settings if you have only the composite cable installed (the standard cable for the Xbox 360 Core System). In this case, the picture will be set to the standard resolution for a television in your country:

✔ 480i in the United States and Canada

✔ 576i for PAL countries (such as the United Kingdom)

Audio

Here you can choose between analog and digital output. In general, you will use analog output unless you purchased a digital audio cable separately.

For information about setting the audio options on your Xbox 360, see Chapter 9.

Language

The Language page lets you choose the language that your Xbox 360 Dashboard uses. This setting can make it easier to navigate and use the Xbox 360 Dashboard if your preferred language is different than your console's default language.

Depending on where you live, you may be able to choose from these languages for your Xbox 360 console:

Chinese	German	Korean
English	Italian	Portuguese
French	Japanese	Spanish

This language selection affects only the default language in the Xbox 360 Dashboard. This setting will not affect the languages in your favorite games. You have to select language options for the games within the menus for the games themselves.

Changing the Language setting is easy. Follow these steps:

1. **Access the System blade, highlight Console Settings, and then press A.**

2. **Use the direction pad to highlight the Language page (see Figure 6-3) and then press A.**

3. **Navigate to the language of your choice (by using the left analog stick or direction pad).**

4. **Press A.**

The language setting doesn't change the *region code* for the games or DVDs that you play. Your Xbox 360 is designed to play only games and DVDs for the region where it's sold. You can find out more about regions in Chapter 5.

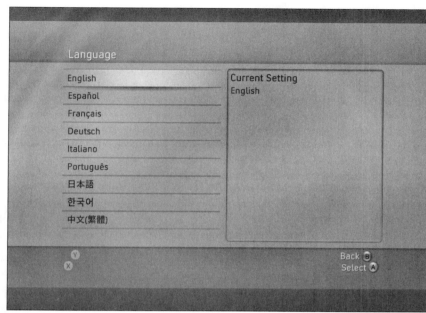

Clock

The clock settings are fairly straightforward. They're accessed from the Console settings page at the System blade.

Date and Time

At the Clock menu, highlight Date and Time and then press A. The Date and Time option accepts your settings for

- ✔ Current calendar date and year (for example, 11/22/2005)
- ✔ Local time

The date and time are used in time stamps of saved games, so you can see when exactly you made that save game.

Time Format

Time Format switches the Xbox 360 console's time display between

- ✔ 12-hour time display (AM/PM)

  This is the usual display in the United States.

✔ 24-hour time display

In the United States, you may hear 24-hour time called military time.

Time Zone

Time Zone tells your Xbox 360 console your local time zone. Your time zone depends on where you live.

If you and your Xbox 360 travel together, change the *time zone* when necessary, not the actual time setting. This setting automatically corrects the clock *hour* without changing the *minutes* setting.

The common time zones for the *United States* and *Canada* are

✔ Eastern (New York, Montreal)

✔ Central (Chicago, Winnipeg)

✔ Mountain (Denver, Edmonton)

✔ Pacific (Los Angeles, Vancouver)

Daylight Savings

Daylight Savings Time is a government policy that adjusts local time to allow an extra hour of daylight in summer afternoons.

In Xbox 360, Daylight Savings should be turned on if your location participates in daylight savings time. Your Xbox 360 console will automatically adjust the time when your community changes its time.

Locale

Locale lets you set the location where you're playing games from a list of 27 countries.

This setting doesn't change the region code, which is explained earlier in this chapter's "Language" section. You can't change the Locale to use Region 1 games on a Region 2 console, for example.

The Locale setting is mostly used with Xbox Live for such details as

✔ The currency displayed on Xbox Live marketplace

✔ Wireless networking protocols in different countries

Auto-off

If you enable the Auto-Off feature, your Xbox 360 turns off after 6 hours of inactivity.

You can keep your console running all day, but turning off the console when you're not using it saves power. And who doesn't want all the power you can get?

Screen saver

The screen saver automatically dims the Dashboard after 10 minutes of no input from you.

Enabling the Screen Saver option can help protect your TV if it's prone to *burn-in* when the same bright picture is left on-screen for a long time. You can find out more about this TV problem in Chapter 8.

Remote control

The Remote Control page lets you toggle between two options:

- ✔ Xbox 360 Media Remote
- ✔ All Channels

Xbox 360 Universal Media Remote

The Xbox 360 option sets the Xbox 360 console to ignore all remotes but the Xbox 360 Universal Media Remote control.

If you have a Windows Media Center PC, use the Xbox 360 Media Remote option if *both* of these are true:

- ✔ Your Windows Media Center PC is in the same room as your Xbox 360 console.
- ✔ You want to control the PC *separately* from your Xbox 360 console.

All Channels

On the Remote Control page, the All Channels option sets the Xbox 360 console to work with *either* of these remote controls:

- ✔ Windows Media Center PC remote control
- ✔ Xbox 360 Universal Media Remote control

Setting the All Channels option lets you use the Windows Media Center PC remote as your primary controller for multimedia content on your Xbox 360 (such as recorded TV shows and music).

System info

The System Info page contains important data about your Xbox 360 console.

You can't *change* the settings on the System Info page. The information displayed here relates to the version numbers of system software updates and the console ID.

Two numbers appear at the top of the System Info page:

- ✔ **Console serial number.** You need this serial number if you either

  - • Talk to technical support
  - • Fill out the details on the registration card that comes in the Xbox 360 box to register your Xbox 360

- ✔ **Console ID number.** This number is sent to the server when you log on to Xbox Live.

Write down your serial number and console ID and keep them in a safe place. If somebody logs on to Xbox Live after your system is lost or stolen, the police may be able to track the console down for you.

Family Settings

The family settings are where you can control access to content played through the Xbox 360.

We describe in detail how to set up parental controls in Chapter 11.

Console Controls limits the playable content by requiring a code, which you type using the controller.

Restricting games

Setting a pass code for playing games on your Xbox 360 console that have a rating that you deem inappropriate is easy:

1. **Navigate to the System blade by using the left analog stick on the controller.**

   The System blade opens and lists the display items.

2. **Highlight Family Settings and press A.**

3. **Choose Console Controls and press A.**

   If you already have a pass code set, you will need to enter it again to access the Console Controls menu.

   The Console Controls menu appears.

4. **On the Console Control menu, select Game ratings.**

   Now you can choose the game ratings you will allow to be played on this Xbox 360. (Chapter 11 covers game rating systems in greater detail.)

   Every Xbox 360 game includes a *content descriptor* along with the rating. This descriptor illustrates specific content — such as violence, strong language, and suggestive themes — that is found in that specific game.

5. **Select an option in the Game Ratings menu and press B.**

Chapter 11 provides details on game ratings. (If you select All Games, any game put in the Xbox 360 will run.)

When you press B to exit the Game Ratings menu, the Set Pass Code menu option appears automatically.

If you don't want to set a new pass code, scroll down to the Done option. If you have changed a setting, you will be prompted to accept the new changes. Select Yes to save the new settings.

6. **If you want to set or change the pass code, scroll down to the Set Pass Code menu option and press A, then press a sequence of *four controller buttons* to be your pass code.**

   This code is a four-button combination that you select by using the direction pad, left and right triggers, left and right shoulder buttons, the X button, and the Y button. For example, you could set a code by pressing *left Directional pad, right Directional pad, up Directional pad, down Directional pad.*

   You will be asked to *repeat* your pass code to make sure it's what you want.

Make sure you write down and save your pass code. If you forget the code, you have to contact technical support to reset the console. You can find contact information for support at www.xbox.com/support.

The Console Controls page options include

- ✔ Game ratings
- ✔ DVD movie ratings
- ✔ Access to Xbox Live
- ✔ Xbox Live membership creation

✔ Original Xbox games

The appendix at the end of this book shows how to play your old favorites with Xbox 360.

✔ Set pass code

You can't set a pass code *before* you set at least one of your own *Game Ratings, DVD Ratings,* or *Access to Xbox Live* restrictions.

Memory

The Memory page lets you access the storage devices connected to your Xbox 360. When you choose the Memory option and press A, you're presented with a list of memory storage devices attached to your Xbox 360. The All Devices option lets you look at all the content stored on a memory device plugged into your Xbox 360.

If you're looking for an item, such as a music track or saved game file, and don't remember where it is, use the All Devices option.

Original Xbox games require a hard drive with Xbox 360. Those games were created with the expectation that a hard drive would be available. (All original Xbox consoles have a built-in hard drive.) You can't copy content from a non-memory device — such as a USB flash drive — onto an Xbox 360 memory device. Devices attached to your Xbox 360 are read-only.

Memory units

Memory units can store

❘ ✔ Saved games

❘ ✔ Profiles — including your Gamer profile and Xbox Live profile

Hard drives

Hard drives hold

❘ ✔ Content downloaded from Xbox Live

❘ ✔ Music copied from CDs that you own

❘ ✔ Game saves

The hard drive isn't included with the Core System, but it is included with the loaded Xbox 360 System package.

Managing memory

For the most part, memory use is pretty transparent.

If you have a hard drive or a memory unit, profiles and game files are saved there automatically.

The only difference is that you may run out of space on a memory unit and need to swap cards to play different games. The memory unit available at launch holds 64MB of data — enough to hold your profiles and several game saves (sizes of these files vary with each game, and also with how far you have progressed through that game) — compared to the hard drive, which has nearly 20GB of available space.

Copying saved games

One of the common memory tasks that you might need to perform is to copy a saved game from a memory unit to a hard drive. Follow these steps:

1. **Attach the hard drive to the Xbox 360.**

   Chapter 1 gives instructions for attaching a hard drive.

2. **Insert your memory unit into a slot in the front of your console.**

3. **From the Dashboard, use the direction pad to navigate to the System blade and then press A.**

4. **Highlight Memory and press A.**

   The Storage Devices page opens.

5. **Choose the memory unit you inserted in Step 2 and press A.**

6. **Choose Games from the Memory Unit page and press A.**

7. **Select the profile associated with the saved game.**

8. **Choose the game save you want to copy and then press A.**

9. **Choose the target you wish to copy your game to.**

   Your game is copied to the target you choose.

The hard drive options lists a Music setting. This option's only purpose is to delete the music from the drive. Be careful, or you might have to re-rip your CDs!

Managing devices

On the Storage Devices page, pressing the Y button brings up the Storage Options screen. This screen lets you

✔ **Rename the selected storage device.**

Renaming is a great way to keep the memory units straight if you have more than two.

✔ **Format the selected storage device.**

Formatting wipes a storage device clean. You can't get the content on that storage device after it's gone.

You can get most of your Xbox Live content back when you re-create your profile and log on.

Network Settings

The Network Settings options, which are covered in Chapter 3, can help if you experience connection difficulties when trying to access Xbox Live, if you're creating a network of linked Xbox 360 consoles, or if you want to connect to the network in a temporary location.

You must have an Internet broadband connection to connect your Xbox 360 to Xbox Live. These connections come in many forms, but a high-speed connection is usually through a digital subscriber line (DSL) or TV cable system connected to your phone or cable. (In either case, you need to order services from your phone company or cable provider.) The modem is normally connected to one of the following: your PC, a network router, a wireless router, or even directly to your Xbox 360. Any one of these connections might require specific settings that you access through the System blade's Network Settings page.

You can see the Network Settings page in Figure 6-4. Take a look at each of these options in case you need to test or tweak your setup.

Test Xbox Live Connection

This option's name tells you all about it: Selecting Test Xbox Live Connection and pressing A on the Xbox 360 controller opens the Test Xbox Live Connection page shown in Figure 6-5.

When you open the page, tests start running automatically. As they run, the results appear on the page. The More Info option next to each test gives you details. If you get an error for any of the network issues listed, you can use the More Information option to retrieve troubleshooting help.

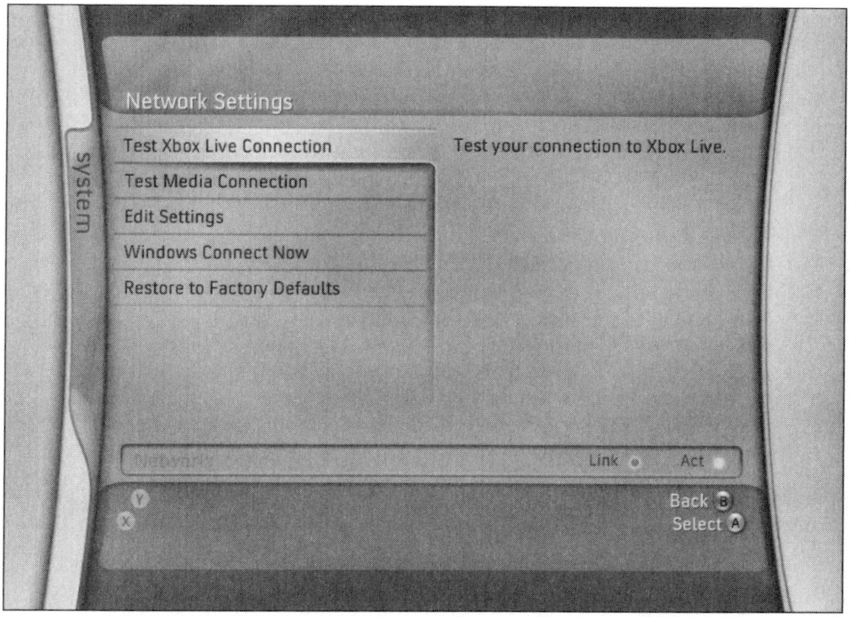

Figure 6-4:
The Network Settings page offers test options for your network.

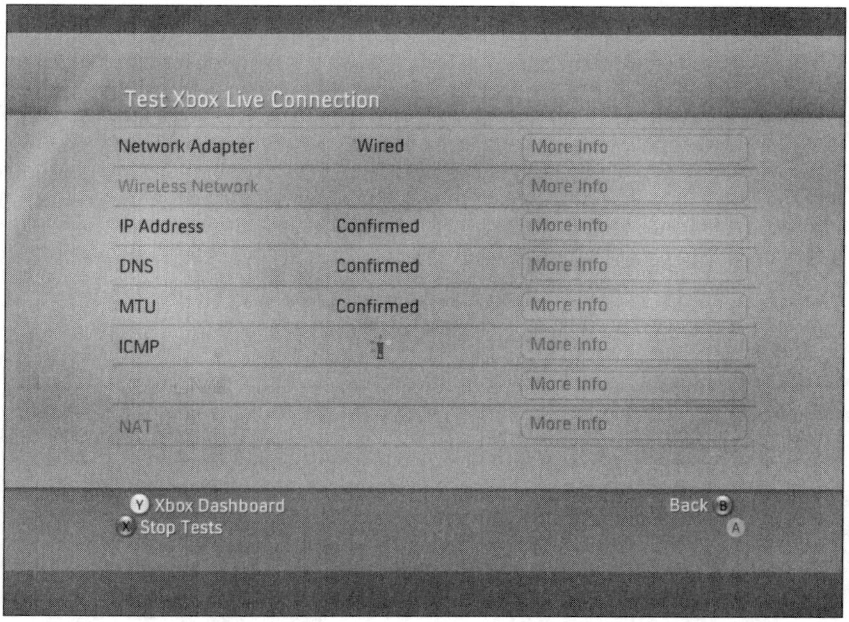

Figure 6-5:
Tests being run for Xbox Live on the Xbox 360.

Test Media Center Connection

The Test Media Center Connection option works the same way the Test Xbox Live option does, but offers fewer tests. The Media Center tests run only against your local area network — not the Internet.

Xbox Live requires a high-speed Internet connection, but using your Xbox 360 with the Media Center PC does not. If you have a home network, you can connect to your Media Center PC from your Xbox 360.

Edit Settings

The Edit Settings page provides access to all the possible Xbox 360 network settings. You can see the Network Settings page in Figure 6-6.

Tweak this option if either

- ✔ You're having trouble with the console's default settings
- ✔ Your Internet service provider requires information to connect to your modem

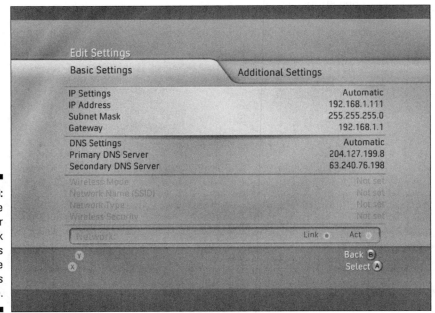

Figure 6-6:
Change your network settings through the Edit Settings page.

Network connections as easy as 1-2-3

Windows Connect Now is a brilliant Windows XP feature for network setup. It basically works like this:

1. You configure a computer for network access on your wireless home network.

   This usually includes adding security in the form of a wireless encryption key.

2. The network settings transfer to a *USB flash drive* for use on your Xbox 360 (or other computers on your network).

3. The rest of the network machines are configured by inserting the flash drive into their USB ports.

If your Xbox 360 network settings are giving you trouble, check out w w w . xbox.com/connect. This page has troubleshooting information for routers, wireless networks, and even the high-speed Internet service providers that are supported by Xbox Live.

Windows Connect Now

Xbox 360 supports *Windows Connect Now*, so you can use a USB flash drive to configure your Xbox 360 for networking.

Creating a Windows Connect Now flash drive

A Windows Connect Now flash drive can transfer a Windows XP PC's network settings to any other USB devices that can be networked (including your Xbox 360 console).

Windows Connect Now requires a correctly configured Windows XP computer on your network. This might involve entering information such as a wireless encryption key so your computers can talk to each other.

Follow these steps to create a Windows Connect Now flash drive from a networked Windows XP PC:

1. **Insert a USB flash drive into the Windows XP PC.**

   If you *lose* this USB flash drive after you have formatted it as a Windows Connect Now device, anyone who finds it may be able to get security access to your home network.

2. **On the computer, choose Start➪Control Panel.**

3. **Start the Wireless Network Setup Wizard.**

   • If you're in Windows XP view, choose Network➪Internet Connections➪Wireless Network Setup Wizard.

   • If you're in classic Control Panel view, double-click Wireless Network Setup Wizard.

4. **Follow the wizard's prompts to copy your networking settings to your USB flash drive.**

   When you finish the Wireless Network Setup Wizard, you're ready to set up your Xbox 360 for networking with Windows Connect Now. The following section shows you how.

Configuring an Xbox 360 console

With a Windows Connect Now flash drive from a wirelessly networked Windows XP PC (as created in the preceding section), you can quickly set up your Xbox 360 console for networking. Follow these steps:

1. **On the Xbox 360, navigate to the System blade by using the left analog stick.**

2. **Open the Windows Connect Now page on the Xbox 360 from the Network Settings page.**

3. **Insert the USB flash drive into your Xbox 360.**

   Your wireless network settings are picked up and applied automatically. Your Xbox 360 wireless connection is set up and ready to go.

Restore to factory defaults

There are a few reasons to restore your networking settings to the factory defaults:

  ✔ You got a new router for your network.

   Sometimes resetting the network and letting the Xbox 360 determine the new settings is easier than fiddling with the various settings yourself.

  ✔ You are troubleshooting a networking issue and want to start with a clean slate.

  ✔ You need to clean an Xbox 360 console that someone has brought over.

   Use a USB flash drive to set up the console; then run the reset when the guest leaves.

Selecting the Restore Factory Defaults option does just what it says, so use it carefully. It eliminates network information such as your

 ✓ Wireless network encryption protocol

 ✓ Specific network configuration

If you reset your wireless connection, you must either reenter your WEP key or reinsert your USB flash drive via the Windows Connect Now steps described in the previous section.

Computers

The Computers setting lists your possible connections to Windows PCs (including Windows Media Center PCs). These connections are made through Windows Media Connect.

Chapter 13 shows you how to connect your Xbox 360 to a Windows Media Center PC, and Chapter 5 talks about connecting to other Windows PCs.

Listing connected PCs

To see a list of connected computers, follow these steps:

1. **Access the System blade and then scroll down the menu list.**

2. **Select Computers and press A.**

    The listed computers are Windows PCs that your Xbox 360 has connected to through your home network.

    This also is part of the process of *disconnecting* a PC from your Xbox 360 console. The following section shows all the steps to disconnect a PC.

Disconnecting PCs

To disconnect a Windows PC from your Xbox 360 console, follow these steps:

1. **Access the System blade and scroll down the menu list.**

2. **Select Computers and press A.**

    The listed computers are Windows PCs that your Xbox 360 has connected to through your home network.

3. **Select a listed Windows PC and press A.**

    The PC disconnects from your Xbox 360 console.

Resetting your console

Because storage on the Xbox 360 is optional, clearing it is as simple as removing or formatting the hard drive (formatting is described in this chapter). To secure your own settings, privacy, game files, and content, you should format your hard drive if you ever want to sell either your hard drive or your Xbox 360 console with the hard drive attached.

Initial Setup

The Initial Setup option starts the Xbox 360 setup sequence; Chapter 3 describes the sequence in detail. Selecting Initial Setup and then pressing A

- ✔ Starts creating a new gamer profile
- ✔ Sets the Xbox 360 console's locale

You can run the Initial Setup program any time you need to start over from scratch with your settings. Existing profiles aren't harmed.

Chapter 7

The Games Blade

*T*he Games blade is like your personal trophy room. In it you can view past glory, play games on Xbox Live Arcade, enjoy game demos, and watch trailers. In this chapter, we take you through the different parts of the Games blade and show you how to read the information it contains.

Features in this chapter require an Xbox 360 hard drive or an optional memory unit. (The loaded Xbox 360 System included a hard drive.) Chapter 18 covers memory devices.

Saying Hi to the Games Blade

You can see the Games blade in Figure 7-1. The tabs open pages for

- **Achievements:** Show which games you've finished and the awards you've earned in each game

- **Played games:** Games you've started but maybe haven't gained any awards in

- **Xbox Live Arcade:** Lets you launch the games you've purchased on Xbox Live Marketplace

- **Demos:** Usually samples that give a taste of game play

- **Trailers:** Reveal a bit of a game's plot and let you see what the game looks like

The difference between a trailer and a demo is that the trailer lets you sample the game by watching it, while a demo lets you play it.

Figure 7-1:
The Games blade lets you track started games and achievements.

The following sections take you through each page.

The Games blade features a DVD tray button at the bottom of the list. The tray button is important because you'll use this to restart your game if you decide to get out of the game without removing the disk. For example, pressing the Guide button in the middle of the Xbox controller brings up the Guide, which can get you out of any game or demo. Press Y to switch to the Xbox Dashboard. (Chapter 3 details that part of your console.)

After you leave a game with a game disc in the tray, the words "Play Game" appear on the tray button on the Games blade. (You see this option on every blade in the Dashboard when you press the power button.)

Follow these steps to start, from the Dashboard, a game already in the tray:

1. **Highlight that tray button by pressing up and down on the left analog stick.**

2. **Press A.**

What's great about getting back to the Dashboard without taking out the game? You can do all sorts of cool stuff — watch media files, play arcade games, control your Media Center PC — and switch right back to your favorite game without having to reload the tray!

Save before you cut out of a game to get to the Dashboard or you'll most likely lose your place when you restart.

Listing Your Achievements

The Xbox 360 is all about games, and the Achievements page shows off what you've done. What's an achievement?

- ✔ Finishing a game
- ✔ Getting a high score
- ✔ Beating a game at an extremely hard level

The Achievements page

When you're logged in to your profile, your most important achievements on the Xbox 360 are immortalized on your Achievements page.

You can find out more about profiles in Chapter 3.

Showing off your achievements

If you're an Xbox Live member, all those hard-earned points and awards appear on your Gamer Card, which we tell you about in Chapter 4. Friends and foes alike can see what you're made of.

If your profile's on a memory card, you can access achievements two ways:

- ✔ Directly from the memory card
- ✔ Through Automatic Xbox Live update (if your friend has an Xbox Live connection and membership)

If you don't want a game showing up in your public achievements page, just create a local profile, as described in Chapter 3, and play the game with that profile.

Reviewing Played Games

The Played Games page, shown in Figure 7-2, tracks the saves, downloads, and achievements you've made.

Figure 7-2:
The Played Games page tracks your progress.

The Played Games page lets you see instantly

✔ Games you've been playing

✔ Games you've finished

Don't be surprised if this information spurs an occasional, "Oh yeah, I loved playing that before I started work on my day job. I should finish it," or "Somebody just beat my fastest lap time in *Project Gotham Racing 3,* I need to get back behind the wheel and show them what I'm made of."

Game Summary page

You can select games from the Played Games page and get more details; the Game Summary page is shown in Figure 7-3.

The Game Summary page shows possible achievements for the games you've been playing. Follow these steps to see it:

1. **Navigate to the Games blade using the left analog stick.**

   The Games blade appears.

2. **Use the left analog stick to highlight Played Games, then press A.**

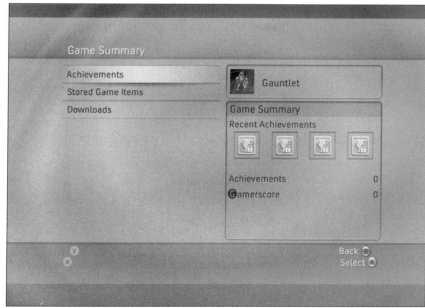

Figure 7-3:
The Game
Summary
page lets
you dig
deep into
your history.

3. **Select a game from your list, then press A.**

4. **Select the Achievements item, then press A.**

   This brings up the blade in Figure 7-4, which shows the possible achievements for the game and your progress toward those achievements.

Figure 7-4:
The possible
achievements
for *Hexic
HD* on the
Xbox 360.

5. **Highlight an achievement, then press A.**

   Details appear. For example, the Achievement Description for Cluster Buster on *Hexic HD* informs you that 25 combos across all of your games are required to unlock the Cluster Buster in the game.

Pressing the Y button usually re-sorts achievements by score.

Stored Games page

The Stored Games page lets you

✔ Navigate your storage devices

✔ Move or copy game data between hard drives and memory units

You can use this feature to

✔ Back up games you've been playing to a memory unit

✔ Move games between consoles

You can carry your game saves to a friend's house on a memory unit, then copy it back to your hard drive when you get home.

To copy game content to a memory unit, follow these steps:

1. **Use the left analog stick to open the Games blade.**

   The Games blade appears.

2. **Use the left analog stick to highlight Played Games, then press A.**

   The Game Summary page appears.

3. **Use the controller to highlight Stored Game Items, then press A.**

4. **Choose the game save location, then press A.**

   The game is usually on the hard drive, but you can also copy game content between memory units.

5. **On the Hard Drive (or Memory Unit) page, highlight the Games item, then press A.**

   The Select Profile page appears.

6. **Choose the profile containing the content you want copied, then press A.**

   The Select Game page appears.

7. **Highlight the game, then press A.**

   The Game Content page appears.

8. **Highlight the item you want to copy, then press A.**

   A screen like the one in Figure 7-5 appears.

9. **Choose the target for your copy, then press A.**

   At this point, your game is copied to the new location. If you want to get back to the Game Summary page, press B until you're there.

Some items can only be moved and not copied. For example, game profiles have to be moved because you don't want them to get out of sync between consoles. If you want to carry your profile to a friend's console, you need to move the profile to a memory unit and then move it back to your hard drive when you get home.

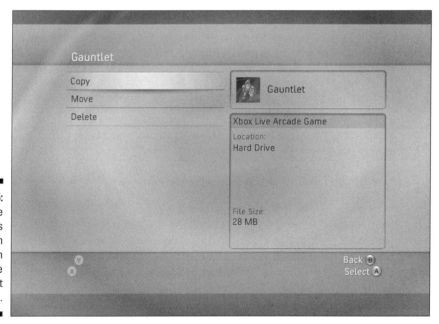

Figure 7-5:
The game page lets you perform an action with a game content item.

If you're really into saving games, you can use two hard drives for backing up your games. Follow these steps:

1. **Copy your game to a memory unit.**

2. **Switch the hard drives in the console.**

   Chapter 2 shows how to switch hard drives.

3. **Copy the file from the memory unit to the hard drive.**

We tell you more about storage devices in Chapter 6.

The Downloads item on the Game Summary page lets you download and manage items you've gotten from Xbox Live Marketplace. You need to log into Xbox Live before you access the content on this page.

Playing Games on Xbox Live Arcade

The Xbox Live Arcade option on the Games blade lets you access games you've purchased and downloaded from Xbox Live.

At launch, the loaded Xbox 360 System includes the Xbox Live Arcade game *Hexic HD* on the hard drive. (*Hexic* isn't included with the Xbox 360 Core System because that system doesn't include a hard drive.) Designed by the creator of classic puzzler *Tetris, Hexic* is a terrific challenge, perfectly balanced to keep you playing for *just . . . one . . . more . . . game!*

Xbox Live Arcade is an Xbox Live store that lets you purchase games that are played directly from the Xbox 360 hard drive. You can find out more about Xbox Live Arcade in Chapter 4.

Highlighting the Xbox Live Arcade option and pressing A brings up the screen in Figure 7-6. From here you can

- ✔ View your games
- ✔ Download new games
- ✔ Review the games you last played

To download new games and content from Xbox Live Arcade, you need at least a (free) Silver Xbox Live Membership.

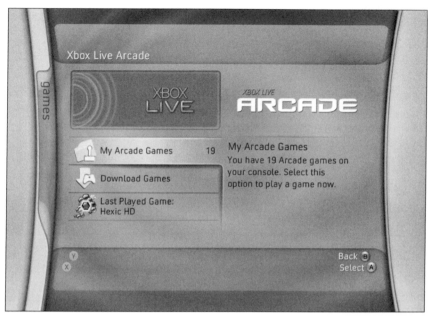

Figure 7-6:
Track the
Xbox Live
Arcade
game you're
playing.

My Arcade Games page

My Arcade Games shows your Gamerscore and achievements for each Xbox
Live Arcade game you own.

To see game details, follow these steps:

1. **Highlight the My Arcade Games item on the Xbox Live Arcade page
   and press A.**

   The My Arcade Games page appears.

2. **Highlight a game and press A.**

   The Game Details page appears, as shown in Figure 7-7.

3. **Use the Game Details page.**

   You can

   • Start the game

   • View details of your game experience

   • Delete the game from your hard drive

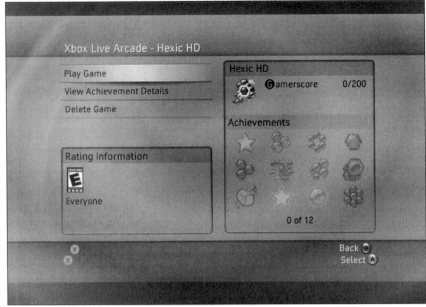

Xbox Live Arcade - Hexic HD

Play Game

View Achievement Details

Delete Game

Rating Information

E

Everyone

Hexic HD

Gamerscore   0/200

Achievements

0 of 12

Back

Select

Figure 7-7:
The Game
Detail page
in Xbox Live
Arcade is
your launch
pad.

This page also highlights the Achievements you've made in the game and shows the ones that you still have waiting for you to earn.

If any of your friends have played the same game, it will display their scores in a leaderboard setup that's sure to encourage bragging rights.

Download Games page

The Download Games item on the Xbox Live Arcade page opens a page that lets you download and install new games from Xbox Live Marketplace, including

- Card games, like *Hardwood Solitaire*
- Board games, like *Bookworm Deluxe*
- Puzzles, like *Bejeweled*
- Action games, like *Ricochet — Lost Worlds*
- Classic titles, like *Pole Position* and *Galaga*

The Xbox Live Arcade game choices are updated all the time, so check in often.

The Play Game option on the Xbox Live Arcade page takes you directly to the launch page for the last Xbox Live Arcade game you played. Use this option to jump right back into the action when you fire up your Xbox 360.

To launch an Xbox Live Arcade game or demo that you own, follow these steps:

1. **Highlight the My Arcade Games item on the Xbox Live Arcade page and press A.**

   The My Arcade Games page appears.

2. **Highlight a game and press A.**

3. **Highlight Play Game and press A.**

Playing Demos and Viewing Trailers

As an Xbox 360 owner, revel in the fact that you can download and view great content from your own living room. Nowhere is this feature more apparent than when you hit the Games blade and grab some game demos.

The difference between a trailer and a demo is that a *trailer* is like a movie of the game; a *demo* is more like a test version of the game. You can watch the trailer, but you can't really play it. Demos are all about playing.

Playing demos

Game demos are a hard-core gaming staple. You can find new demos on Xbox Live and download them directly to your console. Play a level and decide whether you want to get out of your house and go buy it — or at least get out of your chair and go order it online.

1. **Navigate to the Games blade using the left analog stick.**

   The Games blade appears.

2. **Use the left analog stick to highlight Demos and press A.**

3. **Select the Demo you wish to play from the list and press A.**

You can also get demos with the *Original Xbox Magazine (OXM),* which includes an optional content disk with every issue. Chapter 14 shows how to order *OXM.*

Watching trailers

Window shopping was never so easy. Get a sneak peek at upcoming games' ads. Download trailers from Xbox Live by way of the Games blade:

1. **Navigate to the Games blade using the left analog stick.**

   The Games blade appears.

2. **Use the left analog stick to highlight Trailers and press A.**

3. **Select the trailer you want to watch from the list and press A.**

Part III

Xbox 360 in Your Entertainment System

The 5th Wave   By Rich Tennant

Well, I'm impressed. I didn't know the Xbox 360 came with a media adapter for thoracic surgery.

In this part . . .

This part holds the key to seeing how the Xbox 360 fits into your home entertainment system. And if you don't have a home entertainment system, the Xbox 360 makes a great first component! Read about the different video and audio standards that help maximize your gaming experience; then stay tuned to see how to customize the Xbox 360 to make it your very own.

Chapter 8 helps you navigate the often-confusing world of high-definition television. Here you can read about television types and connectors and how to choose a great TV for your Xbox 360 game playing experience. Chapter 9 discusses the considerations associated with picking an audio system for your Xbox 360. Mull over the different audio connectors and what you should think about when choosing a new audio system.

We end with Chapter 10, which covers customizing your Xbox 360 so that it fits perfectly into your home entertainment system — and shows off your own personal style.

Chapter 8

HDTV, EDTV, Plain Old TV

*E*ven if you have some technical know-how, you may find buying a new TV today a truly scary experience. You can find a huge variety of TVs at your local home electronics store, and with new technologies in the works, choosing the right TV gets more complicated all the time. In this chapter, you can find out more than you probably want to know about TVs. But if you're in the market for a new TV, you may gladly look this chapter over. If you're reading this book, you probably want to know the best kind of TV to use with the Xbox 360. But in the end, you want to make your TV-buying decision based on what works best for your home and for your own personal needs and desires, not just what TV works best for your game console.

For a very in-depth look at video options for your home entertainment system, you can take a look at *Home Theater For Dummies* and *HDTV For Dummies,* by Danny Briere and Pat Hurley (Wiley Publishing, Inc.).

Television Basics

When you go TV shopping, you probably notice that TV options are more complicated than they were just ten years ago. You can buy many different types of TVs, and those TVs come in a huge range of prices. Because this book talks about the Xbox 360, I assume that you plan to use your new TV for your new console.

Almost any TV works with the Xbox 360. With some older TV sets, you may need extra equipment to connect the Xbox 360 to the TV, but the TV you own now most likely can work fine with the Xbox 360. You do have some options to create the absolutely best gaming experience that you can afford.

Video performance

TVs have become more complex over the years, and you have a lot more options beyond just plain broadcast-quality TV. When you shop for TVs, you need to keep two main concepts in mind:

- The aspect ratio of the screen (widescreen or standard)
- Whether the TV can display HDTV or EDTV content (and what specific resolutions of HDTV it supports)

Widescreen and standard screens

TVs, at the moment, have only two possible display ratios — 4:3 or 16:9. These numbers refer to the ratio between the width of the screen and the height, so the 4:3 screen looks relatively square, and a 16:9 screen looks quite a bit wider than it is high.

You generally hear 16:9 screens and shows being called *widescreen,* and most video content uses this display as the standard format these days. Movies are generally filmed in a widescreen format, though not always precisely 16:9, and many new TV shows are being broadcast in 16:9 widescreen, as well. Of course, you want to know about the Xbox 360 — the Xbox can produce either 16:9 or 4:3 output. You only have to tell it what type of TV you have (see Chapter 6 for more information on changing the system settings).

Generally, most TVs can display either 4:3 or 16:9 formatted video, but if the screen itself doesn't match the format that you want to display, you get black bars across the top and bottom (an appearance called *letterboxed*) or along both sides (known as *pillowbox*). These black bars appear because the screen is reduced in either height or width to make it match the display format of whatever movie or show you're watching. So, if you watch a 4:3 TV show on a widescreen TV, you get to see nice black bars along the sides, and if you watch the widescreen version of a movie on a 4:3 TV, you end up with bars on the top and bottom.

To show standard TV programs in a 16:9 aspect ratio, most widescreen TVs offer some kind of zoom feature. This feature resizes a 4:3 picture to better fit the wider screen. Different TVs have different options, but you can find three types of zoom on TVs available today:

- **Straight zoom:** This zoom increases the size of the 4:3 content until it fills the entire width of your display. With this zoom, the content gets scaled up by about 25 percent, which cuts off the top and bottom of the picture. Most shows still look great in this view.
- **Wide zoom:** This zoom stretches the image in width only. Because the height doesn't change and the width stretches to fill the display, you don't lose any part of the picture. But with this type of zoom, the image distorts, making objects seem a bit wider than they normally look.

✔ **Stretch zoom:** You can find this third type of zoom in some cases, such as in certain models of Sony widescreen TVs. With this zoom, the height doesn't change, and instead of stretching the center of the image, the left and right sides extend to fill the entire 16:9 area. This more complicated type of zoom leaves the central action alone and stretches only background items.

If you plan to watch some 4:3 content on your widescreen TV, make sure that your TV has a zoom feature.

Even if you watch mostly standard-ratio (4:3) programs, I definitely recommend that you consider getting yourself a widescreen display if you're in the market for a new TV.

You can already get movies on DVD in widescreen, many TV shows on the major networks broadcast in widescreen, and Xbox 360 games look even better when you display them in 16:9 format.

Display resolutions

The *resolution* of a TV display describes how much detail the TV can show in both the vertical and horizontal areas of the display.

Higher resolution numbers mean that the TV displays more detail.

Your TV's display resolution may depend on

✔ The TV's technology

✔ The country where you live

Standard broadcast TV

Your TV's standard broadcast TV system depends on where you live:

✔ In the United States and Canada, standard broadcast TV (NTSC, or *National Television Standards Committee*) has

   • 480 vertical lines of resolution

   • 640 horizontal lines of resolution (maximum)

NTSC is *interlaced,* which means that on each scan of the TV screen, only half the lines are drawn at a time. If you never see a better resolution, you may think this resolution looks fine. But after a while, the interlaced nature of the display leads to interline flicker, especially in content with rapid motion.

Video geeks sometimes describe the NTSC standard with the shorthand *480i,* which describes interlaced content that has 480 lines of vertical resolution.

✔ In countries that use PAL *(phase alternate line)* TVs, such as the United Kingdom, standard broadcast TV has

- 576 vertical lines of resolution

- 720 horizontal lines of resolution (maximum)

Standard PAL video is *interlaced*, so video geeks sometimes identify it with the shorthand *576i*.

This book isn't intended for countries that use the *SECAM* TV system. However, the following sections about *EDTV* and *HDTV* generally apply in all countries, including SECAM countries.

Extended Definition TV (EDTV)

EDTV *(Extended Definition TV)* may sound similar to HDTV, but EDTV doesn't have all the capabilities of HDTV.

If you have an HDTV, you have all the capabilities of an EDTV and much more. You can skip to the following section to see the extra capabilities of HDTV.

Depending on your country, an EDTV (Extended Definition Television) display may support

✔ *480p* progressive-scan video (in the United States and Canada)

✔ *576p* progressive-scan video (in PAL TV countries, such as the United Kingdom)

EDTV uses the same resolution as your country's standard TV system, but with *progressive* scan instead of interlacing. *Progressive* formats draw every line, top to bottom, on every refresh. EDTV is a definite improvement over regular TV, but it doesn't have the quality of HDTV content.

Your *DVD player* operates internally with progressive scan (either 480p or 576p), and then *downconverts* to 480i or 576i for a standard TV if necessary.

High Definition TV (HDTV)

HDTV *(High Definition Television)* hardware and content support at least one of the following video formats:

✔ 720p

720p content has a resolution of 1280 x 720 pixels, and because it's in a progressive format, it gives you an extremely smooth picture free from annoying motion artifacts.

720p is the internal resolution of games in your Xbox 360 console, so we recommend using it for Xbox 360 if you can. Almost all "HDTV" and "HDTV-ready" TVs work with 720p video.

✔ 1080i and 1080p

Both of these 1080-line formats have a display resolution of 1920 x 1080, but one is interlaced (1080i) and the other progressive (1080p).

Most HDTVs can use 1080i video. In 2006, almost no TVs can handle *1080p*. You may be able to find TVs and content in 1080p format in the future.

Connection options

You can find a wide variety of inputs and outputs on a TV, and the options change all the time. Table 8-1 lists the various types of connections that you may find on your TV (or TVs that you're thinking about buying) in order from lowest quality to best.

Table 8-1	Xbox 360 Video Connections
Type	**Description**
RF/Coaxial	Standard antenna input, designed to accept a coaxial cable connector
SCART (analog)	Unified analog audio/video connector for standard TVs (usually in the United Kingdom)
Composite	Single RCA jack (usually colored yellow)
S-Video	A 4-pin round connector (like a PC keyboard jack)
Advanced SCART	RGB video connector for HDTVs (usually in the United Kingdom)
Component	Three RCA jacks, usually colored red, blue, and green
VGA	Standard, 15-hole connector that you normally use for connecting a video source to computer monitors

You can use an external switchbox to get around a shortage of connectors, but avoid this type of setup if you can. (Switchboxes can reduce your picture quality.) The best connection method for your Xbox 360 depends on your TV.

HDTV connections

If you're connecting an Xbox 360 to an HDTV (or an "HDTV-ready" TV), we recommend using one of these options:

✔ **Component video**

Use the HDAV video cable. It's included with the loaded Xbox 360 System package, and it's available separately for the Xbox 360 Core System package.

Hey, what happened to Vport?

You may have a TV with a *Vport* connector for the original Xbox console. (These TVs sometimes are called *Xbox Ready*.) When Xbox 360 went on the market, a Vport cable wasn't available for Xbox 360. If there isn't an Xbox 360 cable for Vport when you buy your system, you have a couple of alternatives:

✔ We recommend connecting *component video* (the red, blue, and green jacks) directly from Xbox 360 to your TV.

✔ If your TV doesn't have component video jacks, you may have to use a standard TV connection, such as S-Video or the yellow composite video jack.

RCA sells an adapter for Vport and component video (RCA GP650XB), but the jacks on the RCA adapter can't directly connect to the component video jacks on the Xbox 360 HDAV cable. You may be able to find component-video cable adapters to stick the jacks together, but the results may not be significantly better than a standard S-Video connection.

Chapter 6 shows how to set up Xbox 360 after you connect component video

✔ **VGA adapter** (optional for any Xbox 360 console)

This connector works with some HDTVs and most computer monitors.

✔ **Advanced SCART Cable** (optional for any Xbox 360 console)

Connects RGB to compatible HDTVs (usually in the United Kingdom).

The SCART *adapter* that attaches to composite Xbox 360 cables isn't for HDTV. If you have an HDTV, skip the SCART *adapter* and use either

• Component video (red, green, and blue jacks on the HDAV cable)

• The optional Advanced SCART *cable*

Some HDTVs have other advanced digital video connectors, such as *DVI, HDMI,* and *FireWire* (IEEE 1394). Currently, Xbox 360 doesn't support those connections. You may be able to find adapters to make Xbox 360 work with these video connectors, but we don't recommend it.

If you're looking for a new HDTV, *HDMI* is the most popular digital connector for other home video devices. A TV with *two* HDMI input jacks is well equipped for the latest digital video gear. (Firewire is frequently used for digital *computer* video devices.)

EDTV connections

EDTVs can use *component video* (the red, green, and blue jacks).

The HDAV video cable is the best option for an EDTV. Use the "HDTV" switch position on the cable if you connect Xbox 360 component video to an EDTV.

Chapter 6 shows how to set up Xbox 360 after you connect component video.

Most EDTV and HDTVs are also compatible with the following *standard* TV connections.

Standard TV connections

Standard TVs may have several connection options.

Many TVs (including HDTVs and EDTVs) often have some of the following standard TV connections on the *front* of the TV. It's a handy way to temporarily connect your Xbox 360 (especially if you're a guest) if you don't need maximum video performance.

If you don't have an HDTV or an EDTV, we recommend using the *first* option that works with your standard TV from the following list:

✔ **S-Video connector**

This cable works with *digital audio* (see Chapter 9).

This is the best standard TV connection for an Xbox 360. You can get this connector as an optional accessory for any Xbox 360 console.

Children (or careless adults) may have trouble with this connection. All S-Video connectors have delicate pins that can be smashed if you don't carefully line up the pins and the socket.

✔ **Composite video connector**

This is the *yellow* video jack on the cable that comes in the box with most Xbox 360 consoles.

If you have the Xbox 360 HDAV video cable (the component video cable with red, green, and blue jacks), you can use the yellow composite video jack with standard TVs. Just flip the switch to "TV" on the cable.

✔ **SCART adapter**

This is a combined audio/video connector (usually seen in the United Kingdom). If your TV has a SCART connector, you probably received a SCART *adapter* with your Xbox 360 console. This adapter uses standard composite video (the yellow video jack).

✔ **RF antenna jack**

Make a list, check it twice

In addition to the most important device, your Xbox 360, you may want to now make a list of all the devices that you plan to connect to the TV and then try to imagine what devices you may add to your system in the future.

Taking my personal system as an example, I have these devices hooked up to my main TV:

✔ Digital cable box (component video)

✔ A DVD player (DVI)

✔ A Media Center Extender (s-video)

✔ Xbox 360

At this point, I'm completely out of High Definition connections, so I can't add any new HD devices. I may even remove my DVD player (because the Xbox 360 now supports progressive output of DVD movies), so I may end up with an open input.

Video technology

The following sections describe types of TV displays you can find for sale today. Each type has pros and cons that you need to consider when deciding what type of set you want to buy.

Direct-view CRT

CRT stands for Cathode Ray Tube. The CRT is a glass jar that shows the TV picture on the flat end. (That's why they're called *direct-view TVs*.)

CRTs usually are the least expensive TVs of a given size, but their volume and weight mean that the largest CRT screens are about 40 inches.

If you're considering a new TV, think about getting a flat-screen CRT. A good flat-screen CRT makes a great display for the Xbox 360:

✔ You get a good viewing angle on a flat screen, so people from around a room can see the picture well.

✔ Direct-view CRTs are usually very bright, so this type of TV makes a good choice for brightly lit rooms.

Projection TV

Projection TVs usually use a small, powerful video light source projected onto (or through) a screen.

Projection TVs rely on a *reflected* picture, so they work best in darkened rooms (such as dedicated home theaters).

The main differences between *media projectors* (front-projection TVs) and rear-projection TVs are the *packaging* and the *screen:*

✔ Media projectors (front-projection TVs) use a video source that projects the picture onto a screen from across the room (like a movie projector.) These are similar to the projectors you may see for group Powerpoint presentations (some models are exactly the same projectors).

Some media projectors don't have TV speakers. You may need a separate sound system.

✔ Rear-projection TVs package the video source inside the a box and project the picture onto the screen from behind.

Rear-projection TVs can be both bigger and lighter than big direct-view CRT TVs because

• Projection TVs have much less glass inside the cabinet.

• Projection TV cabinets can be made of light materials (because the cabinet supports much less glass).

There are several good video systems to drive projection TVs.

CRT projection

Many rear-projection TVs are based on CRT technology. The tube is used as a light source that projects the picture on a screen on the TV.

Projection TVs are relatively light, but they can be *really* big. You may find them hard to move around.

DLP TV

DLP TV cabinets can be lighter and smaller than most CRT-based projection TVs. If you look at a DLP TV in a store, you often can't tell whether it's a flat-panel type display (such as a plasma TV). If you look at the back of a DLP TV, you can see a box that extends a foot or so in the back.

The size of the box is much smaller than the display, so you can easily hide the box in a room corner.

The resolution of DLP projectors ranges from 720p up to 1080p.

Some people see a rainbow effect when they look at a DLP display. Consider having the different members of your family take a good look at the unit in the store before you bring it home. (Few people have this problem, but you want to keep everybody happy, right?) This rainbow effect is overcome in sets that use *three* imagers or chips. Each is filtered by a red, green, or blue filter that are converged on the screen.

LCOS TV

LCOS uses a reflective technology not unlike the DLP. It may become less expensive than DLP, but current models aren't particularly cheaper.

Flat panel TVs

So what's cooler than a big TV that hangs on the wall? A big TV that hangs on the wall and lets you play *Halo,* of course!

If you want a flat panel TV to save space, consider a *DLP rear-projection TV* to save money. DLP TVs can snuggle pretty close to the wall.

If you crave a "true" flat panel TV, you have a couple of options. They're both great displays for an Xbox 360.

Some flat-panel displays don't have TV speakers (just like most computer monitors). If you need built-in TV speakers, make sure they're, well, *built in.*

LCD TV

Manufacturers use an LCD, or liquid crystal display, to create a very flat screen with high resolution. You can find this technology in flat-panel computer monitors. LCD TVs come in a huge range of screen sizes and prices.

Plasma TV

Plasma TVs have thin panels that don't look too different from flat-panel LCD TVs, though plasma TVs tend to be a little thicker. Plasma TVs, used for both HDTV and EDTV, display a picture by exciting phosphors with plasma gas.

Depending on how you use your TV, a plasma TV may be either great or not so good:

- **Great:** Plasma usually makes black in movies look more black than an LCD flat panel TV. You may get more of a movie-theater experience in a dark home theater.

- **Not so good:** Plasma TVs can *burn-in* a "ghost" picture on the screen if you constantly show the same image. (It may take thousands of hours, but it's possible.)

If you leave one of the Xbox 360 blades up for a long time without any input, a *screen saver* kicks in. The screen saver redraws the screen with a varying picture in order to prevent burn in. You can adjust the screen saver in the System blade, which you can read about in Chapter 6.

TV sound systems

Audio connections into your TV generally use only one type of connector: stereo RCA jacks, with one pair of stereo jacks per video input. Your Xbox 360 comes with a video cable that also connects to most TV sound systems.

Your TV sound system may be okay for a small room at low volume, but Xbox 360 sound can be too much for any TV to match. Chapter 9 shows how to get the best possible Xbox 360 sound with your TV or a separate audio system.

Thinking about a New TV

You have to consider several factors when choosing a new TV for gaming and home entertainment on your Xbox 360. As with anything, you have to make a series of trade-offs when choosing the display that you think works best for your Xbox 360. The most expensive TV that you can buy may not be exactly what you're looking for.

How much can you spend?

You probably have to keep in mind how much you can spend on a new TV. When you start to plan your new TV purchase, take a look at your budget and consider why exactly you're getting the new TV. Plan on spending a reasonable amount of money for the features and quality that you're looking for.

Table 8-2 shows the price range for the TV types that you can read about in this chapter. You can use these prices as a rough guide to narrowing down your choice.

Table 8-2	Television Price Range by Type	
Television Type	_Picture Size (diagonal)_	_Price Range (approximate)_
Standard Television (CRT)	8"–36"	$75–$500
High Definition CRT	27"–36"	$400–$1,050
LCD (HD and ED)	14"–50"	$300–$6,000

(continued)

Table 8-2 *(continued)*

Television Type	Picture Size (diagonal)	Price Range (approximate)
Projection Television (HD and ED)	42"–65"	$900–$3,000
DLP Projection	40"–55"	$1,000–$5,000
LCD (HD and ED)	43"–70"	$2,000–$6,000
LCOS	50"–80"	$2,500–$10,200
Plasma (HD and ED)	40"–65"	$1,800–$10,000 and up

In Table 8-2, the Standard TV type includes any CRT-based TV that isn't an HDTV. The High Definition CRT represents a direct-view CRT TV with HDTV capability.

As you begin to budget for a new TV, take into account accessories and cables that you may need to put it all together.

If you're spending more than a few thousand dollars on a new TV or home entertainment system, you may want to hire a professional media consultant. He or she can help you choose the right display and other components for your needs, and he or she can probably help you assemble your home theater system, too.

Obviously, you need to consider whether your new TV has high definition. For the most part, the only TVs that you can buy without either HDTV or EDTV are CRTs that cost under $500. Many of the newer non-CRT TV types that you can find today have HDTV capabilities. Some of the lower priced, and smaller, Plasma and LCD TVs are the exception to this rule. If you're looking for HD and not ED, make sure that the box says HDTV.

Getting the TV's specs

You have to take into account how much space you have for the TV and how much the TV weighs. (How much the TV weighs usually translates into how much trouble you have when you want to move it again.)

The biggest TVs that you can buy are the larger rear-projection CRT-based TVs. These TVs usually come with high definition and a widescreen. You can't move them around very easily, though. But for screen size, you can't beat the price.

The second-largest TVs are the direct-view CRTs. The CRTs that have a flat screen weigh the most because they use a lot of extra glass in the CRT tube to make the screen flat. You may find moving some of the extremely heavy large flat-screen CRTs a big pain. These types of TVs usually do have very good picture, and they cost less than the LCDs and plasmas.

DLP TVs usually have big screens, but they have small back ends, compared to a CRT. You can't hang a DLP TV on a wall, but when you place it against a wall, the display portion of the TV sits only about a foot or so away from the wall, obscuring most of the box behind it.

Lighting

A display projects light. If you have a display that projects a lot of light, you can play games on that display in a bright room and still see all the details of your game.

The only display technologies that need fairly dim lighting are the rear-projection, CRT-based displays and the media projectors. For these types of displays, you need to play in a room where you can shut out a lot of the outside light so that you can get the best picture possible.

For very bright rooms, direct-view CRT and DLP make excellent choices. Both of these display types are very bright, and you can usually see the display very easily in bright lighting conditions. Plasma and LCD displays are good choices, too, but make sure that the display you're considering is bright enough for the room that you want to place it in.

When comparing TVs by their specifications, look for brightness in lumens — a higher value is better.

Making your TV fit your room

How big is the room in which you want to put your new TV, and how far away from the TV do you want to sit?

The farther you sit from the display, the larger you probably want your display. But you don't want a TV that's so big you can see the individual lines and dots that create the illusion of a real picture. If you have a very small room and a very large display, you may find staring at the screen for a long period of time uncomfortable.

If you want to sit close to a huge TV screen, you require the most sophisticated (and expensive) TV technology. Picture quality can vary with many factors, but in the following sections I give you guidelines to finding the largest TV screen for your space.

HDTV screen size

If you're considering an HDTV (or a computer monitor), the distance to the screen should be at least *two times* the diagonal screen size.

For example, if it's 8 feet (96 inches) to the screen, you shouldn't get an HDTV screen much larger than 48 inches. (A top-of-the-line 50-inch HDTV probably would be okay, but a 60-inch screen probably is too much TV for the space.)

Standard TV screen size

If you're considering a standard TV, the distance to the screen should be at least *three times* the diagonal screen size.

For example, if it's 8 feet (96 inches) to the screen, you shouldn't get a standard TV screen much larger than 32 inches.

Viewing angle

The *horizontal viewing angle,* expressed as a degree value, describes how far to either side of the TV people can sit and still see the picture properly.

Check the viewing angle that a particular model allows. Many rear-projection TVs don't look their best if you're sitting much outside the width of the screen.

Projection TVs have relatively narrow viewing angles, but usually you can count on a minimum "audience width" at least as *wide* as you are *far* from the TV. For example, if you're 8 feet straight back from the center of the screen, everyone on an 8 foot sofa usually sees a darn good picture.

For normal home TV viewing, the *vertical* angle (looking from above or below) usually doesn't make much difference for any TV set unless you're already too close (that is, less than the *minimum* distance that's required for the picture to look good).

If your TV salesperson doesn't know the viewing angle of their TV sets, do your own research online at a site like www.crutchfield.com. This site lists viewing angles for almost every TV that they sell.

Getting the TV that works for you

When you're considering a new TV, you need to think about its primary purpose in your home. If you use your TV mostly for watching TV programs, then you may find a widescreen distracting. On the other hand, if you invest in a high-definition DVR and high-definition cable or satellite service, get a TV that can give you the most that you can get from that technology. EDTV falls into a separate category because it will never be able to display a full HDTV signal nor is it typically narrow screen.

Using a Computer Monitor

Computer monitors actually make pretty good displays for the Xbox 360. They can do high resolution, and you can use the monitor's VGA connector to hook up the monitor to the Xbox 360. You can buy the VGA connector add-on separately.

If you want to play your games through a PC, you can hook up the composite cable directly to a PC's video capture card. But if you use this hook up, you can't display the video in high definition. You can also purchase special boxes that let you play composite video through a monitor, but as with the video capture card method, you can't display in high resolution.

Recording Your Games for Fun and Posterity

You can have a lot of fun recording your Xbox 360 games. You can't record games directly to the Xbox's hard drive. (Though some games may let you save individual game runs, like races.) You can record your Xbox 360 games to share with others in a few different ways. All of these recording methods involve using the composite output of your Xbox 360 and saving the data either to a tape or digitizing the video and sound to a PC.

Recording to tape

You can most easily record your games by simply plugging your composite cable (the yellow plug) into your VCR and playing the game through the VCR. You can pop in a video tape and press Record, and you can record your games for a couple of hours. You can record games through your VCR without thinking much about it, and when you fill a tape up, you can just eject the full tape and pop in a new, blank tape.

If you do run your Xbox 360 through a VCR, you can't play a DVD in the Xbox 360 without a certain amount of picture distortion. The content on DVDs usually comes protected with a digital rights management technology called Macrovision. If your VCR detects Macrovision from the source media, it scrambles the signal a bit to discourage recording, or it may even refuse to

The rise of machinima

If you digitize your games and get handy with your movie editor, you may want to know more about an art form called machinima. *Machinima* is a technique for making movies by controlling game characters in a game, recording what you do, and then editing the result to create a real movie. You can find a number of really good machinima series on the Internet, including Red vs. Blue (http://redvsblue.com) and This Spartan Life (http://thisspartanlife.com). (***Warning:*** Some of the content in these machinima videos isn't appropriate for kids.) Creating movies, like these examples, takes a lot of work, but you can have a lot of fun doing it.

record at all. If you want to play movies on your Xbox 360, hook your Xbox 360 directly to the TV.

After you have your games recorded on tape, you can digitize the tape to a PC and edit files to share with your friends. When you take care of business on Xbox Live with your friends, you can always use proof of your dominance!

Digitizing your games

Digitization goes along with the tape method, which you can read about in the preceding section, "Recording to tape," but digitizing may or may not work properly for you, depending on your hardware setup.

Many PCs today have TV capture cards in them. If your PC has such a card and you want to record your games through the card, you can hook your composite cable to the card and use the software that comes with your card to capture the video. This approach works well if you have a lot of hard drive space. You can then use Windows Movie Maker or another movie editing program to make a movie of your work.

You may face an issue with trying to play games through a video capture card — you sometimes get a delay in processing your picture, which can make actually playing the game impossible. Sometimes, you can get around the problems by changing the settings on your capture card. Check the documentation that came with your capture card or the online forums for techniques for recording video-game console data on your capture card.

If your video capture card can't display your game data fast enough, you may have to record to tape first and then use the video capture card on your PC to pull down the data.

Chapter 9

Getting the Best Audio Experience

In This Chapter

▶ Making the most of your 360 experience with great sound

▶ Understanding your options

▶ Choosing an audio/home theater system

▶ Hooking it all up

*T*he blast of an explosion in *Perfect Dark Zero,* the squeal of tires in *Project Gotham,* footsteps coming up behind you in *Quake* . . . these situations are just a few of the experiences that depend on the sound system of your new Xbox 360.

Playing without any audio feedback at all would be pretty unusual, but the right sound system can make your game-playing experience much more enjoyable, helping you feel like you're in the world of the game. This chapter shows the aspects of the Xbox 360 experience that your sound system choices affect, what kind of choices you have, and how best to hook everything up when you're ready to play.

For a more in-depth look at choosing and setting up a home entertainment system, we suggest *Home Theater For Dummies* by Danny Briere and Pat Hurley (Wiley Publishing, Inc.).

If you just got your Xbox 360 today, you're probably itching to get it up and running. This chapter guides you through the two important parts of great Xbox 360 sound:

✔ The "Hooking Up Xbox 360 Sound" section, later in this chapter, shows how to make the best possible connection to any TV or sound system that you have right now. Game on!

✔ If you have the budget and the craving, you can find a shopping guide to bring home the best Xbox 360 sound system that your pocketbook and your home can handle in the section, "Buying a New Home Theater System," later in this chapter. You can then use the section, "Hooking Up Xbox 360 Sound," to connect your Xbox 360 console to your new sound system.

Xbox 360 Game Sound

Sound is a critical element of the current crop of video games, giving you feedback, notification of online events, ambience, and drama:

✔ **Feedback**

Within the game, sounds can tell you

- An event has happened.
- Your health is low.
- Time is almost out.
- The game received your button click.

✔ **Notification**

You can be notified of out-of-game events (such as an invitation from an online buddy) by using sound along with some visual cues.

✔ **Realism**

- *Ambient sound:* Contributes to the background game environment by providing quiet jungle noises, the sound of rain and wind, or crowd noise in a football stadium.
- *Sound effects:* Respond to specific game action. When you hit the gas, the engine gets louder and faster; when a character shoots at you, you hear the gunfire.

Video game audio through the ages

Although sound has always been a part of video games, it never got as much attention as video.

In the first video game consoles, you often couldn't even get audio output in stereo, and the sound quality was nowhere near what records or cassettes could produce. Most of the early gaming consoles (Atari 2600, Intellivision) could produce only a few notes at a single time and used only mono output, so games were quite limited in the music they could produce.

Things didn't get much better after the audio signal left the console. Even high-quality music would sound pretty poor by the time it went into

the TV through the antenna input and out through limited-range TV speakers.

Game cartridges became larger, allowing better audio to be shipped with a game, and consoles kept pace. Stereo output came, and the audio hardware improved with each game console release until the audio output from a gaming console was equal to most home stereo components.

The Xbox 360 represents the current peak of this evolution, supporting 48KHz 16-bit audio. Its audio output equals the best possible sound you can get out of a music CD.

✔ **Drama**

The music in an Xbox 360 game can fit the situation with the depth and audio quality of a full symphony orchestra.

Many Xbox 360 games use music from a full orchestra.

Changing the pace and tone of the music as the action on-screen increases creates an amazing effect that depends on the quality and setup of your sound system.

Hooking Up Xbox 360 Sound

Xbox 360 allows two types of audio connections: analog and digital. Both analog and digital audio connections can give you surround sound or stereo sound, depending on the sound system that you use with your Xbox 360 console.

Your Xbox 360 audio setup applies to both games and DVD videos.

The Xbox 360 audio connection that you want to use depends on the sound system that you connect to your Xbox 360 console:

✔ **Digital audio** is the best option if you have both

- • A sound system with a Toslink digital audio input

- • A Toslink audio cable (which you can get from most stores that sell Toslink-equipped sound systems)

Toslink is the optical version of SPDIF (Sony/Philips Digital Interconnect Format) digital audio. If you have a component with a SPDIF *coaxial digital* audio input, you can try using a Toslink-to-coaxial adapter to connect your Xbox 360 console.

The sidebar, "Digitally different," summarizes the performance advantages of digital audio with Xbox 360.

The following section, "Digital Xbox 360 audio," guides you through the steps of connecting your Xbox 360 console for digital audio.

✔ **Analog audio** is used for most TVs and inexpensive audio systems.

The section "Analog Xbox 360 audio," later in this chapter, guides you through the steps of connecting your Xbox 360 console for analog audio.

Digitally different

If you have a Toslink optical input on your home theater system, you may want to use it with your Xbox 360 system for two important reasons:

✔ Any audio is cleaner through the optical connection.

When a signal travels along any length of electrical wire, it picks up noise (which you hear as crackling, hissing, and popping sounds) from other electrical currents in the area. With good shielding (high-quality cables) and the shortest possible connections, you can reduce noise, but optical cables avoid the noise altogether by getting out of the electricity business.

✔ A Digital connection allows Dolby Digital processing.

Digital Xbox 360 audio

You make an Xbox 360 digital audio connection by using an optical cable (called a Toslink).

Sending sound as pulses of light between your Xbox 360 and your stereo? Deeply, deeply cool.

Digital audio connection

To connect your Xbox 360 to your stereo using a digital cable, follow these steps:

1. **Make sure you're using one of these Xbox 360 AV Cables that connects digital audio:**

   - Component HD cable

   - *Advanced* SCART cable (United Kingdom)

     Digital audio doesn't work with a SCART composite video *adapter.*

   - VGA cable

   - S-Video cable

     This is the only *standard TV cable* that works with digital audio.

2. **Connect a Toslink cable to the connecting plug of your AV cable.**

   You don't get this cable with the Xbox 360, so you need to pick one up.

   Turn the stereo volume down *before* you connect the cable.

3. **Plug the Toslink cable into your receiver.**

The manufacturer sometimes covers this input to prevent dust from damaging the input. Check your input; it may be covered by either

- A plastic shutter that moves automatically when you plug the connector in

- A small square-shaped *plug* in the input

  If the input has a plug, pull it out now.

4. **Switch your receiver over to the digital audio source.**

5. **Fire up the Xbox 360 and pick the appropriate digital output type in the System blade.**

   The following section shows you how.

Digital output options

You can configure the Xbox 360 console's digital output to either digital stereo or Dolby Digital.

Dolby Digital setup

You definitely want this digital connection option if you're connecting your Xbox 360 to a device that either

- ✔ Has the Dolby Digital logo
- ✔ States that it supports Dolby Digital in the manual

Dolby Digital can support *5.1 surround sound* (a system with five full-range speakers plus a subwoofer; you can read about surround sound and subwoofers in the sections, "Surround sound" and "Subwoofer," later in this chapter.)

Dolby Digital (which is also known as AC-3) is the standard audio encoding on DVD movies.

If your audio system uses Dolby Digital, follow these steps to set up your Xbox 360 console for digital audio:

1. **Open the System blade of the Xbox 360 Dashboard.**

2. **Select Console Settings from the list of options and then press the A button.**

3. **Select Audio from the list of options and then press the A button.**

   You see two options, Analog Output and Digital Output.

4. **Choose Digital Output and press the A button.**

   Under Digital Output, you have three choices — Digital Stereo, Dolby Digital 5.1, or Dolby Digital with WMA Pro.

5. **Select Dolby Digital 5.1 and press the A button.**

Windows Media Professional audio

Selecting Dolby Digital with WMA Pro affects the optical output only when you

- Listen to audio encoded in the Windows Media Professional format

- View videos encoded in WMV-HD (Windows Media Video — High Definition), which encode their audio as WMA Pro

- Play sound through a receiver that supports WMA Pro input via optical

Your receiver also needs to support Dolby Digital because enabling WMA Pro automatically enables Dolby Digital as well. The output switches between the two formats, depending on what the content you're viewing or listening to has available.

If your sound system is compatible with Windows Media Professional, follow these steps to set up your Xbox 360 for WMA Pro output:

1. **Select Console Settings from the list of options and then press the A button.**

2. **Select Audio from the list of options and press A.**

   You see two options, Analog Output and Digital Output.

3. **Choose Digital and then press the A button.**

   Under Digital Output, you have three choices — *Digital Stereo, Dolby Digital 5.1,* and *Dolby Digital with WMA Pro* (as shown in the figure).

4. **Select Dolby Digital with WMA Pro and press the A button.**

Consider using the Pro version of WMA when ripping music from CDs onto your PC. You can't get WMA Pro as a format choice when ripping CDs through Windows Media Player, but you can get it when doing your own audio/video authoring by using the Windows Media Encoder. See `www.microsoft.com/windows/windowsmedia/9series/encoder/default.aspx` for more information and to download the encoding software.

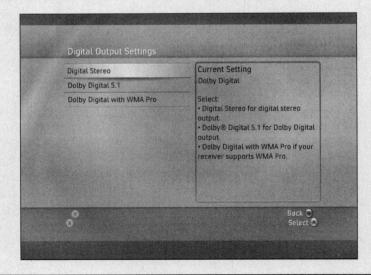

Digital stereo setup

If your audio system uses an optical system but can't use Dolby Digital, follow these steps to set up your Xbox 360 console:

1. **Open the System blade of the Xbox 360 Dashboard.**
2. **Select Console Settings and press the A button.**
3. **Pick the Audio option.**
4. **Pick the Digital Output option.**

   Under Digital Output, you have three choices — *Digital Stereo, Dolby Digital 5.1,* and *Dolby Digital with WMA Pro.*
5. **Select Digital Stereo and press the A button.**

Analog Xbox 360 audio

You make the analog audio connection with a pair of RCA jacks.

Usually, the two analog audio connections are two different colors:

- ✔ **Red** for the right channel
- ✔ **White** for the left channel

This has been the standard connection method since before the original Atari game console was released.

Don't have an optical input? Use analog audio and hook up with the RCA cables.

If you can't use an optical input, you have two ways to make an analog audio connection from your Xbox 360:

- ✔ **Directly to the audio system (receiver)**

  Connecting directly to the stereo system may improve sound quality a little bit. Usually, analog audio sounds better when you reduce the number of connections between the signal's source and its destination.

  To make a direct connection to the audio system, you usually need an extra step when you switch to the Xbox 360 from other entertainment sources (such as a satellite box or a VCR). You have to switch both the TV and the receiver input.

- ✔ **Through the TV's audio input and output to the audio system**

  Extra connections may hurt the sound quality a little. Your TV set can automatically send the matching audio to your sound system when you change video sources (such as satellite boxes and VCRs).

Many TVs that have audio outputs have two options:

- **Variable output:** Adjusts its output volume based on the volume setting on the TV (and the TV remote control)

  We recommend variable output for most situations because it lets you use your existing TV remote to control the volume.

- **Fixed output** (sometimes called "audio out" or "line out"): Volume is not adjustable with the TV remote control

Analog output

If you use analog Xbox 360 audio output, you can choose between two types of output:

- ✔ **Mono** (single-speaker sound)

  If your TV or sound system has just one audio input jack (usually a white jack), use mono analog output.

- ✔ **Dolby Pro Logic II,** which works with most analog sound systems:

  - Standard stereo TV sound systems

  - Two-speaker stereo sound systems

  - Simulated surround sound systems (such as Dolby Virtual Surround and SRS TruSurround)

  - Dolby Pro Logic surround sound

  - Dolby Pro Logic II 5.1 surround sound

    ".1" surround sound systems, like Dolby Pro Logic II, can use a sub-woofer. You can read about subwoofers in the section, "Subwoofer," later in this chapter.

If you don't use a single-speaker mono sound system, skip to the section "Dolby Pro Logic II output," later in this chapter, to set up your multi-speaker analog audio system (even if your stereo TV or sound system doesn't actually use Dolby Pro Logic II).

Mono output

Mono puts all the game sounds through both Xbox 360 analog audio jacks (red and white).

Mono sound technology

When you use mono, it doesn't matter which Xbox 360 audio jack you connect to your sound system. If your TV sound system only has one audio jack (usually white), you may find this the best connection.

If you use mono sound with a multi-speaker sound system (like a stereo TV or a surround sound audio system), you can hear sound from all the speakers, but you can't tell the direction of the sound:

✔ If you're connected to a stereo audio system, Xbox 360 mono audio doesn't tell you whether sounds are on your left or right.

✔ If you're connected to a surround sound audio system, Xbox 360 mono audio doesn't tell you whether

- Sounds are behind or in front of you
- Sounds are on your left or right

Mono sound setup

If you need to use mono sound with your Xbox 360, follow these steps:

1. **Open the System blade of the Xbox 360 Dashboard.**

2. **Select Console Settings and press the A button.**

3. **Pick the Audio option.**

4. **Pick the Analog Output option.**

   Under Analog Output, you have two choices (as you can see in Figure 9-1):

   - Mono
   - Dolby Pro Logic II

5. **Select Mono and press the A button.**

Dolby Pro Logic II output

You may find Dolby Pro Logic II the best analog audio setting if your sound system has

✔ More than one analog audio input channel

   Usually a red input jack and a white input jack

✔ More than one speaker

Depending on the audio device that you connect to your Xbox 360 console, the Dolby Pro Logic II analog output can produce either stereo (two channel) sound or 5.1 surround sound. You may want to choose the surround sound option, even if you only connect to a normal stereo because this choice gives you an output that works for non-surround stereo as well.

After you make your choices, press the B button to go back to the main Console Settings page. The audio option highlights and shows you the current settings that you've chosen for both analog and digital.

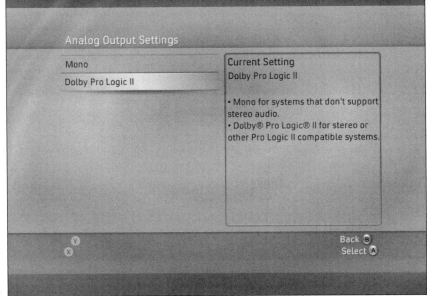

Analog Output Settings

Mono

Dolby Pro Logic II

Current Setting
Dolby Pro Logic II

• Mono for systems that don't support stereo audio.
• Dolby® Pro Logic® II for stereo or other Pro Logic II compatible systems.

Back (B)
Select (A)

Figure 9-1:
You have only two options for analog output, Mono or Dolby Pro Logic II.

You have your audio set up for both games and for DVD movies, so you end up with Dolby Pro Logic II or Dolby Digital for both types of media.

Great Sound Systems

Your perfect Xbox 360 sound system depends on your *budget, equipment,* and *living space.*

You can start using your Xbox 360 without a fancy sound system. If your TV can produce sound, you can be up and running without any other equipment. The preceding sections of this chapter show you your current connection options.

Baseline audio

You can connect your Xbox 360 audio to the TV with RCA cables (included with your console).

If your TV has only one audio input jack, you can still hook up your Xbox 360 if you

- ✔ Set your Analog Output to Mono; see the "Analog Output" section, earlier in this chapter.
- ✔ Connect either of the two RCA plugs from the Xbox 360 into your TV.

The quality that you get from a direct TV connection depends on the audio system in your TV (which might not be too shabby).

Subwoofer

To make the single biggest improvement to any home audio system, just install a subwoofer. Even at low volumes, a subwoofer improves whatever you listen to.

You generally get subwoofers as part of a surround sound system, but you can also get them as add-ons if you start with two speakers.

If your sound system doesn't have connections for a subwoofer, you probably can't add one easily.

If you have a subwoofer, or if you plan on getting one, then you can use a new technology known as Dolby Virtual Speaker. This new audio technology from Dolby can simulate surround sound out of only two front speakers and a subwoofer. A few receivers use this technology, including some from Denon and Kenwood, and you can also sometimes find it in computer software (such as PowerDVD).

When you add a subwoofer, watch your volume carefully if you don't want to disturb other people. Bass frequencies carry farther than high frequencies, so the subwoofer sound goes through the walls to adjacent rooms or apartments more easily.

Subwoofers come in two main flavors: powered and passive.

Powered

Powered subwoofers contain their own amplifier, so they don't place any load on your receiver. You usually hook up this type of subwoofer with a single RCA cable, although with some models, you can also hook your regular speaker output wires up to the subwoofer (and then on to the speakers), and the subwoofer signal comes out of the main signal.

If your receiver has a subwoofer line out, use that line out to connect with a single RCA cable.

You probably want to use a powered subwoofer in most cases:

- It generally provides the best performance and power for the price.
- It leaves your receiver free for mid- and high frequencies.

Sometimes, large front speakers include built-in passive subwoofers, and for many situations in small- or medium-size spaces, those subwoofers are up to the task. In other situations in which you have only small front speakers with limited bass response or you need more power for a larger space, then you want to go with a separate, powered subwoofer and a receiver with a sub-woofer line out.

Passive

Passive subwoofers work just like any other speaker. They don't have any of their own amplification. This type of subwoofer uses a lot of your receiver's power because producing extremely low frequencies requires more power than producing the mid- or high frequencies.

You connect passive subwoofers to your receiver with regular speaker wires.

Sometimes, large front speakers include passive subwoofers built-in, and for many situations in small- or medium-size spaces, those subwoofers can get the job done.

Surround sound

Surround sound describes a wide range of technologies and options. They all have the same goal: creating sound that seems to come from a location that matches what you're watching.

This concept is just an extension of the stereo sound that has existed for many years. Audio from a recording (video or audio) doesn't all come from the same direction because sound doesn't behave that way in the real world.

You don't need surround sound to play Xbox 360 games, but it certainly can improve the effect. When you hear sound coming from all around you, it can really make you feel like you're right inside the game's environment.

Speakers

To produce a surround sound effect similar to the setup in a movie theater, you need at least five speakers:

✔ **Left and right front speakers,** like a standard stereo sound system

✔ **A center speaker** for dialog

You may want to place the center speaker directly above or below the TV screen so the center channel sounds like it's coming directly out of the screen.

✔ **Two surround speakers** at the side or behind the viewer

The following section, "Connections," describes surround speaker connection options.

Surround sound systems often have a subwoofer for bass sound that can give you lower (deeper) sounds than your other speakers can produce. Very low frequency sound isn't directional, so the subwoofer location doesn't affect the surround sound. ".1" usually identifies a surround system with a subwoofer; for example, a 5.1 surround system has five standard speakers plus a subwoofer.

Connections

Aside from cost, the biggest obstacle to surround sound often involves running speaker wire to the rear surround speakers without making a mess of the room. Your connection options depend on your wallet, room layout, and aesthetic standards.

Wired rear speakers

If you have a continuous wall from your surround sound equipment to your rear speakers, you may be able to

✔ Neatly run the speaker wire along the base of the wall.

✔ Hide speaker wire under the *baseboard* (the trim panel where the wall meets the floor)

✔ Use a special speaker wire (called *super flat* or *tape* wire) that you can't easily see on the wall. You can paint this wire to match the wall.

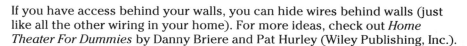

Some flat speaker wires have an adhesive back that sticks straight to your wall.

If you have access behind your walls, you can hide wires behind walls (just like all the other wiring in your home). For more ideas, check out *Home Theater For Dummies* by Danny Briere and Pat Hurley (Wiley Publishing, Inc.).

Wireless rear speakers

Wireless surround speakers may give you the solution you need if

✔ You can't hide wire from your audio equipment to your rear speakers.

✔ You can't connect wires without running across the floor or a doorway.

You can get wireless surround sound speakers from a few manufacturers. They generally fall into three types based on the type of wireless signal they use:

- ✔ **Infrared (IR):** You don't find infrared speakers very much anymore because they have quality limitations that you may find hard to get past and because they work on a line-of-sight basis, which means that the movement of people, furniture placement, and so on can easily disrupt them.

- ✔ **Radio frequency (RF):** RF speakers, which, similar to cordless phones, use the 900 MHz or 2.4 GHz frequencies, are currently the most common type of wireless speaker. I have used RF speakers myself, and they work quite well, although they are prone to interference from other devices operating at the same frequency.

  For 2.4 GHZ speakers, you may have some conflicting devices, like your home wireless network, your cordless phone, or possibly even your microwave oven.

- ✔ **Bluetooth:** Bluetooth-based wireless speakers, which are similar to RF speakers in many ways, are the newest concept, and they're really picking up steam. Bluetooth is described as a short-range technology, but many reviews of Bluetooth-based speakers have found that they work well at any standard home theater distance and often quite farther, as well.

You may want to get RF or Bluetooth speakers at this point, with Bluetooth being the winner for quality and flexibility (Bluetooth is supported by a wide range of devices), but it does cost a bit more than RF.

When setting up wireless rear speakers, you get to avoid the speaker wire, but each speaker probably needs a power connection. Luckily, you can often find a power outlet near your rear speakers much more easily than running speaker wire back there.

You can buy some wireless speakers as part of a set, restricting you to a specific combination of receiver, wireless technology, and speakers. Before you buy such a set, be aware that you won't have any flexibility to change any one part of your system in the future.

Focus on wireless systems that are structured as simple components: the *transmitter* (the part that converts your receiver's output into wireless signals) that hooks up to your receiver with standard line or speaker outputs, and the *wireless receiver* (the part that converts the wireless signal back into outputs that your speakers understand) that sports regular speaker wire connections. A flexible system lets you upgrade your speakers or receiver in the future without having to replace the wireless component, and you can choose a different wireless system while still preserving your investment in the receiver and speakers.

Simulated surround

To get around the hassles of rear speakers, you can simply not use them at all. A number of options produce surround sound out of two (or two plus a surround) speakers. You can find one of the most common marketed as TruSurround (by SRS Labs, www.srslabs.com) or TruSurround XT (an improved form of the original technology). TruSurround allows simulated surround sound from just two speakers, and you commonly find the technology on TVs, DVD players, and even software music players.

Dolby, the folks behind such technologies as Dolby Pro Logic, also has a simulated surround technology available. This technology, Dolby Virtual Speaker (sometime incorrectly called Dolby Virtual Surround in product information), works together with other surround technologies, such as Dolby Pro Logic, to produce the effect of a surround sound system through just two speakers. A few receivers, including ones from Onkyo and Denon, include this technology, and you can also find it on some laptops and TVs. A related technology is called Dolby Headphone, which works in the same general ways as Dolby Virtual Speaker but is specially designed to work with the different space, position, and speaker characteristics of headphones.

Privacy

Need to keep the volume down on your nightly gaming session? The sound of exploding grenades and rocket launchers bothering the folks next door? Kids waking up scared because of the horrible noises coming from the downstairs TV? A couple of audio features may let you play to your heart's content without disturbing the peace.

Headphones

Headphones let you hear everything clearly, while keeping the noise away from everyone else. Traditionally, headphones could only produce standard two-channel stereo sound, but now you also have the option of 5.1 surround sound wrapped right around your head.

What about the Xbox 360's headset?

Before spending time talking about options for headphones, you might be wondering about the Xbox Live headset that plugs right into your controller and is even included in the premium Xbox 360 System. This headset does its job just fine, but it isn't designed to replace your TV's speakers or a stereo system. The Xbox Live headset plays voice chat into your ears, but it doesn't output the rest of the audio coming from the Xbox 360. So if you want to use headphones to listen to your games, you need a regular pair of headphones in addition to the Xbox Live headset. One problem though, is that if you do go out and get a normal pair of headphones to wear, then you can have some trouble wearing the Xbox Live headset at the same time. At this time, I haven't seen any set of headphones out there that could handle the require-ment to output the normal audio output of the game while still providing the microphone and chat audio features of the Xbox Live headset. Unfortunately, you just have to choose either to not chat and wear your headphones or to use the Xbox Live headset and play the main audio through the TV.

Stereo sound

When looking for regular headphones, you need to consider a few important features:

- ✔ Impedance (how much power it takes to drive the headphone properly)
- ✔ Sound quality
- ✔ Size and comfort
- ✔ Cable length and connector type(s)

Impedance really only matters if you're planning to use your headphones with a portable device. If you plan to hook up to your home theater receiver, then the receiver likely has sufficient power out of its headphone jack to handle even full-size headphones. On the other hand, a portable, such as an iPod, isn't really supposed to drive a full-size set of headphones, and sound quality suffers. For reference, the headphones that come with most MP3 play-ers are rated at 32 ohms, and many high-end headphones (from Sennheiser, Grado, and so on) can have impedance ratings from 100 ohms to 300 ohms. Anything with an impedance of 100 ohms or higher may have trouble working well with a portable device.

You probably see sound quality as the number-one requirement, but you can have a hard time figuring out what you're dealing with based on any form of specifications listed in a catalog or on the Web. Some people like to look at the Frequency Response of a set of headphones, which tells the lowest and highest sounds the headphones can produce, but this specification doesn't tell you whether or not those frequencies are output *accurately*. You may want to go to a store that sells a wide variety of headphones and try listening to them yourself with a consistent source material. Taking your own portable music player can work, although if you don't plan to use the headphones with a portable, you may be better off getting the store to plug the head-phones into a good-quality receiver instead. Turn off any bass-boost feature of the source, including any "loudness" feature, because you can't get an accurate idea of the headphone's ability to reproduce low frequencies with those features running.

For more information on headphones, including reviews and news, check out the headphone-focused site: www.goodcans.com.

You may find headphones, especially ones that you want to wear for long periods of intense gaming, quite uncomfortable. Looking at the weight of various pairs can give you an idea of how they feel on your head over time, but as with sound quality, you probably just want to go to a store and try on a variety. If you can't go on a personal shopping trip, read as many reviews of headphones as you can; reviews often cover how comfortable the headphones are.

For wired headphones, you need to have sufficient cable length to comfortably reach your preferred seat, with enough slack that the cord can run along the floor and back to the source component. You also need a connector that matches the output of your receiver, TV, or whatever device you want to hook the headphones to. For portables, some TVs, and very few home theater receivers, you need a ⅛-inch jack (the standard headphone size); most receivers use a larger (¼-inch) jack. Regardless of what type of connector you get, you can find adapters to convert ¼-inch to ⅛-inch and vice versa. Just make sure you buy a stereo adapter.

Surround sound

If headphones work for you, but you want surround sound, you're in luck. You have a couple of paths that you can take to enjoy surround sound:

- ✔ Receivers that support Dolby Headphone output a headphone signal that simulates surround sound through regular stereo headphones.

- ✔ Surround headphones (from manufacturers such as Zalman, LTB Audio, and Acoustic Research) don't just simulate surround sound, they mount up to six speakers into a pair of headphones and output real 5.1 sound right into your head.

If you have or can find the first option, a system that supports Dolby Headphone, then that option makes a great choice because it supports any standard headphone. Otherwise, you can go out and buy a pair of surround headphones, but they can cost you into the hundreds of dollars (some go as high as $1,200, but you can find others available for around $100). Surround headphones have their own base system that you can hook up directly to your Xbox 360 by using an optical cable (Toslink), and some even support wireless connections to the headphones themselves. You get a quite convincing end result, with the headphones accurately reproducing surround effects from an Xbox 360 or a movie. Although a full set of surround speakers sounds better than all but the most expensive surround headphones, not everyone has the space or the money to set up a full set of speakers.

Wireless headsets

In addition to the wide variety of wired headphones from Shure, Grado, and others, you can also find quite a few sets of wireless headphones. Wireless headphones tend to work with either RF (working at frequencies of 900 MHz or 2.4 GHz) or Bluetooth, just like the wireless surround sound speakers that you can read about in the "Speakers" section, earlier in this chapter.

The biggest concerns with wireless headphones are sound quality and range, but when you're evaluating headphones for use with Xbox 360, you probably aren't too worried about range. When playing, you need to be able to see the TV, so you can't really be that far from the source, anyway. Sound quality is a different matter. Remember that 2.4 GHz and Bluetooth systems produce better sound than the older 900 MHz RF headphones that you can find for sale. Wireless headphones come with a base that handles transmitting the audio signal out to your headphones, and you can connect that base to your Xbox's audio output directly or to the output of your stereo.

Dynamic range compression

Dynamic range compression, or DRC (often labeled using a friendly name such as Night Mode), reduces the range of sound volumes that your system can produce. You don't get quieter normal sound, but the maximum volume doesn't increase past a certain point, no matter how loud the source material is.

I find DRC useful because I can't use headphones when playing at night. Wearing headphones might keep the noise from waking up the kids, but it might also prevent me from noticing if one of them woke up crying.

If you plan to do some nighttime listening, then look for DRC in stereo systems.

Make sure you turn off the range compression when you don't need it, such as during the day or when the whole family is watching. Otherwise, you're reducing the quality of your sound system for no reason.

Buying a New Home Theater System

So you just bought an Xbox 360 and you're all excited about the digital audio output and surround sound, but you don't have any home stereo equipment at all. . . . What can you do?

Don't panic, you do have a few options.

At the very worst, you can hook up your Xbox 360 to your TV, which probably sounds anywhere from okay to great, depending on your specific model of television. With that connection made, you're ready to use your Xbox 360, so you remove the temptation to run out as fast as you can and pick up the first home theater system you see. Even the lower-end surround systems cost a fair bit of money, so you don't want to make this decision lightly or quickly.

Now, before you head to the store, you need to give some thought to your audio needs (what you plan to use this system for), your budget, and your timeline.

What do you need your new system to do?

When thinking about your audio requirements, consider these questions:

- Do you need surround sound?

- What devices do you need to hook up to this system?

- Do you need to worry about the volume of the system at night?

- Is wiring up rear speakers a problem?

If you've decided that you don't need surround sound, you may still want to include a subwoofer in your plans. A subwoofer really makes any audio system better. If, on the other hand, you do want surround sound, then you need to make sure your system supports the following minimum specs:

- At least one optical input, possibly more if you have a DVD player (or other audio source) in addition to the Xbox 360

- Several standard, 2-channel inputs for connecting analog devices

- Support for Dolby Digital

You may find the following features nice, but you don't need them for surround sound:

- High bandwidth component video switching

    This feature lets you hook up multiple HDTV signal sources to the home theater receiver, connect output cables to your TV, and then switch between video/audio sources through the receiver.

- Support for Dolby Digital EX (which enables 6.1 and 7.1 surround sound), DTS (5.1 format used by some DVD movies and other sources), and/or DTS-ES (6.1/7.1 version of DTS)

Concerned about waking people up with the sound of explosions? Make sure the system you get has some form of *dynamic range compression,* sometimes known as Night Mode, which you can read about in the section "Dynamic range compression," earlier in this chapter.

In terms of hooking up rear speakers, if you can't hide the wires, and if you (or others in your house) just can't stomach stringing wires across the room to set up rear speakers, then you might want to look into the available wireless surround systems available on the market. Panasonic makes one such system, the SH-FX50, but it only works with their home theater systems. A more flexible option might be the Kenwood wireless speaker system, the RFU-6100, that works with any brand of receiver and any set of surround speakers.

Budget and timeline

Two questions determine whether you can get everything you need all in one shot, or if you need to build up a full system, piece by piece.

- ✔ How much do you want to spend?
- ✔ How fast do you want to be set up?

I just can't wait for good audio

If you want a surround system up and running right away, then you may want to buy one of the many "home theater in a box" systems. These products are a combination of a receiver, a DVD player, and a full set of speakers. You can find some models for under $500.

Don't do it! Leave those products alone and buy yourself the individual pieces. These "home theater in a box" products are often designed as a single unit, combining the DVD player (that you don't need) into the receiver and sometimes even making the speakers so that they can connect to only the receiver they came with. You can set up these systems very easily, you don't have to think much to buy them, and you can be done with all your decision making by picking up a single box. But if you ever want to change things in the future, you might find yourself unable to swap anything out. These types of products don't really support replacing the speakers or just the receiver — they're an all-or-nothing type of system.

The failings of these boxed systems don't mean that packages are a bad idea. Many stores bundle a good home theater receiver with a full set of surround speakers for just a little bit more than the one-box option, and you may want to consider those deals. Because the components may vary in a bundle, the price range can start as low as $500 and go up to $2,000 or more. It all depends on the store and the bundle.

I'm willing to take my time

I call this the incremental approach to home theater. Spread your purchases over time as you find spare cash:

1. Start with the minimum equipment that you need for very good sound:

   • A good receiver

   • A good pair of stereo speakers

   The "Great Sound Systems" section, earlier in this chapter, describes the features that your receiver needs.

   When choosing front speakers, the corresponding surround and center channel speakers from that manufacturer are *timbre matched,* which basically means all the speakers sound the same.

2. When you have some money available, pick up a subwoofer.

   You don't need to worry about matching your subwoofer's manufacturer to your other speakers.

3. Finish with a center channel and rear surround speakers.

   You want these speakers to match your front speakers.

Building your system in stages gives you the biggest bang for the money that you have available.

I can't get a new audio system at all

Many TVs have pretty good sound systems. Some TVs can simulate surround sound with only their built-in speakers.

If your TV has SRS TruSurround, turn it on in the TV's menu. This technology simulates surround sound with only two speakers, taking advantage of the Dolby Pro Logic information in the stereo signal.

For more information

Technologies, prices, and features all change rapidly in the world of home theater and home audio systems, so check out our Web site at www.xbox4dummies.com for additional information and links related to this chapter.

Chapter 10

Customizing Your Console

*Y*ou'll love Xbox 360 for the game play, but you'll love it even more when you make it your own. Make your mark with the information we give you in this chapter.

Faceplates

White isn't for everybody. The fastest and easiest way to trick out your Xbox 360 is by adding a custom faceplate. A *faceplate* is a plastic cover that clips to the front of your Xbox 360, and all kinds are available. The Xbox 360 comes with a plain white faceplate that matches the console.

Figure 10-1 shows the Flames faceplate.

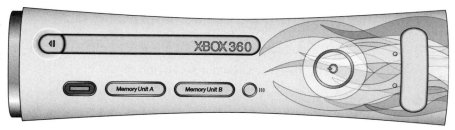

Figure 10-1: A new faceplate is the easiest way to customize your Xbox 360.

The faceplate can either

- Match your other home entertainment devices
- Be a little flashier

LAN parties, described in Chapter 12, are a great reason to get a custom faceplate. Keeping track of your own Xbox is easier if it's customized!

Changing the faceplate is a piece of cake.

Removing the faceplate

Follow these steps to remove the old faceplate from your Xbox 360:

1. **Turn off your Xbox 360.**
2. **Remove any memory cards you have plugged in.**
3. **Put your finger in the slot on the side of the faceplate and pull the faceplate.**

   The slot is by the USB ports. The faceplate should pull off with moderate force.

If the faceplate is hard to remove, *don't force it.* Keep the button pressed and gently rock the faceplate back and forth until it's released.

Attaching the faceplate

Popping a faceplate on is easy if you follow these steps:

1. **Line up the faceplate tabs with the slots on the Xbox 360.**
2. **Push the faceplate into place.**
3. **Check the installation:**
   - The faceplate should look correctly installed, with even gaps.
   - The disk tray should operate normally.
   - The memory units should fit in the memory slots.

If the faceplate doesn't look or work right, pull the faceplate off (following the instructions in the preceding section) and try again.

Dashboard

The Xbox 360 lets you access photos and music from other devices on your home network. You customize your Xbox 360 Dashboard with either

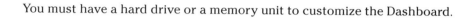

➤ Photos from your own devices or your PCs

➤ Themes on Xbox Live

Each custom faceplate from Microsoft has an associated theme available from Xbox Live.

You must have a hard drive or a memory unit to customize the Dashboard.

Your own photos

You don't have to come home to find your profile decorated with daisies, courtesy of your baby sister. Photo backgrounds are set for each user profile. Figure 10-2 shows a custom Dashboard.

Figure 10-2:
A custom background on the Xbox 360 Dashboard.

Chapter 5 shows how to view photos with your Xbox 360.

To set a custom photo as your Dashboard background, follow these steps:

1. **Navigate to the Media Blade on your Xbox 360.**

2. **Choose Pictures and then press A.**

   This opens a page allowing you to choose which device or PC you want to browse for pictures.

3. **Select the device or computer containing the picture you want to use and then press A.**

   You'll see the photos available on the PC or the device you've chosen.

4. **Use the left analog stick to navigate to the folder containing the picture you want to use and then press A.**

   This opens the folder and show you a thumbnail view of the pictures.

5. **Select the picture and press A.**

   You'll see the picture and a list of options for that picture.

6. **Choose Make Dashboard Background from the list of options and press A.**

Some pictures work better as backgrounds:

✔ Use photos with smooth color transitions.

   It's best to find a picture with big areas of similar color.

✔ Avoid photos that have a lot small details. This makes the text in the dashboard more difficult to read.

Xbox Live themes

Xbox Live provides the easiest way to customize your profile: professionally designed themes. Figure 10-3 shows a game theme purchased from Xbox Live Marketplace. Themes include

✔ Popular games

✔ Designs that match the Xbox 360 custom faceplates

✔ Other designs — the sky's the limit!

Chapter 4 shows how to set up an Xbox Live account. After you do that, you'll be able to access and purchase themes.

Figure 10-3:
A theme
can really
change the
Dashboard's
look.

Look for themes available with the Xbox 360 games you purchase. Some games have theme codes available in the package, and you'll be able to use this code to download a theme based on the game title.

Wireless Accessories

Wireless control can really make playing games on your Xbox 360 more comfortable and convenient, to say the least. Imagine how impressed your friend will be when you hand her a wireless control and sit back, ready for unencumbered play.

Turn on your Xbox 360 by pressing the Guide button in the middle of the controller. You can leave your favorite game in your Xbox 360 and jump right into it when you want to play.

How cool is a wireless controller? Count the ways:

- ✔ Clears the floor for more important things like feet, furniture, and empty popcorn bowls
- ✔ Looks cool on your coffee table
- ✔ Quickly tucks under cushions when your five-year-old cousin comes over

Game controller

The Xbox 360 premium edition includes a wireless controller. (You can buy a wireless game controller separately if you started with an Xbox 360 Core System.)

Use the Xbox 360 wireless controller with either

✔ 2 AA batteries

You can use rechargeable AA batteries in your Xbox 360 wireless controller. However, you must remove those batteries from the controller and recharge them in their own charging devices. The Xbox 360 battery-charging devices work only with the Xbox 360 rechargeable battery packs.

✔ The Xbox 360 rechargeable battery

The Xbox 360 rechargeable battery should let you play about 25 hours between charges.

You have a couple of options for putting the juice in Xbox 360 rechargeable batteries.

Play and Charge Kit cable

The Play and Charge Kit lets you play while the Xbox 360 rechargeable battery charges inside the controller.

While the cable's connected, your wireless controller is powered through a USB cable that also charges the battery. Figure 10-4 shows the Play and Charge Kit cable.

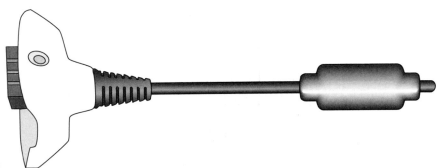

Figure 10-4:
The Play and Charge cable keeps you playing while the controller charges.

The wireless controller always controls the game wirelessly, whether or not you're charging the batteries through the USB cable.

Follow these steps to use the wireless controller with the Play and Charge Kit:

1. **Open the battery door on the wireless controller and remove the battery pack.**

2. **Insert the rechargeable battery pack and replace the cover.**

3. **Plug the large end of the Play and Charge cable into the front of the controller.**

4. **Plug the small end of the Play and Charge cable into one of the USB controller ports on the front of the console.**

   The light on the charge cable will turn from red to green when the battery pack is fully charged.

When the battery is charged, you can unplug the Play and Charge cable and put it away without missing a beat while you're playing.

Quick Charge Kit

The Quick Charge Kit is a battery charger for the Xbox 360 Battery Pack, which is available separately. This kit works only with the Xbox 360 Battery Pack and cannot be used to charge other battery types.

You can use only the Quick Charge Kit or the Play and Charge cable to recharge Xbox 360 batteries for your wireless controller.

If you don't want to bother with the Play and Charge cable, and you don't want to wait while batteries recharge, buy two rechargeable battery packs, alternate charging them in the charger, and swap them when you need to.

Media Center Remotes

An Xbox 360 Media Center Remote is the most convenient tool for

- ✔ Choosing media content
- ✔ Playing DVDs
- ✔ Controlling your Windows Media Center PC through your Xbox 360

The remotes come in two versions.

Universal Media Remote

The full-on Xbox 360 Universal Media Remote has all the functions you need for both Xbox 360 and a complete entertainment system.

Figure 10-5 shows the Xbox 360 Universal Media Remote.

Figure 10-5:
The Xbox
360
Universal
Media
Remote.

This remote has a numeric keypad so you can control

- ✔ Your TV and other components in your home entertainment system
- ✔ A Windows Media Center PC

Small media remote

The small Xbox 360 Media remote is included in some Xbox 360 systems. This remote allows you to navigate the dashboard and provides controls for the basic DVD functions, but lacks a numeric keypad. (So that's obviously why it's smaller!)

This remote is available only as a promotional item in some Xbox 360 packages, and it isn't available separately. After the initial Xbox 360 release period, you may not be able to find a package that includes it.

Part IV
Pushing the Outer Limits

The 5th Wave   By Rich Tennant

"We need to pimp our Xbox 360."

In this part . . .

Tune in here to read about the advanced ways you can use your Xbox 360. First, master the parental control features of the Xbox 360 to control the content that's usable on the box. Got a Media Center PC? You can connect to it from the Xbox 360 to watch TV and recorded television shows. Planning a party? Why not make it an Xbox 360 party?

Chapter 11 shows how to use the parental control features of the Xbox 360 to limit the type of games and movies that can be played on the 360. Chapter 12 tells you about how to make your Xbox 360 the center of a great party in your house. You can network consoles together for great multi-player action, and you can project a huge picture on the wall for life-sized gaming action.

Chapter 13 explains how to use the Xbox 360 with a Windows Media Center PC. The Windows Media Center PC is a special kind of PC that allows you to use the computer in much the same way you use a TiVo or other digital video recorder. By using the Xbox 360 as a Media Center Extender, you can keep the Media Center PC under a desk in the office and view content on the television in the living room.

Chapter 11

Parental Control

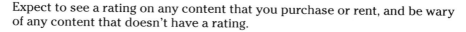

*V*ideo games, computers, music, and TV likely form a large part of your child's life. Each kind of media can be a source of great concern to parents. An Xbox 360 introduces a powerful multimedia system into your children's lives; with that system comes new concerns. This chapter gives you advice and technical options for concerns about violent or sexual game content, exposure to unknown people through the Internet, and the sheer quantity of time spent in front of a TV.

Rating Systems

Most video game manufacturers and movie producers have their products rated. The rating system for your Xbox 360 depends on your country.

Expect to see a rating on any content that you purchase or rent, and be wary of any content that doesn't have a rating.

Unrated games and movies may have shocking violence, language, or sex.

United States

In the United States, a review board — set up by the Motion Picture Association of America (MPAA), who are sent copies of pre-release movies to view and then categorize — provide these ratings. That same rating concept has extended to video games through an organization called the Electronic Software Ratings Board (ESRB).

ESRB ratings

If a game has a range of possible content, it receives the most restrictive rating that applies. In other words, if a game is mostly child-friendly but has a few scenes of intense graphic violence, it's rated based on those violent scenes, not on the average of the whole game.

The ESRB assigns one of six different ratings to a video game; see Figure 11-1.

If you want to browse games by rating or find a specific game's rating, check the Search feature on the ESRB site at `www.esrb.com/esrbratings_search.asp`.

Early Childhood

The safest possible rating is Early Childhood (EC). Games in this category should be fine for children as young as three years old. These games have no violence, sexual content, or even situations where onscreen characters are in danger.

You probably can't find any Xbox 360 games rated EC.

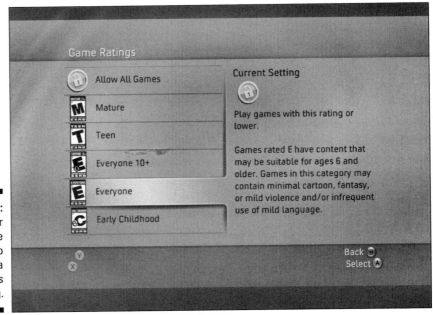

Figure 11-1: Look for these images to identify a game's rating.

Everyone

The Everyone (E) category is misleading. It actually means everyone over six years of age.

A lot of Xbox 360 games fall into this group, including popular titles such as *Project Gotham Racing, RalliSport Challenge,* the *Harry Potter* games, *LEGO Star Wars,* and most sports games, such as *NFL Fever, NHL 06,* and *NBA Street.* Even *Barbie's Wild Horse Adventure* is rated E rather than EC.

When onscreen characters are in unsafe situations (such as when Barbie navigates a cliff), those instances push an otherwise completely safe game into the E category.

Games in this category may contain minimal amounts of the following types of content

- ✓ **Cartoon violence:** Think of a cat hitting a dog over the head with a bone.
- ✓ **Fantasy violence:** Situations are clearly not real-life.
- ✓ **Mild realistic violence:** Smashing cars in a racing game.

Everyone 10+

Everyone 10+ is suitable for kids 10 years old or older. This rating doesn't get used very often. Games in this category generally contain the same elements as games rated E, just with a bit more than "minimal" content. In addition, mild suggestive content might appear in E 10+ games, such as characters with revealing outfits or mild bits of innuendo; such content isn't allowed in an E-rated game.

Think of Everyone 10+ as a bit stronger than an Everyone rating.

Teen

Teen (T) games are aimed at 13-year-olds and older. Teen-rated games increase the violence and may include blood, strong language, or mildly suggestive themes (like those themes that can appear in the E 10+ rating, in the preceding section).

This category contains many titles, including the new Tony Hawk game *American Wasteland, Kameo,* and *Need for Speed.*

Mature

Mature (M) is aimed at "kids" age 17 and older. Games in this category can contain (among other things) intense violence, strong language, and some sexual content. *Perfect Dark Zero, Halo,* and *Quake 4* all fit in this group, as does the infamous *Grand Theft Auto.* The first three games fall into this category mostly for their violent content, but *Grand Theft Auto* hits on every possible style of inappropriate content, including drug references, sexual references, and strong language, along with the standard intense violence.

Adults Only

The most restricted rating in the ESRB system, Adults Only (AO), is reserved for games best left to folks who are 18 and over.

The only Xbox game that I know has received the AO rating is *Grand Theft Auto: San Andreas,* a later game in the *Grand Theft Auto* series. At the moment, no Xbox 360 game has been assigned this rating.

Descriptors

The ESRB rating system includes descriptors that describe game content. Say you decide that games rated M are okay, as long as they don't contain any sexual content. You can pick up a game, look at the larger ESRB rating box on the back, and read the descriptors. *Perfect Dark Zero,* for example, is rated M and has "Blood, Language, Violence," but no mention of sexual content, so you put it in your cart and keep shopping. You pick another M-rated game, *Gun,* and it has "Sexual Themes" listed, so you leave it on the shelf and go pay for your copy of *Perfect Dark.*

You can find a full list of descriptors and their meanings in the following section and online at `www.esrb.org`:

- **Alcohol Reference:** Reference to and/or images of alcoholic beverages.
- **Animated Blood:** Discolored and/or unrealistic depictions of blood.
- **Blood:** Depictions of blood.
- **Blood and Gore:** Depictions of blood or the mutilation of body parts.
- **Cartoon Violence:** Violent actions involving cartoon-like situations and characters. This may include violence where a character is unharmed after the action has been inflicted.
- **Comic Mischief:** Depictions or dialog involving slapstick or suggestive humor.
- **Crude Humor:** Depictions or dialogue involving vulgar antics, including "bathroom" humor.
- **Drug Reference:** Reference to and/or images of illegal drugs.
- **Edutainment:** Content provides user with specific skills, development, or reinforcement learning within an entertainment setting. Skill development is a main part of product.
- **Fantasy Violence:** Violent actions of a fantasy nature involving human or nonhuman characters in situations easily distinguishable from real life.

✔ **Informational:** Overall content of product contains data, facts, resource information, reference materials, or instructional text.

✔ **Intense Violence:** Graphic and realistic-looking depictions of physical conflict. This may involve extreme and/or realistic blood, gore, weapons, and depictions of human injury and death.

✔ **Language:** Mild to moderate use of profanity.

✔ **Lyrics:** Mild references to profanity, sexuality, violence, alcohol, or drug use in music.

✔ **Mature Humor:** Depictions or dialogue involving "adult" humor, including sexual references.

✔ **Mild Violence:** Mild scenes depicting characters in unsafe and/or violent situations.

✔ **Nudity:** Graphic or prolonged depictions of nudity.

✔ **Partial Nudity:** Brief and/or mild depictions of nudity.

✔ **Real Gambling:** Player can gamble, including betting or wagering real cash or currency.

✔ **Sexual Themes:** Mild to moderate sexual references and/or depictions; may include partial nudity.

✔ **Sexual Violence:** Depictions of rape or other sexual acts.

✔ **Simulated Gambling:** Player can gamble without betting or wagering real cash or currency.

✔ **Some Adult Assistance May Be Needed:** Intended for very young ages.

✔ **Strong Language:** Explicit and/or frequent use of profanity.

✔ **Strong Lyrics:** Explicit and/or frequent references to profanity, sex, violence, alcohol, or drug use in music.

✔ **Strong Sexual Content:** Graphic references to and/or depictions of sexual behavior, possibly including nudity.

✔ **Suggestive Themes:** Mild provocative references or materials.

✔ **Tobacco Reference:** Reference to and/or images of tobacco products.

✔ **Use of Drugs:** The consumption or use of illegal drugs.

✔ **Use of Alcohol:** The consumption of alcoholic beverages.

✔ **Use of Tobacco:** The consumption of tobacco products.

✔ **Violence:** Scenes involving aggressive conflict.

Use ESRB's Web search feature to look by both rating and descriptor. Using ESRB's search, you can filter your list based on criteria. For example, you can find all T-rated or E-rated Xbox 360 games that do not have any "Intense Violence."

Movie ratings

The MPAA has five movie ratings categories:

- **General** (G): Suitable for all audiences.

- **Parental Guidance** (PG): Some violence, drug use, strong language, or situations result in this rating. A movie with this rating may be inappropriate for a child, so the parent(s) may want to research or view the movie first.

- **Parental Guidance Strongly Recommended** (PG-13): Games or movies with this rating are probably not suitable for children under 13. Even for kids 13 and older, an adult may want to be present when the kids are playing or watching.

- **Restricted** (R): Anyone 17 years old or kids with a parent or guardian can see these films. Violence throughout a movie, nudity, sexual content, and drug use may all merit this rating.

- **NC-17:** This rating limits access to 18 years and older only — no exceptions! The official definition of this category, from the MPAA's own guidelines, is any content that most parents would consider inappropriate for their children under the age of 18. Violence, sex, drug use, or other content that is present in very strong forms throughout a movie usually warrants this rating.

MPAA movie ratings are only a starting point. To find out more about a movie, specifically whether you think it's suitable for your children, the Web has several resources:

- **Kids-in-mind** (www.kids-in-mind.com): This site lets you see information about a wide variety of movies.

    Each movie is rated on three areas:

    - Sex and nudity

    - Violence and gore

    - Profanity

    The three individual ratings, given as values from 0 to 10, combine to give you a three-part value for each movie. Here are a couple of examples:

    - *Batman Begins* (MPAA rated PG-13) is rated 2.6.3 (low sexual content, fairly violent, not much profanity).

    - *Herbie: Fully Loaded* (a G-rated family movie) is rated 3.3.2.

    Each movie has a full content review, where you read real content examples. The review discusses the movie's messages and poses potential discussion topics. The site itself responds slowly and has some very annoying ads. *Hint:* Mute the sound before visiting because many of the ads have voiceovers.

✔ **Nick Jr.** (`www.nickjr.com`): Nickelodeon's site for younger folks includes a video and movie guide under their Parenting section. This guide doesn't dig into every single image and scene, but it does give you a quick Yes or No answer to the question of suitability for specific age groups.

Unlike most other sites, these reviews take into account that some movies are too slow-paced or too complicated for a younger viewer, even if the content is completely safe.

Other countries

If you aren't in the United States, your country has its own systems for rating game and movie content.

Canada

Canada uses the ESRB game ratings along with the MPAA ratings for movies. The actual DVD that you buy in Canada is probably labeled with a different rating, though — one from the Canadian Home Video Ratings Association — which you generally find as a sticker on the packaging. You don't get the information on this rating on the DVD itself, so you need to set your parent control settings by using the MPAA ratings.

Australia

Game and movie ratings are combined into a single system in Australia, one created and managed by the Office of Film and Literature Classification (OFLC). When you set up your Xbox 360 in Australia, the full OFLC information is available to control the use of games, but Xbox 360 can't restrict movies if you live in this country.

The OFLC classifies content into categories based on the level of impact that its content is expected to have on the average viewer, focusing on violence, sex, nudity, language, and drug use. You can find the available ratings listed below, followed by the impact description used in the official OFLC guidelines (`www.oflc.gov.au`):

✔ **General (G):** Very Mild

✔ **Parental Guidance (PG):** Mild

✔ **Mature (M):** Moderate

✔ **Mature Audiences 15+ (MA 15+):** Strong

✔ **Restricted 18+ (R 18+):** High

✔ **Explicit 18+ (X 18+):** Very High

Descriptions, such as *mild* and *very mild* might seem hard to turn into a specific rating for any particular movie or game, but all the currently available ratings systems are similarly vague. In the end, you (or your parents, if you aren't an adult) might need to view a few games in different categories before picking the right level for content viewing and playing restrictions.

Great Britain

Games in Great Britain are rated using the Pan European Game Information (PEGI) system, which classifies games by a combination of age and descriptors. The age classifications include 3+, 7+, 12+, 16+ and 18+, and the content descriptors are Fear, Drug Use, Sex, Violence, and Bad Language. All in all, PEGI's rating system isn't all that different from the ESRB system used in the United States, but Great Britain implements the system quite differently, using an online form that allows the game or movie publisher to determine a proper rating based on their answers to a series of yes/no questions. This approach means that if you're interested, you can very clearly see what type of content leads to what PEGI rating just by looking at the online form (available at www. pegi.info). For example, if a game or movie includes "Violence towards vulnerable or defenseless humans," it receives an automatic 18+ age rating and a descriptor of Violence.

The British Board of Film Classification, the BBFC, generally rates movies in the U.K., and they can also rate games. The BBFC classifies content into one of a long list of categories, including

- **Universal and Universal Child** (U and UC): Indicates that the content should be acceptable to almost anyone, with UC specifically indicating that the content is particularly suitable for preschool children. A game with this rating is free of bad language, contains only mild violence at the most, and has a reassuring outcome from any action.

- **Parental Guidance** (PG): Indicates that the content is generally acceptable to anyone but that some scenes might not be suitable for young children. Games that get this rating can have nudity only in a "natural" (as opposed to sexual) context; can have violence only if justified by a fantasy, historic, or comedic theme; and can't contain ongoing frightening content.

- **12(A):** Indicates that the content is suitable for children aged 12 or older. Specific restrictions prevent someone younger than 12 from renting or buying content with this rating or from viewing it in a theater unless accompanied by an adult. Content with this rating can include occasional strong language, implied sexual activity, brief nudity in a sexual context, and a wide range of violence.

✔ **15:** Limits access to only children age 15 and older and allows for all but the strongest types of inappropriate content. Drug use is allowed as long as it isn't shown as positive. Sexual activity also gets a pass under this rating, provided it isn't shown with too much detail.

✔ **18/R18:** The two strongest ratings, limiting this content to adults only. Games in the 18 category can contain almost any type of violence, drug use, and language; however, if the sexual content is too detailed or explicit, it gets an R18 rating. R18 is a bit more restrictive and is intended mainly for games and movies focused on sexual activity.

Singapore

Although Singapore has its own system for rating movies (and for games, as well), the Xbox 360 doesn't detect this system. So, if you're in Singapore, you can't use the parental control features to limit DVD and game playback.

Controlling Access

Each parent makes different decisions about what games his or her children play and movies they watch. If you're worried about your kids making that decision without your input, then you might want to investigate the Xbox 360 parental controls. The parental control system blocks access to material rated beyond certain limits by requiring a password. This way, you can watch any movie of any rating yourself and give permission for specific movies or games.

Remember two important rules about Xbox 360 parental controls:

✔ **Settings apply to the console, not to individual profiles.** Restrictions apply to absolutely anyone who uses your Xbox 360 console, including you.

You can access any material if you know the code, but you must enter that code every time.

✔ **If you lose your code, all is not lost.**

When you set the pass code, you also set a pass code reset question/answer (for example, "What is your favorite color?"). If the parent fails to correctly enter the pass code when trying to enter the Console Settings area, he or she can enter the answer for the reset question to clear and then re-create a new pass code. If the parent forgets the new pass code, too, then he or she can call customer support to get the console-specific reset code that clears the Flash settings. Clearing the pass code doesn't erase profiles, saved games, downloaded content, or any other vital info.

When creating your pass code, don't pick a pass code reset question that your children know the answer to (like, "What is your pet's name?").

To get started with parental controls, follow these steps:

1. **Open the Xbox Dashboard.**

If you aren't already in the Dashboard, you can get to it by starting the Xbox 360 without a game or movie in the DVD drive or by ejecting the current disc. You can also get to the Dashboard by pressing the Xbox Guide button on your controller or remote and then pressing the Y button when the Guide appears.

2. **Choose the System blade with the controller.**

3. **Choose the Family Settings option.**

4. **Choose the Console Settings option.**

The console settings apply to the entire Xbox 360, not just a specific user.

By default, the console settings give you full access to Xbox 360 features and content:

- You can play any game.

- You can watch any movie DVD.

- You have access to Xbox Live.

- You don't need a pass code to change any of the settings.

The following sections show how to set up your pass code and change some settings.

Picking a code

If you modify a parent control, you must set a pass code. Follow these steps:

1. **Access the Console Settings screen.**

The preceding section tells you how to access this screen.

2. **Choose the Set Pass Code menu option.**

You're prompted to enter a four-button pass code, as you can see in Figure 11-2.

3. **Press any Xbox 360 controller button or pull a trigger.**

4. **Select a pass code reset question and then enter its answer.**

This question and answer helps you if you ever forget your pass code. See Figure 11-3.

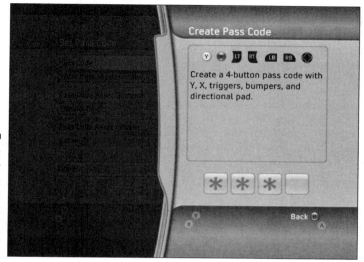

Figure 11-2:
Enter your
pass code
by using the
Xbox
controller
buttons.

If you forget your pass code, you can reset it by using your reset question.

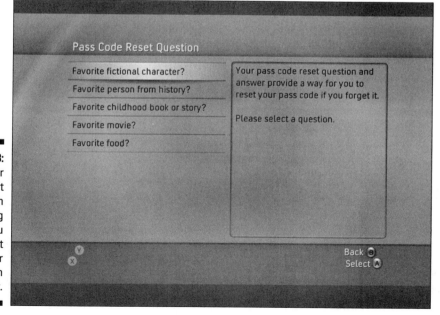

Figure 11-3:
Make your
reset
question
something
that you
know but
your
children
don't.

Movies

The Console Settings screen offers the DVD Movie Ratings option, which in turn lists movie ratings. Those ratings match the ratings system in your country. (See Figure 11-4.)

The ability to block movies based on their rating depends on that rating being encoded onto the DVD. Most DVDs sold in the United States and Canada are rating-coded, but a particular movie (or a pirated copy of almost any movie) might not have the proper information encoded. A disc without rating information isn't blocked.

MPAA ratings, such as G for General, are used in the United States and Canada.

Setting a limit in the Console Settings screen means that one or both of the following screens show up when you insert a DVD movie exceeding your specified rating:

- **A dialog box from the DVD itself:** Says that your DVD player (the Xbox 360) has parental controls running and gives you the option to stop playing the DVD (kicking you out to the Dashboard).

- **An Xbox 360 slide-out dialog box:** Appears along the side of the screen and prompts you to enter the pass code.

    The movie plays normally if you enter the code; otherwise, you end up back at the Dashboard.

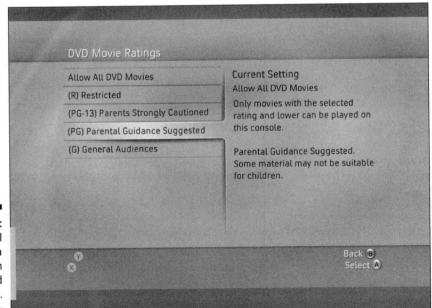

Figure 11-4:
Limit all movies at a certain rating and above.

DVD Movie Ratings

Allow All DVD Movies

(R) Restricted

(PG-13) Parents Strongly Cautioned

(PG) Parental Guidance Suggested

(G) General Audiences

Current Setting
Allow All DVD Movies

Only movies with the selected rating and lower can be played on this console.

Parental Guidance Suggested. Some material may not be suitable for children.

Back B
Select A

Games

ESRB ratings control game access in the parent control options. Follow these steps to restrict access to games of a certain level or above:

1. **Access the Console Settings screen.**

   The "Controlling Access" section, earlier in this chapter, tells you how to access the screen.

2. **Choose Game Ratings.**

   Game Ratings is the first option on the Console Settings screen. When you select it, a list of ratings, like the list you can see in Figure 11-1, appears.

3. **Choose allowed ratings.**

4. **Press the A button to accept your settings.**

Xbox Live

Xbox Live is a general term used to describe all of the Internet functionality of the Xbox 360, including its ability to play games with players scattered all around the world. Through the main system-wide family settings, you can control certain aspects of Xbox Live, blocking the creation of new accounts and/or blocking the use of Xbox Live altogether. You also have access to a special set of Xbox Live family settings. Xbox 360 controls Xbox Live through a different system than the rest of the parental controls although you do find some overlap. At the main Family Settings screen, which you can see in Figure 11-5, you can go into the Console Settings area to access all the system-wide settings. Or, you can go into the Xbox Live area to set up restrictions on your children's Xbox Live accounts.

If your kids don't do any online gaming, you can simply restrict the access at a console level. The setup gets more complicated — but also more configurable — if you allow your children to use the Xbox Live system. You control access to Xbox Live by

✔ **Setting up your own account** on Passport (and Xbox Live, if you want) first (before the children).

✔ **Creating each child account** that you want to have, associating each one as a child of your account. See details on those steps in the following section, "Creating your children's account(s)."

At any point after you create the accounts, you (as the owner of the parent account) can go into the Family Settings, Xbox Live area and adjust the settings for each child account.

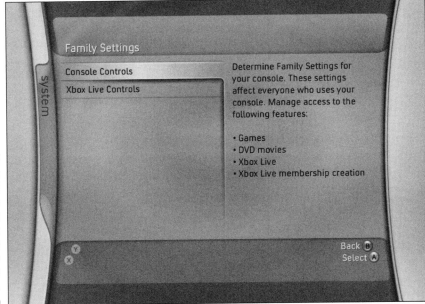

Figure 11-5:
You can find
Xbox Live
settings in
the System
blade's
Family
Settings
area.

✔ **Blocking the creation of new Xbox Live accounts** in the Console
Settings area.

Make this setting by choosing the Access to Xbox Live and Xbox Live
Membership Creation options on the Console Settings screen. This
action makes the pass code necessary to connect to the Live service or
to create a new Xbox Live membership.

Creating your children's account (s)

When you sign up your children — or if they attempt to sign themselves
up — you have to enter their birth dates (see Figure 11-6).

If your child enters the real date and he's under 18 years of age, the sign-
up process asks for the parent to finish the steps from that point on (see
Figure 11-7).

At this point, you (the parent) need to provide your Passport credentials —
unless you already have an adult account on the Xbox 360, in which case, you
just use that passport information. After you create the association between
the parent's account and the child's new account (see Figure 11-8), the Xbox
Live option under Family Settings becomes useful.

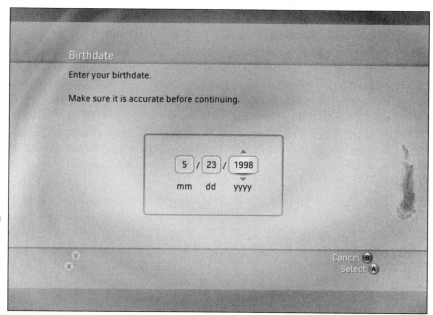

Figure 11-6:
Xbox bases
Child status
on birth
date.

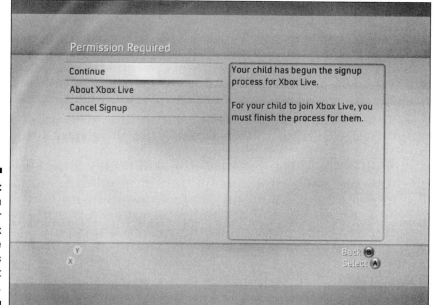

Figure 11-7:
Signing up a
child (under
18) for Xbox
Live
requires
adult
involvement.

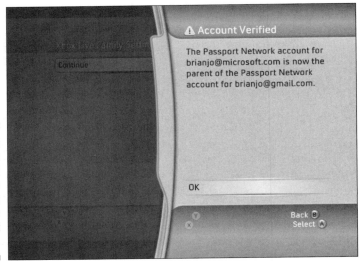

Figure 11-8:
You can create child accounts only with an adult's passport account.

When you set up your child's account

✔ You might want to start with a Silver membership. It's free (see Figure 11-9), and you can upgrade to a Gold account later without having to re-create the child account.

Figure 11-9:
Silver memberships are free, and you can upgrade them to Gold memberships.

✔ When choosing an Xbox Live Zone, you can help ensure that your child ends up playing in games with appropriate language and the right age range of players by picking the Family Zone (see Figure 11-10).

Adjusting Xbox Live settings

After you create your accounts, go to the Family Settings screen (from the System blade in the Dashboard) and choose the Xbox Live menu option. This option brings up a list of child accounts that you can select from. After you pick the child account whose settings you want to adjust, you need to enter in the passport account password for the parent account (see Figure 11-11).

After you (the parent) log in, you can configure one of several Xbox Live options, including

✔ **Online Gameplay:** Control what types of games the child can play against other people on Xbox Live.

✔ **Privacy and Friends:** The most critical section, in our opinion. These options control who your child can add to her friend list, who she can chat with, who can see her gamer profile, and who can see her online status.

✔ **Content:** Allows you to restrict what additional materials (new game updates, custom graphics for your Xbox 360 Dashboard, and so on) your child can download onto your machine.

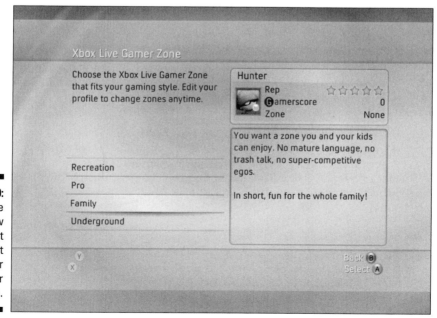

Figure 11-10: Xbox Live Zones allow different rules about player conduct for each zone.

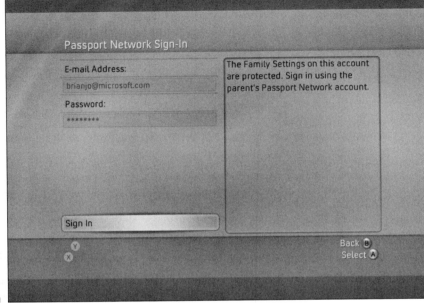

Figure 11-11:
To adjust
Xbox Live
settings for
a child
account,
the parent
needs
to log in.

Online Gameplay

You have two options for Online Gameplay: Xbox 360 games and Original Xbox games. You can configure whether your child can go online with only new games (that support all the new Xbox Live concepts, such as Zones) or also with old games from the first Xbox.

You might want to choose the most restrictive option that allows for the games that you want your child to play online. If that game list includes both old games (such as *Halo 2*) and new ones (like *Project Gotham Racing 3*), you end up having to turn on both settings.

Privacy and Friends

Figure 11-12 shows you this page, where you can control whom your child can have on his friends list and whom he can interact with online. This control goes beyond gaming; you might find the chat features of Xbox Live just as worrying as chatting directly on the Internet.

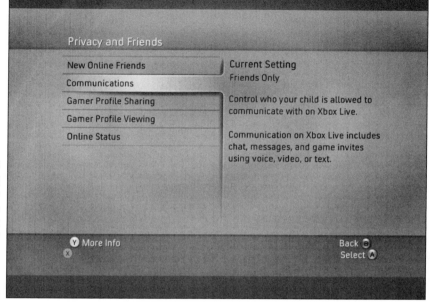

Figure 11-12:
Use Privacy
and Friends
to restrict
whom your
child can
interact with
online.

As with the Online Gameplay options in the preceding section, you might want to lock these options down as tightly as you can and then open them up later if you decide to. Here are your Privacy and Friends options:

✔ **New Online Friends:** This controls the addition of people to your child's friends list. Because that list forms the basis of many other security restrictions, you might want to use this option, which requires parental involvement to add a friend to a child's list. Suggest to your child that he gather all his friend's gamertags, and then the two of you can add them together in one sitting. From time to time, you have to add more names as additional friends get Xbox Live accounts, but you can do the bulk of the additions at one time.

✔ **Communications:** This controls whom your child can chat with, send messages to, and receive messages from. You can block this altogether, but you might want to restrict it to Friends Only and then carefully monitor the contents of your child's friends list. (See the previous bullet.)

✔ **Gamer Profile Sharing/Viewing:** Sharing controls monitor who can see your child's gamer profile (which can contain a lot of information about your child's habits and interests), and Viewing controls monitor whose profiles your child can see. In both cases, you might want to restrict these options to Friends Only. This setting means that people on your child's friends list can view her profile and vice versa, but no one else can see or be seen.

✔ **Online Status:** This controls who can see when your child is online and what he's doing (what game he's playing, and so on). This is potentially private information, so you might want to restrict access to Friends Only.

Family Rules

No matter what technical features regulate the use of an Xbox 360, PC, or TV, parents ultimately determine and enforce the rules. You decide what your children watch or play, regardless of the rating. Use the parent controls in this chapter merely as a way to ensure that you're the one making the final call.

These tips can help you keep your children from the wrong type of content or from overusing the Xbox 360 (or any other technology):

✔ **No computer/TV/Xbox 360 in the kids' bedrooms:** You can know what they're doing much more easily if they're in a main room.

If they need a computer for homework and they do that work in their bedroom, consider limiting the range of time in which you allow Internet access.

If you're not sure how to turn off Internet access, check out the online administration site for the firewall or router that connects to your Internet source. That source might be a DSL or cable modem.

✔ **No shutting the door:** If you have the computer in a room with a door (such as a den or a home office), institute an *Open Door policy*. When the kids are in there using the computer, let them know that they need to always keep the door open.

✔ **No ten-hour entertainment marathons:** Set time limits on any technology that you feel your kids might abuse.

• **Set a single time limit for the day across all technologies.** For example, limit to one hour per day of "screen time," whether it's TV, Xbox 360, or a PC.

• **Set a different time limit for each technology.** If you're willing to tackle the tracking, of course. You can make the limit conditional on your kids doing other tasks (such as homework or chores). Didn't help out around the house? That hour of time watching TV or playing Xbox 360 goes away.

The earlier you put rules in place, the more easily you can enforce them. If you're considering an Xbox 360 or if you just purchased one, have the rules discussion before setting up the console.

A bunch of gadgets and software can help you monitor your children. We haven't talked about them here because they should only help you with your existing rules. If you're interested in some form of technical assistance, we recommend a few steps:

- Check out MSN Premium at `http://join.msn.com/premium/overview`.

  This works over your existing Internet broadband connection and provides a bunch of family-focused features.

- Find out more about the router or firewall that sits between your home PC and the Internet.

  If you have one PC, you need to run at least a firewall on that computer, such as the built-in firewall in Windows XP SP2. The router logs Web traffic, which you can use much more reliably than software installed on individual PCs. You can also block certain sites by using your firewall, but you might find doing so a bit of a pain. You could probably more easily specify all the sites that you *can* visit.

- Visit `www.xbox4dummies.com` for more tips and links on parental controls.

Despite the large number of Web sites, software, and gadgets, we can suggest only one really successful measure: Make sure it all happens out in the open. Put your computer in the living room. Don't put a TV in the bedroom. And no matter how busy you are, try to be in the same room when your kids are watching TV or playing games. Whether you're cleaning, reading, or chatting, just being in the room has benefits beyond controlling their behavior; it also means that they don't feel isolated and reinforces that they're part of a family.

Chapter 12

LAN Parties

*P*laying games by yourself is great, but sharing them with good friends changes the experience in a nearly tangible way. In this chapter, we show you how to link multiple Xbox 360s, both with wires and without. You read about the ways you can set up TV for optimized display in a busy, crowded environment, and we talk about fun, alternative displays you can use projectors, which completely change the way that gaming on the Xbox 360 feels in unique and wonderful ways.

What's a LAN Party?

Most home Internet connections have limited bandwidth. High-speed connections work great for a few Xbox 360s running at the same time, but potential connectivity problems crop up as you add more consoles. You can get the most speed by connecting in a LAN configuration. When you play, the information that goes back and forth between consoles isn't slowed down by round trips to the Internet.

A LAN (local area network) isn't necessarily connected to the Internet. A *LAN party* is a gathering of gamers who network their consoles and play at high speed. The parties can range from a couple of systems to hundreds of systems at public shows and events. LAN parties have been around ever since geeks started playing games on computer networks.

Although game consoles are becoming more popular at LAN parties, most of the larger LAN parties feature networks of PCs. PC LAN parties are absolutely fun and a great time. People bring custom game rigs, featuring the latest video cards, motherboards, memory, and high-end CPUs. It's amazing to see how much work people put into creating a gaming rig. A negative is that some people can spend thousands of dollars on the latest equipment, to great advantage. Although winning's the name of the game, losing to somebody with a rig much better than your own might leave you wondering whether that person's really a better player.

This is where a LAN party of Xbox 360s becomes the great equalizer. You know that everyone is running the same game on the same system. Some players might have an advantage when it comes to the display, but for the most part, everybody at an Xbox LAN party is starting at the same point.

This chapter covers the Xbox 360 settings for the type of LAN party you might have at home, hosting as many as a dozen Xbox 360s.

Play Games with Your "Real" Friends

As gaming geeks ourselves, we know you don't do enough of some things: Eat fresh fruits and vegetables, get enough sun, and (especially) talk to each other face to face. LAN parties are your chance to get face time.

Why the Xbox 360 makes an excellent LAN party console

A couple of important features make the Xbox 360 an excellent console for party play.

The price is right

An Xbox 360 costs about the same as a high-end video card. Of course, you can spend a lot more on accessories, but the console itself is just a fraction of what you need to spend on a custom PC for gaming. Even with an Xbox 360 Core System, you get

- A high-speed Ethernet port
- A great controller
- The ability to hook up to nearly any TV

Add a memory card or a hard disk for just a little extra storage, and you've got a very powerful gaming system.

Multiple players per box

You can have up to four players on each Xbox 360 in the house. Friends who don't have one can still join in the fun.

System link configuration

The Xbox 360 comes with an Ethernet port. You can *system link* consoles, meaning you can create a network of Xbox 360s, allowing for private play. System link connects the consoles through a switch or a hub. With system link, you aren't playing through Xbox Live: The consoles talk to each other directly. This configuration is a definite no-brainer.

This chapter shows you how you can connect multiple Xbox 360s without any configuration fuss whatsoever.

Everybody is running the same system

The great equalizer: When you're playing with your friends and you're all on the same system, there's one less excuse for getting beat. However, players with a widescreen HDTV might have a slight advantage because their peripheral game vision is better than players on a standard TV.

Fewer security issues

Players in big, public PC LAN parties need to worry about PC security. Although security usually isn't an issue at a small house party, it's something that you need to think about when you're connecting your PC to an unfamiliar network.

Xbox 360 security is tight enough that you can plug into any network you want without worrying about the console's data. You need to be in control of the console itself to access any of the data.

Even if you're playing with friends, protecting your account with a pass code is a good idea. You don't want somebody connecting to Xbox Live when you're out of the room and sending "funny" messages to everybody on your buddy list!

Planning your party

This section help make you the host with the most. You want to make sure everybody has a good time, right? We can help you plan your party

Write it down

Ask yourself questions about the kind of party you want.

What kind of crowd?

Consider whether you're hosting hard-core gamers or casual non-gamers. Non-gamers need fun while the hard-core players concentrate on competition:

✓ **Dedicated gamers are easy to please at a party.**

- Set up a good network.

- Give everybody a comfortable place to sit.

- Fill the fridge with soda.

You're all set.

✓ **Non-gamers are tougher to please.**

- Consider a non-gamer co-host.

  If you want to play a lot during your party, make sure everybody is taken care of. Trying to do this yourself and play at the same time leads to misery.

  Schedule your games so you have time to walk around and talk to everybody.

- Set up a party game station or two.

  If you want your non-gamer friends to share the joy of gaming, set up an Xbox 360 with casual games so they can jump in and play. Check out Xbox Live Arcade for good games people can play without having to mess around with discs.

  Think about setting up a couple of dance pads and a dance game. And make sure to get your camera ready for that!

How many people?

People at a LAN party need more room than during a regular party. Equipment's going to overtake the room and wires might run everywhere, not to mention the people trying to play.

✓ **If people bring their own monitors,** identify enough spots around the house that have space for

- An Xbox 360 console

- Players

- A small television

✓ **If you're letting people connect to your existing TVs,** just make sure that you have

- Enough space for the number of people who are going to be playing at each TV

- A place for somebody to plug in the Xbox 360 console

A TV that doesn't have a *composite video jack* (the yellow jack) probably can't connect to the video cables that come with an Xbox 360 console.

How many Xbox 360s?

Are you having multiple players per Xbox 360, or is everyone bringing her own?

You need one display per system, which means you need space for each of the TVs or monitors you're hooking up to. Many more flat panels than big TVs will fit into your house. With that in mind, up to four people can play on each system, which means you can have a great casual LAN party with four Xbox 360s and 16 people.

Game choice and schedule

You need one copy of the game for each Xbox 360 at the party. You can rent games from most of the major movie rental chains, such as Blockbuster.

Plan on playing the type of game that most of your friends like to play for most of the time during the party. Schedule breaks where you can play games you wouldn't usually play together. Who knows — you might find something new that you like!

A game schedule might look something like this:

8:00 – 8:30	Network setup.
8:30 – 9:00	Warm-ups and testing connections. (Test the network games to make sure the systems are all communicating with each other.)
9:00 – 11:00	Perfect Dark Zero Deathmatch.
11:00 – 12:00	Project Gotham Racing 3.
12:00 – 2:00	Halo 2.
2:00 – ??	Whoever is still awake can decide!

First-person shooters

First-person shooters are usually the first choice for LAN parties. Many hardcore gamers play this kind of game. They let you get tons of players in the same game, at the same time — sort of the LAN party's purpose!

Racing games

Racing games are great for LAN parties. They're not everyone's cup of tea, but a few races can be a lot of fun, particularly if they are more arcade-style (*Need for Speed: Most Wanted,* for example).

Fighting games

Fighting games are a lot of fun, but the games are usually one-on-one.

I need full power, Scotty!

More Xbox 360s means the need for more power. The Xbox 360 is rated at 5 amps (which, compared with a laptop computer at about 1.5 amps, is quite high). When multiple consoles are to be used, make sure to check that the amps are available in your circuit box.

Each breaker in your circuit box includes on it a number of amps that it supports. Breakers are rated at 10, 15, 20, 25, or more amps. So, with each the Xbox 360 requiring 5 amps, be sure to plug the consoles into separate outlets around the house in order to lessen the load on just one circuit. Your circuit box should already have labels that tell you which breakers correspond to which outlets in your house.

Remember: Your TVs, lights, and other devices also draw power from those circuits. This is an important consideration if you're going to hook up three or more Xbox 360s, thus drawing 15 or more amps on a circuit.

If you're going to play fighting games in a LAN party, create *elimination brackets* (like a basketball tournament) so you can figure out the night's ultimate champion.

Sports games

Sports games are always fun, but they lend themselves to a lot of one-on-one play. Consider creating elimination brackets and tracking the ultimate winner.

Alternative games

You might plan for a hardcore night of first-person shooter play but then find everybody gravitating toward the games you never expected. Games in this category include

- Dance and music games
- Timed puzzle games
- Poker

System Link

System link gets two or more Xbox 360 consoles talking to each other for home game play.

You can tell whether an Xbox 360 game supports system link by checking the label on the back of the game box.

This chapter shows you how to make system link connections through either

- **Xbox 360's own direct networking accessories:** You can directly connect Xbox 360 consoles with either

  - **System link cable or crossover Ethernet cable:** You can directly connect two Xbox 360 consoles with this cable.

  - **Wireless networking adapters:** You can directly connect two or more Xbox 360 consoles in an ad hoc network if they have wireless network adapters. (They can also connect through a regular wireless home network.)

- **Standard home network equipment:** You can use

  - **Routers:** You can connect up to 32 Xbox 360 consoles through routers. (Most home networks use routers.)

    A router is the best way to connect Xbox 360 consoles if you want to use them with Xbox Live.

  - **Network switches:** You can connect up to 32 Xbox 360 consoles through a network switch if the switch has enough Ethernet jacks.

  - **Hubs:** Technically, you can connect up to 32 Xbox 360 consoles through a hub, but we don't recommend connecting more than 4 consoles with a hub.

Networked Xbox 360 consoles can play *different* games at the same time. For example, two consoles can play the same game, and two other consoles can play a different game. They can all communicate through the same network.

Here's how to connect your consoles.

Direct Xbox 360 connections

Xbox 360 consoles can directly communicate through Xbox 360 cables and wireless network adapters.

You can't directly connect Xbox 360 consoles to each other (without other network equipment) if *either* of these statements is true:

- You want an Xbox Live connection.
- You have more than two Xbox 360 consoles, and you don't have wireless network adapters for them all.

System link cable

The *system link* cable directly connects two Xbox 360s. The system link cable is a crossover cable. Its wires are arranged so you don't need an Ethernet device.

You can use the same Xbox 360 console jacks to either

✔ Directly connect two Xbox 360 consoles with a system link cable

✔ Connect as many as 32 Xbox 360 consoles through standard Ethernet home networking equipment (as shown later in this chapter)

The system link cable is great when you want to put two Xbox 360s together. It's light, and you don't have to carry any extra equipment. Just plug in the cable, and the two Xbox 360s "see" each other. Pop copies of the same system link-compatible game into each Xbox 360, and you're set!

Xbox 360 consoles automatically disable their other communication capabilities when you connect them with a system link cable:

✔ You can't connect to Xbox Live.

✔ You can't connect to your home network or a Media Center PC.

✔ If an Xbox 360 wireless network adapter is installed on your console, it's automatically shut off when you connect the console with a system link cable (or an Ethernet cable for a wired home network).

Xbox 360 consoles must be within 50 feet (15 meters) of each other to connect with a system link cable.

Wireless network adapters

Connecting consoles for system link play is usually easier if every Xbox 360 has the wireless adapter attached. (The Xbox 360 Wireless Adapter is described in Chapter 3.)

System link through the wireless adapter is known as an *ad hoc connection*. In ad hoc Xbox 360 networks, wireless adapters talk directly to each other, not through a central wireless access point.

You can use the same Xbox 360 wireless network adapters to either

✔ Directly connect in an ad hoc network

✔ Connect through a standard wireless router or wireless home network (as shown later in this chapter)

For a direct system link using wireless network adapters, follow these steps on *each* Xbox 360 console:

1. Make sure the wireless adapter is connected to each Xbox 360.

2. **Check your network settings in the System blade for confirmation that your wireless adapter is connected and active.**

   The workgroup name for the system link connection should be Wireless Channel.

3. **Place a game in each Xbox 360 console.**

   The game must be system link-compatible.

4. **Follow the game's instructions for playing a system link game.**

All Xbox 360 console wireless network adapters must be within range of each other to read recognize the network. This range with on such factors as

- ✔ Distance between devices
- ✔ Thickness of the walls

If your signal strength appears too low, try either

- ✔ Moving the consoles (or just the transmitters) closer together
- ✔ Removing potential signal blocks, such as closed doors

Standard network connections

Xbox 360 consoles can communicate through several kinds of standard Ethernet-based network equipment.

If you don't already have a home network, you can easily find an affordable router for your LAN party. A *wired* router is both less expensive and more reliable: a key factor when your LAN party spills into multiple rooms or occupies multiple floors.

You might be able to link Xbox 360 consoles to Xbox Live through the same home network, but try to get everyone to connect at least 15 minutes before you want to play. This gives the consoles time to download game updates from Xbox Live.

Home networks and routers

If you have a home network, it's probably a LAN. Most home LANs share a high-speed connection to the Internet. A home network usually is based on a *router* that assigns addresses to each computer on the network so they can talk to each other.

A wireless router usually makes a lot of sense when some Xbox 360 consoles have wireless network adapters and other consoles are wired. Most wireless routers also have connections for wired devices, so you can

✔ Connect wirelessly Xbox 360 network consoles to the router through the wireless network connection.

✔ Connect the other Xbox 360 consoles directly to the router with Ethernet cables. Each cable connection requires both

• A separate Ethernet cable for each console

• A separate Ethernet jack on the router

Limit the number of consoles that you connect to Xbox Live at a LAN party. The average cable or DSL Internet connection can reliably handle only a few connections simultaneously before performance begins to suffer.

A router-based home LAN works fine for connecting Xbox 360s, and the connection is completely automatic. When each console is plugged in to the network, it is automatically assigned an address on the network that allows them all to function without a hitch.

If you're connecting a new Xbox 360 network through a router, allow at least five minutes to make network connections before you start playing.

The steps to connect each Xbox 360 console through your router-based network depend on whether the console uses wired or wireless network connection.

Wireless router connection

Xbox 360 consoles are simple to connect wirelessly through a router-based network.

If you're connecting an Xbox 360 to the network with a wireless network adapter, you might need to add an encryption key to the Xbox 360 in order to connect the console to the network. (Chapter 6 shows how to add a WEP key by using Windows Connect Now.)

To wirelessly connect Xbox 360 consoles through a router or a router-based home network, follow these steps:

1. **Make sure that the wireless adapter is connected to each Xbox 360.**

2. **Check your network settings in the System blade for confirmation that your wireless adapter is connected and active.**

   The Xbox 360 network settings automatically detect the router and configure it. If any errors are detected, follow the onscreen instructions.

Wired router connection

Follow these steps to add a wired Xbox 360 console to your router network:

1. **Plug an Ethernet cable from the port on the back of the Xbox 360 to an open slot on the router.**

2. **Check your network settings in the System blade for confirmation that the connection is secure and active.**

   The Xbox 360 network settings automatically detect the router and configure it. If any errors are detected, follow the onscreen instructions.

Network switches

A *network switch* sends each signals directly to the Xbox 360 console that needs it, without using IP addresses.

If you're shopping for network hardware, you can probably buy a router for just a little more money than a network switch.

To connect Xbox 360 consoles with a network switch, follow these steps:

1. **Place a network switch where it can be connected to all your Xbox 360 consoles via Ethernet cables.**

   All your Xbox 360 consoles must be within five feet (two meters) of the switch.

2. **For each Xbox 360 console:**

   a. Connect an Ethernet cable from Xbox 360 console to the switch.

   b. Insert a copy of the game you want to play with that console.

   The game must support system link.

3. **Follow the in-game instructions for playing on a system link connection.**

If you also have a router that's connected to the Internet, you might be able to connect your Xbox 360 consoles through the network switch to Xbox Live. Connect the network switch port that's marked *Uplink* (or something like it) to your router. Your router will assign addresses to each Xbox 360 connected to the network switch; you should be able to get onto Xbox Live.

Hubs

A *hub* sends every signal to all the Xbox 360 consoles connected to the hub. Each console must receive every network signal and then decide whether to use or ignore that signal. (Technically, this is a cheap but inefficient way to run a computer network.)

To connect Xbox 360 consoles with a hub, follow these steps:

1. **Place a hub where it can be connected to all your Xbox 360 consoles via Ethernet cables.**

   All your Xbox 360 consoles must be within 50 feet (15 meters) of the hub.

2. **For each Xbox 360 console**

   a. *Connect an Ethernet cable from Xbox 360 console to the hub.*

   b. *Insert a copy of the game you want to play with that console.*

   The game must support system link.

3. **Follow the in-game instructions for playing on a system link connection.**

We don't recommend using a hub with more than four Xbox 360 consoles. The signal between those consoles gets slower with each addition.

Going Mobile

Of course, every LAN party needs *guests*. And it wouldn't do to show up empty-handed, would it?

Put on your traveling shoes and get ready to see the world, Xbox 360 style!

What the well-dressed guest is carrying

What's the best way to prepare for LAN party play when you're the *guest?*

The answer is a backpack. If you're planning to take your Xbox 360 on the road a lot, fill a backpack with all your stuff. When you get to the LAN party, you can set up and play. Why waste time messing around?

Contents vary from person to person. The list in Table 12-1 should get you started.

If the best Xbox 360 connection option for your home TV or monitor requires a special connection cable (see Chapter 8), put the cable that came with your Xbox 360 console in your travel pack. The video cable that came with your Xbox 360 console works with most TVs.

You can often find a composite video jack on the front of a TV. It's a handy connection when you're a guest looking for a fast Xbox fix. Chapter 2 shows how to connect.

Table 12-1	Your LAN Party Kit
Item	*Function*
Backpack	A backpack or a large laptop computer case with a padded storage area.
Game pack	A sturdy CD case for carrying your games.
Network router	A device for connecting computers.
Ethernet cable	Bring extra Ethernet cables if you have the space. Parties often need more than they have on hand.
System link cable	One system link cable for playing at a friend's house.
Wireless network adapter	Using wireless network adapters gives you better freedom to position your Xbox 360 console without having to worry about keeping it wired to the router.
Wired controller	Reduce the risk of interference when you play at large LAN parties.
Power strip	Stay powered up when electric outlets are scarce. Remember, you need at least two power outlets (one for your Xbox 360 and one for your TV), so with just a few people at your LAN party, you'll need more outlets than the room you're gaming in is likely to have.
LCD monitor	If you have money and space, LCD monitors are light and sharp. Hooking up to the monitor with a VGA cable makes for a really good experience, especially if you get a widescreen LCD. (Chapter 8 shows the LCD video connection.)
Extra controller	Add a friend on the fly.
Video connector cable	The cable that came with your Xbox 360 console works with most TVs. You might need special cables for VGA, S-Video, SCART, or RF antenna connectors (see Chapter 8).

Baby, you can drive your Xbox

A long road trip in your future? If you're lucky enough to be traveling in a car kitted out with a video screen, you can plug in your Xbox 360 and make the time fly by.

If you want to use your new Xbox 360 on the go, here's what you need to know:

✔ Pack the Xbox 360 carefully for the trip. You'll need the Xbox 360 console, the power supply, the controller, and the A/V cable.

✔ You'll also need a *power inverter*. This device plugs in to the car's lighter socket and converts the power to the kind that runs household appliances — like your Xbox 360.

You plug the Xbox 360 power supply in to the power inverter.

✔ Most mobile video systems have a *composite video jack* (the yellow video input jack). Check the vehicle (or video system) owner's manual for instructions on connecting and using the video input.

Chapter 2 shows how to connect Xbox 360 to devices with composite video. When it's all connected, power up and start playing!

Remember: *Don't drive while you play.* (It reduces your score.)

Take me to Partytown

If you're looking for LAN parties, try asking at your local games retailer. They might have their own list of local LAN events, or at least point you to more information in your local area.

To find (or publicize) LAN parties, check out

```
http://lanparty.com
```

Chapter 13

Windows Media Center Extender

*T*he built-in Media Center Extender software is one of the key new Xbox 360 features. This chapter explains exactly what Media Center is, what the extender software provides, and how you can get set up with your own Media Center.

What Is Media Center?

This product's full name is Windows XP Media Center Edition 2005, but you can call it Media Center Edition — or better yet, MCE. MCE is a Windows XP version with features that make it perfect for using as an entertainment hub — the kind of computer that's a lot of fun at a party.

Digital video recorder

MCE's core feature is a digital video recorder (DVR). Media Center's capabilities are similar to

✔ TiVo (a popular DVR in the United States and Canada)

✔ Fancy set-top boxes for cable or satellite TV

Media Center TV channels

If you're considering Media Center (or any other DVR), check how it works with your available TV channels. Your retailer should be able to tell you exactly which of your available channels is compatible with the DVR you're considering.

In the United States and Canada, a Media Center can be equipped to directly record

✔ Standard broadcast TV channels

✔ High-definition broadcast TV channels

✔ Unscrambled cable channels (the cable channels you can see on most TVs without using a special cable box)

If you have satellite TV or a cable box, Media Center uses *infrared transmitters* (essentially remote control outputs controlled by the media center system) to change the channel on your satellite or cable box, then records directly from the box. (It works, but it's a bit of a hassle. The Media Center interface will walk you through a series of steps to set up the transmitters.)

Media Center can't record high-definition channels from cable or satellite. If you are interested in recording high-definition cable or satellite channels, you may need a DVR system available directly from your cable or satellite provider.

DVRs let you

✔ Record TV shows directly to their hard drive

Some DVRs may not be able to record all the channels you pay for. The sidebar "Media Center TV channels" describes channel options for Media Center PCs.

✔ Watch recorded shows

DVRs seem like VCRs without tapes but include many advanced features, such as

✔ Pause and rewind live TV

DVRs automatically record what you're watching, so you can back up if you miss something or pause the program if you need to grab a snack or answer the phone.

✔ Record shows automatically by title

Tell it that you want to record all episodes of a series, and the DVR grabs the episodes.

✔ Display TV listings

An onscreen TV schedule lets you find shows to both

- • Set up for recording later

    You'll probably find this much, much easier than programming a traditional VCR.

- • Watch live (selecting a show that is currently playing will automatically switch to that channel)

✔ Play and record different programs simultaneously

Because a DVR is digital, it can

- • Start playing a recording before the recording is finished
- • Play a recording while a new show is recorded

MCE's DVR features also support advanced functions:

✔ Using multiple TV tuners

Tuners are the hardware in a TV, DVR, or other video device that let you watch a specific channel. One tuner is required for each live channel you're watching or recording. Multiple tuners means that the Media Center can tune to multiple channels at the same time. With two tuners you could

- • Record two shows at once

    Watch a recorded show while taping two others: TV junkie nirvana!

- • Watch one channel while recording another

- • Watch live TV on two different TVs at one time

The "Extenders" section, later in this chapter, shows you how.

✔ Movie listings

MCE provides listings just for movies, so you can see a small poster of all the upcoming or currently playing movies on your TV.

✔ Extended show information

For any show in the listings, MCE lets you see beyond what's normally shown; some of that information is shown in Figure 13-1. You can view the credited actors, a full plot description, and reviews. If you want even more, select an actor's name, then read his biography, look at other shows he's acted in, and more.

Digital recording is only one trick in MCE's bag. The Media Center application also provides access to your photos, music, and custom software programs.

Music and photo features

MCE's photo and music features are a great way to browse through music albums (CDs) or photo slideshows — all through your TV and using a remote control. Of course, your Xbox 360 has music and photo capabilities. See Chapter 5 for more information on those features.

Custom applications

Custom Media Center applications can provide almost any type of feature you can imagine, including

✔ Online news

✔ Weather reports

✔ Full movie downloads from sites like MovieLink

✔ Music downloads from Napster

Figure 13-2 shows one of my favorite add-ins, My Netflix. I can connect to the online rental site, add movies to my rental queue, or just browse the available DVDs.

An *add-in* is a program that is designed to work inside another program. Available add-ins are discussed in the "Third-party applications" section, later in this chapter.

Figure 13-2:
Add features that take advantage of the Internet and your PC.

Extenders

Extenders come in three forms:

✔ Hardware extenders from Linksys and Hewlett-Packard

✔ The new Xbox 360

✔ A software extender that runs on the original Xbox

Xbox Extenders come into play if either

✔ You use more than one monitor or TV with your Media Center.

✔ You don't want your PC in the living room.

Extenders share the features of the MCE PC with other locations in the house. For example, you can hook up your MCE PC to a large-screen TV in your living room, then hook up an extender in the upstairs bedroom TV and another one in the family room TV. The extenders all have to be on the same network as your Media Center PC, which can be done with a wired or wireless network system.

Now all three locations (the living room, bedroom, and family room) can use Media Center features, including DVR, music, photos, and custom applications. All of your content is stored in a single location, but you can view and schedule recordings from any one of the locations.

Figure 13-3 shows one possible system setup that provides access to

✔ Live TV in two rooms at once (one room per installed tuner can watch live TV)

✔ Continual access to your library of recorded shows, videos, music, and photos in all three spots in the house

Even if you don't have multiple TVs, you might be in the same situation I'm in. My Media Center PC is in my home office, but everyone watches TV in the family room. An extender makes all the content viewable on the family room TV.

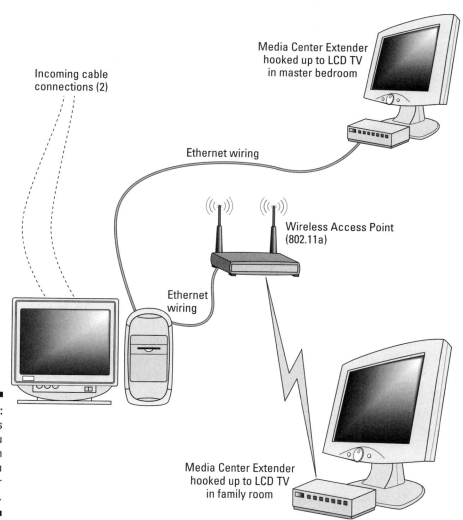

Incoming cable
connections (2)

Media Center Extender
hooked up to LCD TV
in master bedroom

Ethernet wiring

Wireless Access Point
(802.11a)

Ethernet
wiring

Figure 13-3:
Networks
give you
freedom
when you
set up your
system.

Media Center Extender
hooked up to LCD TV
in family room

Extenders for the original Xbox

When I first set up my own Media Center system, I used the Xbox software extender with the original Xbox. I switched to the Hewlett-Packard hardware extender because I wasn't happy with the software extender's noise and lack of a power button on the remote control. The new Xbox 360 fixes the following limitations of the original Xbox software extender:

✔ The original Xbox could not be turned on or off via remote. If you wanted to watch a show from the Media Center, you had to get up from the couch and turn it on. This might seem like pure laziness, but every other TV or movie-watching technology has a remote with an on/off switch.

✔ The extender software was built like a game. Because the software wasn't installed, you had to put in the disc whenever you wanted to use it. This created another minor inconvenience: the need to switch your Halo 2 disc with the Media Center Extender software whenever you wanted to watch TV. Even if the Xbox were already on, a trip from the couch was required!

✔ That Xbox is darn noisy, which can really effect the enjoyment of movies and shows.

✔ While the MCE user interface (UI) looks amazing on the PC (including background animations, subtle shading, and other effects), with the first-generation extenders, it looks . . . okay. All the effects, including animations, are missing, and the resolution is a lot lower than on the PC.

Moving to Hewlett-Packard's hardware extender solved the first two problems for me, and the UI still looked better than competing DVRs, so I was okay with that solution.

The Xbox 360 has the following improvements over previous Xbox extenders:

✔ Remote on/off

✔ Extender software built in and accessible anytime via the Xbox Dashboard or remote Start button

✔ High-definition output of the UI (the interface is shown in high-definition, but the TV output is still only at normal resolution)

✔ UI graphic effects appear in the Xbox 360 extender view

✔ Noise and heat reduction

Setting Up the Xbox 360 as an Extender

You won't be disappointed if you decide to use your Xbox 360 as a media extender, and setting up isn't difficult.

Before trying to set up the Xbox 360 side of this system, make sure your media center is working as expected. Your Media Center PC and your Xbox 360 need to be up and running.

Follow these steps to set up your Xbox 360 as a Media Center Extender:

1. **Bring up the Media Center UI and make sure you can watch live TV.**

   This confirms that the correct drivers are installed and working for the tuner card(s) you have installed in your system.

2. **Go to www.xbox.com/pcsetup and install the extender software.**

   If your PC displays a Media Center Extender Setup screen with Enter Setup Key across the top, skip Step 3.

3. **Click Start⇨All Programs⇨Accessories⇨Media Center⇨Media Center Extender Manager.**

   This brings up a dialog box like that shown in Figure 13-4. The dialog box lists all media center extenders set up to connect to your PC, which may be none at this point.

Figure 13-4:
Configure
the extender
list with the
Media
Center
Extender
Manager.

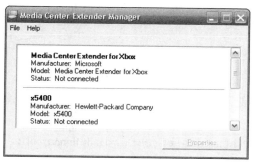

On the Media Center Extender Setup screen, you can

- Add new extenders

  This is exactly what you want if you are setting up your Xbox 360 as an extender.

- Remove extenders

- Update the software on your hardware extenders

- Name individual extenders

- Configure extender IP address information

4. **Click File⇨Add a New Extender.**

   The full-screen setup wizard launches and prompts you to enter a setup key. See Figure 13-5.

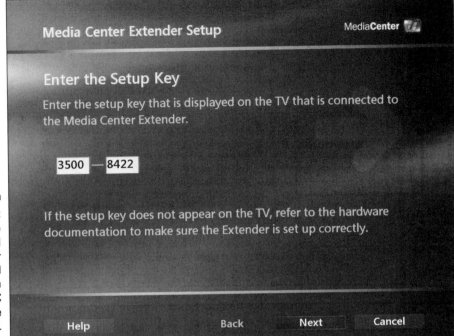

Figure 13-5:
The setup
wizard
binds your
console and
Media
Center PC
with the
setup key.

5. **Press the button in the middle of your Xbox 360 controller to open the Guide.**

6. **Use your Directional pad (arrow to the left or right) to go to the Media blade.**

7. **Choose the Media Center menu option.**

   The Media Center option, at the bottom of the features list, normally launches you into the Media Center UI. If this is your first time using the feature, a dialog box appears and displays an eight-digit setup key.

8. **Enter that key into the PC's setup screen, then press the A button on your Xbox controller or remote.**

9. **On your PC, choose Next.**

   The two machines should attempt to connect. If they connect, the Media Center UI will appear on your Xbox 360.

   If the connection fails, confirm the network settings on both the Xbox and the PC. You should also check out the help file for the Media Center Extender Manager because it contains a useful section on Troubleshooting. To access the help file, select the first menu option from the Help menu of the Media Center Extender Manager application (on your PC).

Comparing Media Center with TiVo

You may wonder how Media Center stacks up against its most visible competitor, TiVo. They provide common features, but differences abound.

The compelling differences between TiVo and Windows Media Center are

- Capability

  The Media Center Edition is more powerful than a TiVo, and Media Center works well with your Xbox 360.

- Price

  TiVo costs much less than a Media Center PC.

- Simplicity

  TiVo's reduced (or focused, depending on your point of view) feature set is simpler to use and easier to set up.

Before you buy any DVR, make sure it records all the channels you want. The sidebar "Media Center TV channels," earlier in this chapter, describes channel options for Media Center PCs.

TiVo, the household name in DVRs

In the United States and Canada, TiVo is synonymous with digital video recording (DVR), and it is the leader in the market, so any decision to go with Media Center as your DVR should only be made after comparing it with TiVo's product.

Positives

The features that have made the TiVo into one of the hottest consumer electronic devices around include:

- TiVo is very easy to use.

- TiVo doesn't depend on your network or PC setup to function.

- TiVo has a large community following and buzz; its name is the "cool" one in the DVR field.

- TiVo devices are relatively inexpensive.

  If you sign up for at least a one-year subscription (TiVo's work with an active subscription that you can pay for on a month-by-month or lifetime basis), you can get a TiVo for less than $200 with available mail-in rebates.

- TiVo devices include unique features, such as the thumbs-up/thumbs-down concept and recording based on habits.

Negatives

Okay, so the TiVo rocks, but here are a few of the areas in which it could use some work:

- ✔ Upgrading the TiVo (to increase storage space, for example) is difficult and generally voids your warranty.

- ✔ A two-tuner TiVo doesn't currently exist, so you can only record one show at a time.

- ✔ TiVo requires a monthly subscription or a one-time permanent license to download listing data. Prices at the time this book was written were $12.95 per month or $299 for a lifetime. In a multi-room scenario, each additional TiVo is another $6.95 a month!

- ✔ Multi-room viewing is more complex.

  Each TiVo stores its content locally, so you have to know which device contains the show you are trying to watch.

Media Center Edition 2005 (with the Xbox 360)

Media Center is a very different type of system, but it can still compare point-by-point with the TiVo product.

Positives

As a PC-based solution, Media Center offers many capabilities that the TiVo cannot:

- ✔ Media Center lets you add hard drives or memory without additional fees, with only standard PC technical knowledge required.

- ✔ Media Center has no subscription fee.

- ✔ Media Center can support these tuners at the same time:
  - One or two analog tuners
  - An additional over-the-air high-definition TV receiver

- ✔ Everything's presented in the same UI, regardless of which room you're in.

- ✔ Media Center lets you add features through add-in applications.

- ✔ Because the Media Center is a full-blown PC, you get standard Windows XP features.

Negatives

Media Center certainly has some limitations, so here are a few items that you should be aware of before making your decision:

- ✔ Media Center is a full-blown PC.

  It requires a network connection between itself and the extender(s) in use, a much more complicated system as a whole than a consumer device.

- ✔ Media Center is pricier than a TiVo.

  If you're planning on purchasing a PC, a Media Center PC may cost *less* than a standard PC and a separate TiVo DVR.

Getting Windows XP Media Center Edition

If you want your own MCE PC, start shopping around. Visit `www.xbox4 dummies.com/mediacenter` for a link to most of the available systems and compare cost and features.

I'm a big fan of Media Center systems that look like they belong in an entertainment center (instead of on a desk), such as

- ✔ Alienware

  `www.alienware.com`

- ✔ Hewlett-Packard Digital Entertainment Center

  `http://poweredby.hpidea.com/mediacenter`

Using Media Center through Your Xbox 360

The following sections let you in on the secrets of using your MCE with your Xbox 360. Of course, if you already have MCE, most of this is already burned into your brain — but you might pick up a couple tricks you hadn't seen before.

No matter what you're doing — watching a DVD, playing a game, or using the Xbox Guide — you can get to the MCE interface by either

- ✔ Pressing the green start button on either of the remote controls, as shown in Figure 13-6
- ✔ Accessing the Media blade's Media Center menu option (at the bottom of the list of choices)

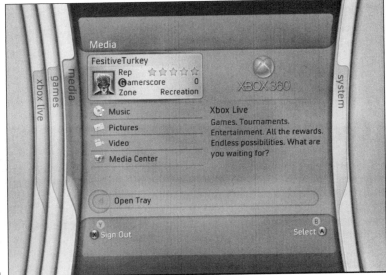

Figure 13-6: Press the green start button to jump into the Media Center user interface.

Watching TV

If you select My TV from the main Media Center screen, three icons appear next to the menu, as shown in Figure 13-7. When you're in My TV, these icons represent links to commonly used features:

- ✔ **Remote control icon:** Recorded TV is available from the first icon, which takes you to a screen listing your upcoming recordings and already-recorded items.
- ✔ **TV icon:** Click this to watch live TV. Pressing B on the controller takes you to live TV if you're already in the Media Center UI.
- ✔ **Movie reel icon:** Takes you to the Movies section, which is described in the "Looking for movies" section, later in this chapter.

On all other top-level menus, icons represent recently viewed items.

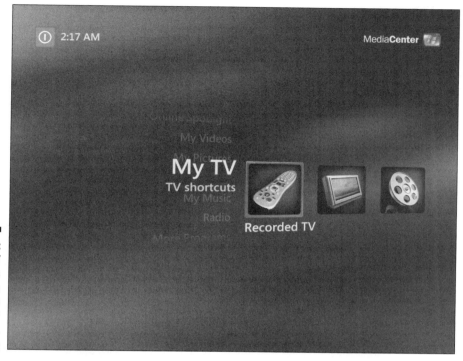

Figure 13-7:
The My TV
menu gives
you access
to the three
main TV
subfeatures.

No matter what you're watching, the core features are accessible through either of the Xbox 360 remote controls. Using the standard DVD-style buttons on the remote, you can pause, fast-forward, and rewind whatever you're watching.

For live TV, you can fast-forward only after you've rewound or paused long enough to be behind the live feed. (Unless you've found a coaxially connected wormhole to the future.)

Scheduling a recording

To schedule a recording with MCE, follow these steps:

1. **Open the Media Center UI.**

2. **Press the Y button on your controller.**

   The Guide appears on the screen.

3. **Browse the listings and select a show.**

4. Press the rec (record) button to set the recording:

- Press the rec button once to record just this show.

  If you're recording a single show, a single red disc appears next to the show in the Guide.

- Press the rec button twice to record every episode of this series.

  If you're recording every episode, three red discs appear next to the show in the Guide.

Figure 13-8 shows the Guide, with the *Kim Possible* series set to record and an episode of *Martha* set to record only a single showing. Icons indicate the status of any pending recordings:

✔ Red circles indicate shows set to record.

✔ Exclamation marks are problems that may prevent recording, such as

- Shows scheduled at the same time
- Lack of space

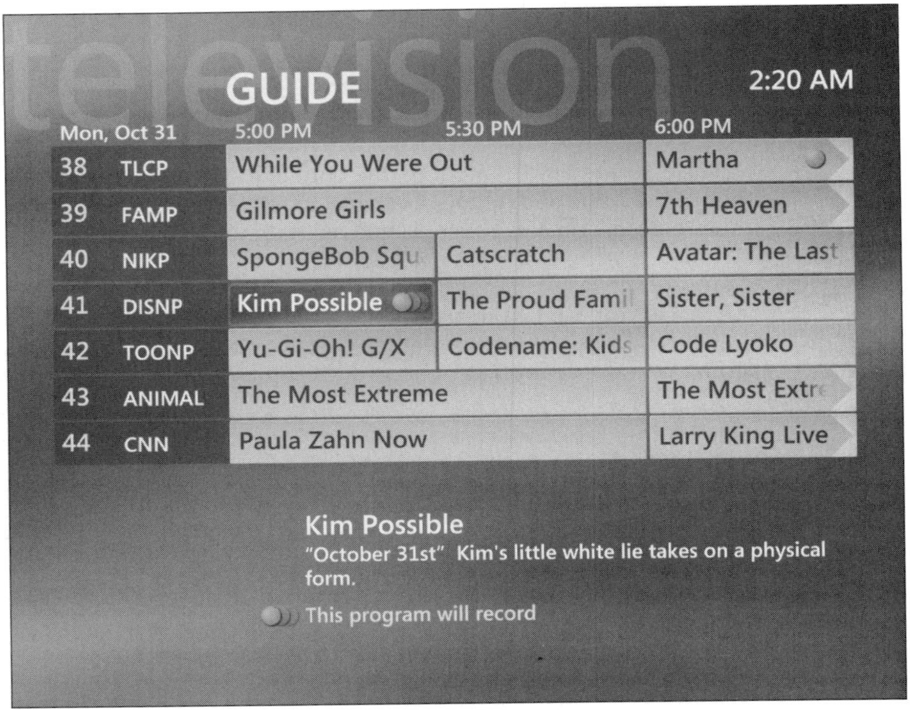

GUIDE 2:20 AM

Mon, Oct 31		5:00 PM	5:30 PM	6:00 PM
38	TLCP	While You Were Out		Martha
39	FAMP	Gilmore Girls		7th Heaven
40	NIKP	SpongeBob Squ	Catscratch	Avatar: The Last
41	DISNP	Kim Possible	The Proud Fami	Sister, Sister
42	TOONP	Yu-Gi-Oh! G/X	Codename: Kids	Code Lyoko
43	ANIMAL	The Most Extreme		The Most Extr
44	CNN	Paula Zahn Now		Larry King Live

Kim Possible
"October 31st" Kim's little white lie takes on a physical form.

This program will record

Figure 13-8:
Icons
indicate the
status of
any pending
recordings.

Looking for movies

One of the first MCE features that really impressed me was the new Movies option under My TV. The option takes you to a view (see Figure 13-9) that displays mini posters of all the movies, both currently playing and upcoming.

I like to pick Top Rated and view "by star rating" to see a list of all the highly rated movies coming up in the next few weeks. You'll be surprised at how many great movies are available on your TV with channels like AMC, Showtime, or TBS. If you want to watch something right now, the default On Now view is a handy way to browse through everything that's in progress.

Figure 13-9: The Movies feature shows off your Media Center's advanced functions.

Viewing the spotlight applications

The main MCE menu offers Online Spotlight, a submenu that provides a bunch of Internet-based applications optimized for use with a remote and a TV.

This functionality really separates MCE from the other DVRs on the market, so make sure you dig around in here to find something you enjoy. From here you can

- Check out the latest news from MSNBC.
- View movie previews or download entire movies from Movielink.
- Connect to music services such as Napster.
- Listen to archived radio shows from National Public Radio (NPR).

Third-party applications

Media Center can host applications, exposing them as additional features in the MCE UI, which is the purpose of the Other Programs menu option. In here, you can find all the installed add-ins, which include a few games and utilities even in a basic installation, and this is where any add-ins you download and install will be accessible.

To find add-ins written by other folks, visit the MCE community site www.thegreenbutton.com. You might find these add-ins useful:

- mceWeather at www.cbuenger.com
- My Netflix at www.unmitigatedrisk.com/mce
- My Movies at www.mymovies.name

If you're into developing your own computer programs, then creating add-ins for MCE can be a really fun hobby. Check out http://msdn.microsoft.com/mce for more info.

For more information

Check out this book's Web site at www.xbox4dummies.com for additional links and information about the Media Center features included in the Xbox 360. You can also find a link to information about Windows XP Media Center Edition PCs and how to get one for yourself.

Part V
The Part of Tens

The 5th Wave
By Rich Tennant

"Amy surfs the web a lot, so for protection we installed several filtering programs that allow only approved sites through. Which of those nine sites are you looking at now, Amy?"

In this part . . .

We take you on a tour of Xbox 360 Web sites, tell you about some great games for the Xbox 360, provide tips for parents of gamer kids, and offer tips on how to make some good friends online. Finally, we conclude with some great accessories for your Xbox 360.

Chapter 14 shows you ten great Xbox 360 Web sites. Here you'll find sites that have the latest Xbox 360 news, support information, and stats for the games you and your friends play. Chapter 15 discusses ten great games for your Xbox 360. There are bound to be hundreds of titles for the Xbox 360 over time, but these are a few to start with.

Chapter 16 has tips for parents who want to let their kids play games but who are also concerned about the types of games the kids play and the amount of time they spend playing. Chapter 17 tells you about meeting friends online. If you're going to play with other people, it's best to play with people who are the same kind of player you are. We give you tips for meeting the right kind of people online.

To finish, Chapter 18 lists ten great accessories that you should get for your Xbox 360. Some of these accessories aren't included with the Core System, so you can use this chapter as a reference to determine whether you want to purchase these accessories separately.

Chapter 14

Ten Great Web Sites

*T*he great thing about the Xbox 360 is that it's more than just a gaming system. If you're interested, you can join a thriving online community that has

✔ The latest news

✔ Users who want to

- Talk about the Xbox 360

- Help you solve the problems that might crop up

In this chapter, I suggest ten Web sites that offer the second-best Xbox 360 information available (aside from this book, of course).

www.xbox.com

Xbox.com should be your first stop when looking for information online. Here, you find the latest information on the system and games, plus technical support and forums, where you can ask questions and talk to other gamers about your favorite titles. Figure 14-1 shows a shot of the site.

Figure 14-1:
Xbox.com
is your first
online stop
for all things
Xbox 360.

Xbox.com becomes an especially good resource as you look for news about the system and game releases. Looking for something to play? Xbox.com features a database of all of the games released on the system. Using this database, you can view screen shots, short movies, and descriptions of the games you're considering purchasing.

To find a game on Xbox.com, follow these steps:

1. **Go to** `www.xbox.com/games`.

2. **Enter the title in the Search box.**

   If you don't know the title, you can enter some descriptive text.

3. **Choose the game you want to find out about from the resulting list.**

   On the games page, you can find out all sorts of information about the game you're interested in, including

   • Number of players supported

   • Game rating

   You can see this information in the Product Info panel as shown in Figure 14-2

Say Hi to TriXie while you're there!

TriXie is one of Xbox.com's most recognizable celebrities. The site has tons of stories by TriXie where she provides a lot of useful information about Xbox gaming. (Here's her smiling face!)

Xbox gamer profiles are one of the more interesting features TriXie works on. TriXie is great at finding some interesting gamers on Xbox Live and asking them questions about their favorite games and their lives. That can't be easy, so hats off to TriXie. You can either

✔ Meet TriXie at

    www.xbox.com/trixie

✔ E-mail TriXie at

    xlmail@microsoft.com

Figure 14-2:
The Product Info panel provided important game information at a glance.

Product Info

Call of Duty® 2

Developer: Infinity Ward
Publisher: Activision
Genre: Shooter
Release Date: 11/22/2005
Console: Xbox 360
Xbox Exclusive
$59.99

Game Rating: T (Teen)
Blood, Mild Language, Violence

Players 1-2
System Link 2-16
HDTV 720p
Players 2-16
Friends
Voice

| 480i | 480p | 720p | 1080i |

All Xbox 360 games support high-definition resolutions up to 720p and 1080i.

The Games section has the complete catalog of Xbox and Xbox 360 games available to date. This is an extremely valuable resource if you're a compulsive game collector or looking for information about a game that you think you might buy. Each game in the catalog has its own page on Xbox.com.

http://forums.xbox.com

Wait a minute — this is still Xbox.com. The forums on Xbox.com are important enough to deserve their own entry in the top ten.

The Xbox.com forums are divided up by game and technology. You can get help setting up your Xbox if you need it, as well as find a place to hang out and talk to other players about your favorite games. Figure 14-3 shows a shot of the forums page.

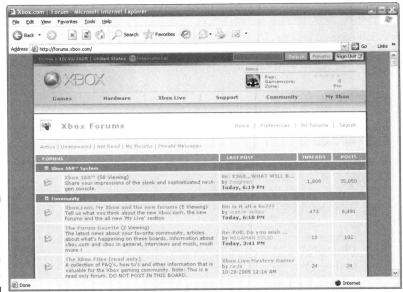

Figure 14-3:
The
Xbox.com
forums
page.

www.bungie.net

Do you play Halo? Do you play Halo 2 online? Then get yourself to Bungie.net and set up an account. In addition to being the hub of all things Halo, Bungie.net has features that make grown gamers cry with joy. If you set up an account there, you can

✔ See your Halo 2 ranking and all the games you've played.

✔ Use the forums to talk strategy with the top Halo players in the world.

Bungie is the Microsoft game studio responsible for creating Halo and Halo 2. They're considered one of the premiere game studios in the world.

Figure 14-4 shows some of my stats page on Bungie.net.

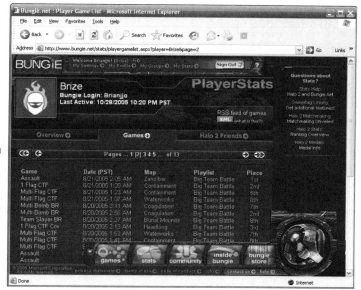

Figure 14-4:
Go to
Bungie.net
to relive the
glory of your
Halo 2
matches on
Xbox Live.

For a full-on description of how Bungie put together such an awesome site, check out the Bungie.net Technical Case Study on MSDN at `http://msdn.microsoft.com/library/default.asp?url=/library/en-us/dnbda/html/bungie.asp`. This case study is pretty detailed, but it gives you a good idea of the work that needed to be done behind the scenes to get the site up and running. (You might even see some of Festive Turkey's early stats!)

www.majornelson.com

Major Nelson is an Xbox.com fixture. In addition to creating content, Major Nelson has an extremely informative blog that gives the detailed scoop on what's going on around all things Xbox.

What's a blog?

Blogs, Web sites with diary-like entries, are usually written by individuals, though sometimes groups of people, companies, and news organizations create them. Blogs usually feature lists of related blogs, called *blog rolls,* and something called an RSS feed. *RSS (Really*

Simple Syndication) is a file format that lets you view the site in an aggregator. An aggregator makes it possible to watch many RSS feeds at once so you can get constant injections of news and information.

A *blog,* short for *Web log,* is a Web site featuring entries displayed in reverse chronological order, sort of like a journal.

Why does Major Nelson know so much? Major Nelson is Microsoft's director of Xbox Live, that's how. Major Nelson writes about anything having to do with Xbox. He updates his blog regularly, and he's often the first person to provide information about breaking Xbox news. Figure 14-5 shows Major Nelson's Web site. Check his site out carefully, there's a lot there to see.

Major Nelson also does a regular podcast. A *podcast* is a sort of Internet radio show. You can download his latest podcast at the Web site.

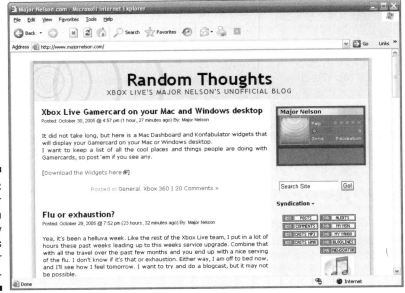

Figure 14-5: Major Nelson.com is run by Xbox Live's Major Nelson.

To get notified when the Major updates his blog, set up an MSN Alert on his Web site by clicking the LiveMessage Alerts button. You can get messages by either

- ✔ E-mail
- ✔ MSN Messenger
- ✔ Short message service (SMS) messages sent to your cell phone

www.joystiq.com

Joystiq.com isn't dedicated to the Xbox, but this great blog *is* about gaming and the gaming lifestyle in general.

Although it's nice to marinate yourself in Xbox completely, there is a world out there, you know.

Joystiq.com features up-to-the-minute gaming news, top game reviews, and a point of view you won't find anywhere else. You'll want to add this site to your favorites so you're in the know. Figure 14-6 shows the Joystiq.com page.

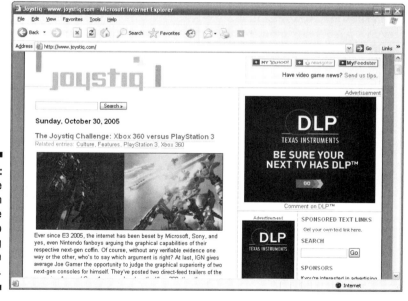

Figure 14-6: The Joystiq.com site is one of the top gaming blogs on the Net.

Like Major Nelson, Joystiq.com is a blog featuring an RSS feed. (As a matter of fact, many of the sites in this chapter feature RSS feeds.)

www.activexbox.com

ActiveXbox.com is a site that's part of the ActiveWin family of sites. Many of this site's writers are based in the United Kingdom, so the reviews and commentary have a distinctly European flavor.

One of the great ActiveXbox.com features is that readers get to comment on individual stories. Got a comment about a review? Go ahead and leave a note.

www.teamxbox.com

TeamXbox.com dubs itself the "Insider's Choice for Xbox Information." This, one of the original Xbox fan sites, has a long history of creating great content and reviews (like most fan sites). TeamXbox.com features forums, reviews, and news because you just can't get enough news about your console. Figure 14-7 shows TeamXbox.com.

Fan sites are Web sites that are created by fans of a particular console or even a particular game. What I like about fan sites is that some gamers are passionate enough about the thing that they love to take the time to build a site around it.

If you're interested in starting your own Xbox 360 fan site, be sure to check out the guidelines on Xbox.com at

```
www.xbox.com/en-US/community/communityportal/
          communitysiteguidelines.htm
```

Figure 14-7:
TeamXbox.
com is one
of the oldest
Xbox fan
sites.

www.officialxboxmagazine.com

Every game console needs at least one magazine. And an official magazine is better than any old magazine, right? I mention the *Official Xbox Magazine* not because it's really that great a Web site. I mention it because this is the place you go to order *Official Xbox Magazine,* which is a great magazine.

Why would you want to order such a thing in this, the day and age of instant gratification and electronic information? Well, mostly it's for the fine writing and the demos that let you try the game out on your Xbox 360 before you buy it. Each month, the magazine features a disc that you can pop into your Xbox to try upcoming games and to get multimedia news and features you won't find anywhere else.

Figure 14-8 shows the Subscribe button. What are you waiting for?

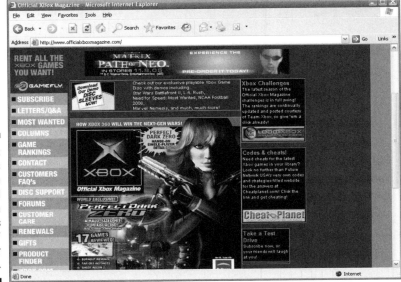

Figure 14-8:
Access
game
demos and
multimedia
features
with *Official
Xbox
Magazine.*

If you order *Official Xbox Magazine,* get the subscription that includes the disc. Playing the game you're reading about is more fun than thinking about what it would be like to play the game.

www.g4tv.com

It's a Web site, it's a TV network, it's a Web site. Whatever you want to call it, G4TV.com is probably one of the coolest ideas in the history of gaming. G4TV.com is also known as "Television for Gamers." Yes, you read that right: a TV channel dedicated to bringing you news about the latest video games. If you really want to be a hard-core gamer, then you have to get this channel. It is to gamers what the Food Network is to chefs (or something like that).

Parents, not everything on G4TV.com is appropriate for kids. Check out the shows your kids want to watch if you're concerned about adult content.

www.xbox4dummies.com

Hey, what's a book without a Web site? Well, it's still a book. But you want to give the author a hard time, right? Go to Xbox4Dummies.com, find out the latest on *Xbox 360 For Dummies,* and read updates and letters from adoring fans (though probably more of the former than the latter).

Anyhoo . . . Duncan and I try to provide as many useful resources for the Xbox 360 as we can at this site, including an updated Top Ten Xbox 360 Web Sites List. Figure 14-9 shows you the Xbox4Dummies.com site.

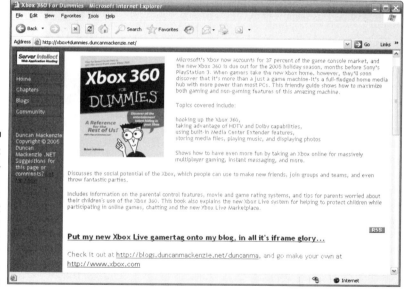

Figure 14-9: Xbox4 Dummies. com has the latest information about *Xbox 360 For Dummies.*

Chapter 15

More Than Ten Great Games

*A*t its heart, Xbox 360 is a game console: Its most important function is delivering the kind of games you want to play. This chapter goes inside the launch line-up of games so you know what to expect from all the newest releases.

Games are released throughout the year, and you can usually find out about the games to expect on retail store shelves by checking sites like `http://ebgames.com` and `http://xbox.com`. New games are usually released in the United States on Tuesdays. Check the Sunday ads to find the best deals on upcoming titles.

The "Original Xbox Games" appendix shows how to play your old favorites with Xbox 360.

Perfect Dark Zero

Perfect Dark Zero takes advantage of all the Xbox 360's high-resolution graphical features. It also delivers an incredible suite of online multiplayer game options. For action gamers looking for a stylish, thrill-packed, and story-driven experience, *Perfect Dark Zero* might be just the game for you.

This game is a prequel to the very popular *Perfect Dark,* which was originally released in 2000 on the Nintendo 64.

Perfect Dark Zero is the story of Joanna Dark and her quest to become the perfect agent. The game is set in the near future, and Joanna takes full advantage of a super-spy's technology to get the job done. In addition to a wide variety of weapons, Joanna has multiple vehicles at her disposal, including a jet pack and a motorcycle. Figure 15-1 shows a screen from the game.

Figure 15-1:
High-resolution graphics abound in *Perfect Dark Zero.*

In addition to a great sci-fi storyline, *Perfect Dark Zero* features great online play:

- ✔ **Multiplayer options,** including four-player split screen and cooperative action. A split screen lets you play against others sitting in the living room with you, and cooperative play lets you play through the single-player game with another player.

- ✔ **Deathmatch** with up to 32 players online. *Deathmatch* is player-versus-player action on Xbox Live.

- ✔ A **multiplayer game** where your team wins points for kills on the other team.

- ✔ **Massive levels** that dynamically change their size to fit the number of players on the map, meaning that you'll never play a live game where the level is so large you can't find an enemy or so small that a large number of players end up in an unwieldy melee.

This game isn't for everyone; it's rated M for Mature. As with any Xbox 360 title, check final ESRB (Entertainment Software Rating Board) rating before letting kids play this game. Chapter 16 has advice for learning about game content.

Kameo: Elements of Power

Kameo: Elements of Power is an epic story that takes place across seven worlds. Kameo is a *shapeshifter,* an elf that can change into different monsters at will. You control Kameo, and you change into different elemental creatures to complete specific tasks throughout the game. *Kameo: Elements of Power* features an engrossing single-player experience, with stunning graphics and even a cooperative mode that lets you play with a friend over Xbox Live.

You have to see this game running to realize how beautiful it truly is. You can even see Kameo inside the monsters she morphs into. Figure 15-2 shows some scenery from one of the worlds in this game.

Figure 15-2:
Kameo: Elements of Power features a number of lush, highly detailed worlds.

Project Gotham Racing 3

Project Gotham Racing 3, also known as *PGR3,* is the third edition of the hyper-realistic street-racing simulation from Microsoft. PGR3 puts you behind the wheel of some of the fastest, hottest, most sought-after cars in the world. Ferraris, Lamborghinis, Aston Martins, and more are all available for you to race around tracks in London, New York, Tokyo, Las Vegas, and Germany's Nurburgring race track.

One of PGR3's revolutions is the introduction of Gotham TV, where you can be the star of races and the envy of friends! Gotham TV introduces an amazing array of new features that include these options:

- ✔ **Spectator view.** At the PGR3 main menu, select Gotham TV.

- ✔ **See races from the best in the world.** Select Heroes Channel.

- ✔ **Watch people from your Friends List as they take part in their own races.** Select Friends Channel.

- ✔ **Your Saved Replays:** Select this option to view the replays of races that you've saved.

- ✔ **Your Saved Photos:** Select this option to view any photos you might have taken during the race. (From the Pause menu, select Photo Mode to take a snapshot of the paused action from any camera angle.)

Top Spin 2

Top Spin 2 is the sequel to the Top Spin tennis game that debuted on the original Xbox. Many fans have been clamoring for this sequel since the first game was released. *Top Spin 2* features a player creator that builds a custom character. You can take your new character on Xbox Live or you can take on one of the game's new professional players, such as Maria Sharapova, Andy Roddick, or Roger Federer.

Figure 15-3 shows a screen from *Top Spin 2.*

Figure 15-3:
Top Spin 2
features
a player
creator and
professional
athletes.

Gears of War

Of all the games shown in the build-up to the Xbox 360 launch that demonstrated the leap to high-definition graphics, Epic Games' *Gears of War* is the one that generated the most enthusiastic ooohs and aaahs. This military horror/action game is visually stunning — clearly pushing the new hardware — and introduces some fresh gameplay in the action genre. You have to take cover from the ravening Locust Horde as you and your squadmates battle for the survival of mankind. In the role of war hero Marcus Fenix, you use the environment — buildings and vehicles — to your advantage, trying to stay alive after the Locusts emerge from the Earth's crust.

Gears of War is built on the latest version of the time-tested Unreal game engine. A *game engine* is the software that creates all the images, objects, and graphics onscreen. Games built with the Unreal engine include all the titles in the Unreal, Unreal Championship, and Unreal Tournament series.

Tom Clancy's Ghost Recon: Advanced Warfighter

In *Ghost Recon: Advanced Warfighter,* you lead your team of special operations soldiers — the ghosts — through military missions that no other team could complete. The Ghost Recon series takes place in the near future — in this case, in the year 2013 — where you're equipped with the very latest tools for finding and eliminating any threat. This time out, the Ghosts do their duty in Mexico City, as the capital is re-created in incredible detail. As with most of the Xbox 360 titles mentioned in this chapter, *Ghost Recon: Advanced Warfighter* looks absolutely stunning on an HDTV. Figure 15-4 is a shot from the game.

Figure 15-4:
Tom Clancy's *Ghost Recon: Advanced Warfighter* features fantastic graphics and online play.

The Ghost Recon series has been a favorite on Xbox Live since the first game ran on the original Xbox. The game features large multiplayer maps and very realistic online combat.

In *Ghost Recon: Advanced Warfighter,* one shot is all it will take to drop you, just like with real combat. Be sure to take cover when you spawn into your first GRAW game on Xbox Live!

Quake 4

The Quake series always set a high bar for graphical quality and gripping first-person action on the PC, and *Quake 4* promises to deliver the same kind of intensity and immersion on Xbox 360. A *first-person shooter* is a game where you see the action through the eyes of the character you're controlling, adding a level of personal immersion in the game world that other views can't deliver. *Quake 4* continues the story from 1997's *Quake 2* of one Marine's struggle against an enemy called the Strogg. (*Quake 3* was a multiplayer-only game.) Now you'll be joined by squadmates, including medics who can heal you so you're encouraged to keep them alive on the battlefield. The legendary development studio, id Software (the company behind *Doom,* one of the most famous PC games of all-time) co-developed *Quake 4* with the help of Raven Software.

Dead or Alive 4

The Dead or Alive series is a classic beat-'em-up franchise in which your character and one other duels in a stunning slugfest of kicks, punches, and throws. Known for its stunning character design, you can expect *Dead or Alive 4* to deliver a visual experience you've never seen before. Hand-to-hand fighting is the heart of the game, with each of the combatants employing his or her own unique attacks. Stringing together a combination of attacks (or combos) by using a variety of button presses unleashes incredibly powerful hits that not only move perfectly fluidly but deliver devastating damage. Figure 15-5 shows a scene from *Dead or Alive 4*.

Dead or Alive 4 introduces some new characters, including

- *Eliot,* a blonde male who fights in the Keii Ken style
- *Kokoro,* a black-haired girl who fights in the Hakkyoku-Ken style
- *Mystery Wrestler,* a masked woman clad in white

Figure 15-5:
Dead or Alive 4 continues the tradition of beautiful scenery and fast gameplay.

Dead or Alive 4 on Xbox Live features fast, multiplayer action. Xbox Live can host a large number of spectators in online tournaments.

Halo Series

Halo holds a special place in the hearts of Xbox gamers. It's said by some (Brian, at least) that a console depends on one big title to sell the whole box. For the original Xbox, this title was *Halo*. People loved the first game, which set a new standard for space-based, first-person shooters. *Halo 2* was released in 2004 and showed everyone what an online first-person shooter should look like.

You might wonder why these games are listed among great Xbox 360 games. Given the importance of this series to the fans of the Xbox, Bungie (the development studio behind the *Halo* series) did something special just for Xbox 360 player. It updated the graphics on the games so that they're now rendered in full 720p HDTV glory on the Xbox 360. If you own the Xbox 360 System (with the hard drive), you can put your *Halo 2* disc in the drive and play it all over again with a visual clarity you never thought was possible. Same goes for the original, seminal *Halo*.

At the launch of Xbox 360, over 200 original Xbox games could be played in the new system (as long as you have the hard drive). After downloading the emulator software that allows these select games to be played on Xbox 360, you'll be able to enjoy all those supported original Xbox games in 720p high definition. The "Original Xbox Games" appendix has the details.

Halo

The game *Halo* is pretty much the reason many people bought the original Xbox in the first place. In *Halo,* you play as Master Chief, a Spartan warrior, and it's your job to help save humanity from an alien alliance know as the Covenant. Where do you fight the Covenant? A strange ring in space called Halo. What's Halo for? Who built it? Can you save humanity? These questions and more are answered in *Halo!*

Halo 2

Halo 2 is an original Xbox game. It's also the most popular Xbox game and the top game played on Xbox Live. With so many devoted fans, Microsoft needed to make sure it plays perfectly on the Xbox 360, and it does.

In the single-player game, Master Chief continues his fight with the alien Covenant, who want to destroy the human race.

A huge part of *Halo 2*'s massive success (its launch date of November 9, 2004 is the biggest revenue day in entertainment history, generating over $125 million in sales) was Xbox Live. Statistics for each game played are stored in a database, and a player gains ranks after winning a match or being part of a winning team. You start at Level 1 and can advance to Level 50 (although very few players ever reach that goal). Then you can review your statistics and played games at `http://www.bungie.net`. Figure 15-6 shows one of the features you'll find on the Bungie.net Web site: the ability to see every place you were killed in every online game you've played.

Figure 15-6:
An action map shows what happened in the *Halo 2* games you played on Xbox Live.

To play *Halo 2* online, you need an Xbox 360 hard drive and some software. The "Original Xbox Games" appendix has the details.

Halo 3

If you're a person who bets, don't bet that *Halo 3* won't be the biggest game ever — at least until *Halo 4* comes out.

If you're a *Halo* fan, be sure to keep an eye out for the *Halo* movie. It remains to be seen whether *watching* Master Chief will be as fun as *being* Master Chief, but *Lord of the Rings* director, Peter Jackson, has signed on to be Executive Producer of the new movie project.

Call of Duty 2

Already a hit on the PC, the stunning World War II first-person shooter, *Call of Duty 2* illustrates the power of Xbox 360. Aside from incredible graphics that bring the Russian, British, and American campaign settings to vibrant life, the Surround Sound effects of the battlefield generate an intensity that few other games can match. Your comrades-in-arms yell warnings and alerts of enemy movements and attacks; stand too close to shells exploding, and the screen shudders and blurs to represent your dazed state before the scene clears and you have to get back into the battle. Multiplayer options on Xbox Live add to the value of *Call of Duty 2* and ensure its position as one of the best games available on Xbox 360.

Condemned: Criminal Origins

For a truly original action adventure experience on Xbox 360, this crime thriller is a must-play. On the trail of a vicious serial killer, you take the role of Agent Thomas, investigating crimes in the seediest locations you can imagine and picking up evidence for forensic examination by your partner back at HQ. It may sound like a shirt-and-tie job, but a slew of mentally deranged criminals lurking in the shadows ensures Condemned requires equal parts brawn and brain. Plucking weapons from the environment (pipes, 2x4s, axes) you have to fend off the felons with whatever you can get your hands on.

Condemned: Criminal Origins plunges you deep into a gripping chase that leads into the darkest, most terrifying environments on Xbox 360. With surround sound effects cranked up, every move in the darkness is amplified into a stunning, terrifying experience that you have to witness to believe!

Gun

The wild west is big. It's also wild. And as Colton White, it's your oyster for chasing down the people who wronged you. Now the open landscape is yours to wander, trading bullets with gunslingers, protecting ladies of the night, hunting for food, and even assaulting forts. From horseback or on foot, riding through tumbleweed and coming across frontier towns, the world is truly open for you to explore and uncover its secrets.

Gun delivers a scintillating story that you'll want to pursue until its conclusion, and as that path takes you through wild country and unique encounters, its successful culmination will be all the sweeter. Riding, racing, talking with locals, playing, fighting, and keeping your wits about you ensure that Gun will grip you from its opening scene all the way to its rewarding conclusion.

Full Auto

Fast cars are one thing. Cars mounted with guns are another. Blend them together with a destructible terrain and you've got a game of incredible potential. So sits *Full Auto,* which delivers incredible graphics on Xbox 360 with new gameplay elements that will give every race a unique flavor. Sure, the graphics and speed might be next-generation, but the real leap in technology is the ability to Unwreck.

If you want to cut a corner, you can blow out the masonry with some well-placed missiles. But if you miss a turn and land your own ride in the side of a building, hit the Unwreck to reverse time and give yourself another shot at it. Your Unwreck quota is limited, but can be increased by laying waste to the environment, which includes handy Propane tanks that can cause devastation to your opponents . . . particularly the ones ahead of you in the race.

When you're ahead, however, your rear-mounted weapons can help keep you there as mines and other options keep your opponents from getting near. Explosions and destruction are all in a day's work for the racers of *Full Auto,* and it promises to be one of the most inventive, visceral, and downright explosive games to hit Xbox 360.

Tony Hawk's American Wasteland

One open city, hundreds of opportunities to find new lines, and tons of ways to execute killer moves are at the heart of the next iteration of Tony Hawk's superb ongoing series. Now the City of Angles is fully open for uncovering new lines and spots for killer combos. Travel through sewer pipes to move between districts of the city, but you'll never see a load screen as all the background texture is there for you to explore on your board.

Chapter 16

Ten Tips for Parents

*S*ometimes it's tough to be a parent. Parents want to do everything possible to protect kids, but sometimes parents want to let them test their independence.

This chapter is for you if you're a parent who wants to both

- ✔ Protect your child
- ✔ Allow a positive and enjoyable gaming experience

This chapter doesn't make any recommendations about the values you should reinforce in your children. We provide information and resources you can use to help you both reinforce your own values and protect your children.

Gaming Safely

Most parents have two major concerns when it comes to gaming:

- ✔ **The content in the games that children play.** Parents want to make sure games are appropriate for their kids.
- ✔ **The amount of time kids spend at the console.** Games can be fun and engrossing. A kid (not to mention a big adult) can sit at a game for hours, solving puzzles, collecting points, or trying to boost a character's level.

Content

Content refers to the art, language, action, and ideas that a video game comprises. The content that's appropriate to one parent for their child might be completely different than what another considers appropriate. Ratings systems have been instituted worldwide to help parents determine what type of content exists on a game that they may never play.

Ratings have suggested ages associated with the descriptions, but that doesn't mean you'll consider the content within that rating appropriate. If you understand the rating associated with the game, there's less chance you'll be surprised by something in a game.

Knowing the ratings

Game ratings are designed to help parents (and other consumers) determine the type of content included in a game before purchase. As with all types of popular media, some types of games just aren't suitable for kids.

If you're a parent, making yourself familiar with the different ratings can make it easier to steer your child in a direction that you're comfortable with.

Chapter 11 covers ratings in detail.

Family features

The Xbox 360 lets you to set limits on the types of games and the amount of time spent in each game by particular family members. You can also control the Family Settings for your Xbox 360 console through the System blade shown in Figure 16-1.

Chapter 11 covers setting up parent-controlled profiles on your Xbox 360.

Time

If you let them, kids will spend whole days and nights playing video games. (Some adults have been known to do the same thing. It's just human nature.) Spending too much time at the console just isn't healthy. Humans need exercise and fresh air, among other things.

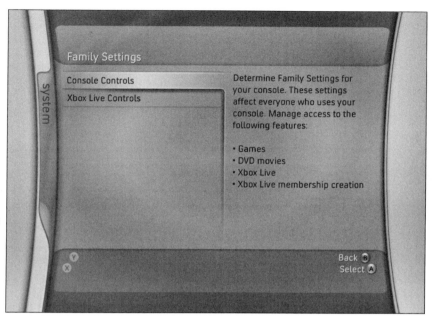

Figure 16-1:
Family controls on the System blade.

Spending hours playing presents a couple of problems:

✔ Sitting in one place, not moving anything but thumbs and eyeballs, just can't be good for a body.

✔ Time spent in front of the console is time that's not spent developing the mind in different ways.

One of the best ways to take control of the Xbox 360 console is to put it in a common room in the house. That way, you can follow the game your child is playing. You might use this common TV for more than Xbox 360, so that automatically limits game play.

Contact

As your child gets older, he or she will want to spend more time playing games with others online. There are issues associated with this that you need to understand and be aware of. There are dangers associated with meeting strangers online. People can say that they are one thing and actually be something quite different.

Controlling voice chat

Xbox Live is a huge, wonderful service that you can play with other Xbox 360 fans from around the world. Unfortunately, not everyone on Xbox Live is using language that you might approve of. On the System blade, you can specify whether voice chat is allowed in online games. Blocking voice chat prevents your child from hearing what other players in a game are saying. This can make playing games more difficult, but it's often the only way to prevent exposure to some pretty rude behavior.

You can control whether a child profile has rights to talk to others on Xbox Live when you create the profile. You can choose to either

✔ Allow anyone

✔ Allow friends only

✔ Disable the voice feature

Figure 16-2 shows voice chat options in a child profile. You can find out more about creating a child profile in Chapter 11.

If your children are a little older, say preteen to teen, make sure they know what type of language you will allow on Xbox Live. For instance, let them know that if they hear somebody swearing excessively or using other unacceptable language, they should simply turn down the volume on voice chat for that session.

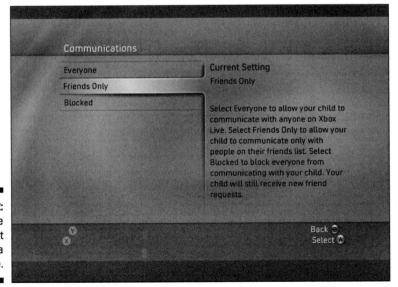

Figure 16-2: Setting the voice chat options for a child profile.

If you or your kids are having trouble with a single individual, you can mute him or her. After you mute somebody, you never have to listen to them again. To mute a player, follow these steps:

1. **Open the player's Gamer Profile in the Guide.**

   Accessing a player's Gamer Profile is discussed in Chapter 4.

2. **Choose Mute from the list of options.**

In cases in which unacceptable language is being used, make sure to report the behavior as described in the following section.

Reporting bad behavior

Sometimes you find people online who aren't nice at all. You occasionally hear strange rants, screaming, and other bad behavior.

You want to let the folks at Xbox Live know about these people when you come across them. You can do this in-game:

1. **Press the Guide button on the controller to bring up the Xbox Guide.**

2. **Navigate to see the recent players in the Community section.**

3. **Find the name of the player you want to provide feedback on in the list and then press X to see his or her profile.**

4. **Choose File Complaint in his or her profile and press X.**

5. **Follow the instructions to provide the feedback you want on the player.**

Keep these rules in mind when giving feedback:

✔ **Be specific.** Make sure you report exactly what you see or hear.

✔ **Be honest.** Don't use feedback for revenge. Gloating, very negative taunting, and abuse are different things, though it might be difficult to see right after an intense game and loss.

✔ **Give *good* feedback, too.** There's an option to provide positive feedback if another player has been a good sport. Go ahead and use it.

Adding exercise

If you're worried about the amount of time the kids are playing video games, why not get them up and doing something in front of their console? Add a dance pad, drums, or a microphone and let the kids dance and sing.

A number of games use a dance pad instead of a hand-held controller. A *dance pad* is a big, flat controller mat whose buttons are places kids step. Dance games work by directing a player to step on different buttons on the pad. As you can imagine, it gets hard to keep up with the game. After 45 minutes or so of that, you're finished without even realizing that you've just completed a workout.

Tracking play time

When it comes to gaming, one of the ongoing discussions between kids and parents is the amount of time spent playing games. Take it from a big, over-grown kid: If you let them, kids will spend all day playing their favorite games. As a gamer, you would like to play all the time. As a parent, you really want more balance. You can bring balance by setting limits and being smart about extended play time. For the purposes of this discussion, *extended gaming* is defined as a session lasting more than an hour without a break.

Extended gaming can lead to some undesirable situations:

- ✔ A child might be kept in a really excited state for an extended period of time. This can lead to crankiness.

- ✔ A child might sit the same way for a long time, potentially causing circulation problems and cramps.

- ✔ Mashing a controller for a while without a break can lead to soreness in the hands.

- ✔ Staring at a screen for long periods can lead to eye strain, headaches, and fatigue.

Some games take many hours to finish. To prevent some of the issues just mentioned, track the time the kids are playing and make sure they're taking regular breaks. A good game break has your kids (and you) doing these things:

- ✔ Set a timer for 50 minutes and take a 10-minute walk when it goes off.

- ✔ When returning from a break, sit in a different chair or position.

- ✔ Look at stuff outside to help refocus your eyes.

- ✔ Get a drink and use the bathroom. Don't hold it!

Tracking friends

Xbox Live helps you screen and view the friends that your child is making online.

Check your child's profile to see who's being added as a friend. Many times, players send friend requests to players who are good or who are simply fun to play with online. You don't know much about these people, other than what you can find out by looking at their Xbox Live profile. You can find out more about how to do this in Chapter 4.

Make sure your child understands what it means to add friends to the buddy list. Come to an agreement about who you find acceptable. If you've got voice chat turned off, the people playing with your child probably don't know his or her age. He or she might be getting requests from individuals older than you'd like. Make sure your kids understand that they don't have to accept friend requests and that they know whom you don't want them playing with regularly (or ever).

Figure 16-3 shows a friend request. By looking at the player's profile, you can tell a lot about this player. A huge amount of time spent playing games rated Mature or higher might indicate that the player is too old to associate with your child in the online arena.

Figure 16-3:
Review a player profile before accepting a friend request.

Communicating with Your Family

Gaming should be a fun experience for both kids and adults. But a number of factors can make it more contentious than fun:

✔ Kids want to play games you find objectionable.

✔ Kids want to play more than you would like them to play.

✔ Kids want the freedom to play on Xbox Live without restrictions.

The best way to handle this is to let your children know your expectations.

Learning about gaming

The gap between what kids know and what parents know about technology is one of the big blocks to good communication. The kids often control the computer at home because the parent isn't comfortable with the technology.

When you talk to your kids about gaming, make sure you have a good understanding of what gaming is all about. Read up on the game ratings systems and learn the ratings of the most popular games out there. This way, when you get asked about a game or you see one in the store, you can recognize it as one you either approve or disapprove of.

To find out more about gaming and the games that are available, you can do the following:

✔ Read game reviews online and in *The Original Xbox Magazine*.

✔ Look at game boxes in the game store and note the game's rating on the back of the box.

✔ Watch the news for stories about gaming so that you're familiar with what's coming out.

✔ Watch game reviews on channels like G4 so that you can see what the trends are in gaming.

✔ If you're concerned about a game, rent a copy and play it yourself. You'll be amazed at how much you'll discover!

If you want to be more active and knowledgeable about gaming, educate yourself about it. If you do this, a couple of things happen:

✔ You know when to say no.

✔ You may be able to suggest a reasonable alternative to the game.

www.xbox.com has

• All sorts of tips, tricks, and information about new and upcoming games

• Forums where you can ask questions about the games you have in mind

Playing together

You almost never have to play alone with the Xbox 360. The rest of this chapter has tips for playing together at home.

Play modes

Most Xbox 360 games let you join your child in a game:

- ✔ Split screen games let up to four family members play at the same time.
- ✔ Cooperative play lets family members work together in a game.

Game types

These games often are fun for parents and children together:

- ✔ **Party.** Party games are usually played with two to four players on one console.

  These games are so short that you can finish them in just a few minutes.

- ✔ **Racing.** Almost all racing games support more than one player. Racing together takes no time at all, and it can be a lot of fun.

- ✔ **First person and role playing.** Cooperative missions are a great way to bond.

  Try cooperative missions if you're interested in letting the kids try a new genre with a higher rating. This way, you can monitor the game more closely as they play, and you'll be able to point out parts of the game that you're less comfortable with them playing.

- ✔ **Puzzle.** Even if you can't have separate players at the same time, it's fun to take turns and help each other with puzzles. You'll find a lot of puzzle and other casual games available on Xbox Live Arcade.

- ✔ **Sports.** Sports games like football, basketball, baseball, soccer, hockey, golf, tennis, and bowling are all great family games.

  Most sports games are rated for everyone, so even the youngest in the house can play with a little help.

Chapter 17

Ten Ways to Make Friends

Back when Grandpa walked five miles uphill in the snow — both ways — to get the latest game releases, owning a console meant either playing by yourself or having friends drop by.

In a console world connected by Xbox Live, you can have virtual relationships with

✔ People who've never been in the same room with you
✔ Friends and family who are far away

Having friends online makes Xbox Live team games better:

✔ Team games are more fun with a friend on your side.
✔ Regular partners usually make a better team.

Xbox Live

The obvious place to make friends for Xbox Live is on Xbox Live. But there's a knack to putting your best foot forward. Get the knack!

Play right

Build your online reputation by playing the way other people want to play.

Follow the Golden Rule

Being part of a virtual community is just like being part of the real world. If you want to make friends, behave in a way that makes people want to hang around with you. How do you do that?

✔ Help teammates win.

✔ Be a good sport, whether you win or lose.

The cool kids got tired of this junk a long, long time ago:

✔ Noise pollution:

- Screaming
- Swearing
- Rude noises

No, I don't want to hear from your armpit.

- Keeping the microphone open with your stereo on

✔ Deliberately hurting your own team:

- Killing yourself
- Killing your own teammates
- Wasting team game assets, like time and vehicles

Your Xbox Live *reputation* (the little stars on your gamertag, described in Chapter 4) indicates what others you've played with think about you. If you've been great to play with, they'll rate you high. If a player acts inappropriately or uses bad language, he might find his reputation lowered by others. The better your reputation, the more friends you'll make online.

Play a lot of your favorite game

The more you play, the better you get. People like playing with good players.

As you play the same game on Xbox Live, you get familiar with players you see each time you play. These people are playing

✔ The same games as you

✔ The same times as you

Write down the names of players you see a lot and then watch them play and listen to what they're saying. If they seem to be about your age and sound like the kind of person you want to play with, send a friend request.

You can see a player's statistics through either

- ✔ Looking at the Xbox 360 dashboard
- ✔ Checking someone's gamertag on the Web by going to www.xbox.com

To get the profile for a gamertag, use the following URL (uniform resource locator) and replace name with the actual gamertag:

```
http://live.xbox.com/en-US/profile/profile.aspx?pp=0&GamerTag=name
```

If you use the preceding URL to see the profile for a gamertag, you represent spaces in the Gamertag with the "+" sign. For example, the following URL produces the Gamer Profile page for "FestiveTurkey," as shown in Figure 17-1:

```
http://live.xbox.com/en-US/profile/profile.aspx?pp=0&GamerTag=Festive+Turkey
```

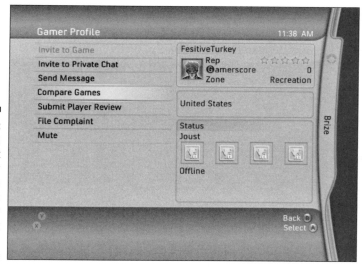

Figure 17-1:
You can check out another player's history on the Web or on Xbox Live.

Play in the right Gamer Zone

Your Gamer Zone indicates how competitive you want to be when you play on Xbox Live.

You can be friends with anyone in any zone, but you should probably try to either

- ✔ Play in the zone where your friends are playing.
- ✔ Encourage your friends to move to the level where you play.

Recreation

Casual gamers want to play a game and maybe chat about what movies are playing in theaters this weekend.

If you're into online gaming for conversation and just having a friend to play with, then the Casual Zone is probably right for you.

Pro

Players in the Pro Zone are most interested in competition:

✔ They expect more skill from other players.

✔ They tend to focus on the game, instead of socializing.

The Pro Zone might be a good fit if you're most interested in

✔ The challenge of the game

✔ Meeting players who share your passion for a particular game

Figure 17-2 shows the gamer profile for a player who competes at the Pro level. The level appears in the Gamer Card.

Figure 17-2:
The Gamer
Card shows
a player's
Gamer
Zone.

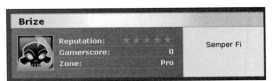

Family

The Family Zone is for players who want to participate in all the fun Xbox Live has to offer, without worrying about language, trash-talk (excessive taunting), and discussions not appropriate for kids.

This is a great zone to set your younger kids up with.

Underground

Underground is generally for people who like to mess around a lot.

If you don't mind being stomped on excessively after being terminated in a game, or if you like to return the favor, this zone might be the one for you.

Groups

Microsoft provides a couple of communication and community-building tools that help you keep in touch with online buddies and make gaming more fun.

Clans

Clans are online teams that compete both formally and informally on Xbox Live. Clans can be a lot of fun, and you can make some pretty good friends on your teams.

Clans often take some commitment. Teams that play in the Pro Zone might have practice several times a week, along with weekly games. This can take a lot of time, but the results may be worth it:

- ✔ You can learn a lot about your favorite game by practicing with your clan.
- ✔ Wins that you rack up with your clan can help improve your reputation.

Not all games support clans and team play. Look for these features on team games like

- ✔ First-person shooters
- ✔ Multiplayer sports games

MSN Messenger

MSN Messenger can connect your Messenger account to your Xbox Live gamertag and get all sorts of interesting features going.

I like the feature that lets me see what my friends are playing on Xbox Live right now. This makes it easy to pick out a game and join in at a moment's notice. Figure 17-3 shows the Xbox Live tab for MSN Messenger. This tab shows who currently is and isn't playing on their Xbox 360.

Playing or working

My boss is one of my Xbox Live friends, and we use MSN Messenger to track what happens on Xbox Live. He came to my office at around 3:30 one weekday and asked if I had an Xbox in my office. He told me that an indicator popped up to let him know I was playing *Halo 2*. I immediately knew what happened: My kids had gotten off the school bus and logged in.

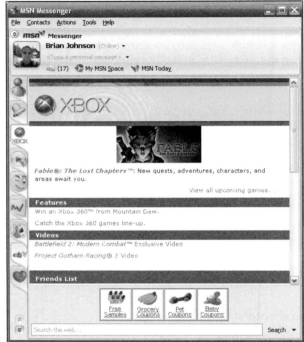

Figure 17-3:
Track your
friends on
Xbox Live
through
MSN
Messenger.

MSN Messenger tells your Xbox friends when you start playing a game on Xbox Live. Be sure that you want to allow that before you join your MSN Messenger and Xbox Live accounts.

Don't add your boss to your Xbox Live friends list unless you want her to know when you're playing games.

Online Communities

Online communities offer some of your best resources for both information about the games you like to play and for making good friends. You'll often make friends through the forums by helping other players and by being an expert resource for the rest of the community for the games you like to play.

Xbox.com forums

New games come out all the time, and with new games come new discussion groups on `http://forums.xbox.com`. Forums offer a couple of really cool things:

- ✔ **Answers to questions:** Check to see whether someone has already answered it, and if not, ask away.
- ✔ **Forum conversations:** Talk to people you're playing with on Xbox Live.

When a new game comes out, often a sticky thread is created, where players post messages with their gamertag listed, asking for people to play with. Sticky threads have a permanent place at the top of the conversation lists and can be a great way to find another gamer.

Figure 17-4 shows a thread on the forums where players list their gamertags.

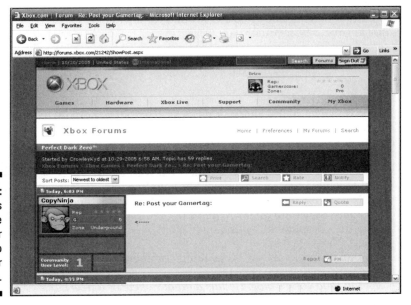

Figure 17-4:
Xbox forums usually have a board for people to share their gamertag.

Discussion boards

Many Xbox 360 sites on the Web feature discussion boards where you can talk to other Xbox Live gamers. Some players even start sites and discussion boards dedicated to their favorite games. Here are some boards you can check out right away:

- ✔ **Team Xbox:** `http://forum.teamxbox.com`
- ✔ **Xbox Users Group Forums:** `www.xboxusersgroup.com/forums`
- ✔ **Xbox Solution Forums:** `http://talk.xboxsolution.com`

You might need to poke around to find just the right community site for you. Some of these sites are fantastic. In addition to letting you talk with other Xbox Live players, these sites share tips for game play, news about Xbox games and publishers, and generally offer a place to be among friends.

You can find more sites like this by searching the Web or by hearing about them secondhand. They tend to come and go, with the good ones building a community and usually sticking around for a while. We'll keep a good list running at `www.xbox4dummies.com`.

Blogs

A *blog* is like an online diary or news site, with the most recent post at the top of the page. Blogs usually let readers leave comments about posts, but the owner is usually the only person who posts to the blog. One of the features that connect blogs is the idea of cross-linking. When one blogger finds an interesting post, she links to that post with a blog entry of her own. In that way, blogs become a very linked community. Blogs are a great way to make friends because bloggers can see who links to them, and they generally appreciate the compliment. When they see something interesting, they'll return the compliment by linking back.

Here's an example of how blogs build communities:

1. *You read John's blog. He has a great review of a new game.*

2. *You link to John's blog, and you say he has a great review.*

3. *John sees people use your link to his blog. He subscribes to your blog.*

4. *When you post a review of a new controller, John links from his blog to yours.*

Blogs and RSS

Blogs usually feature a technology called RSS. *RSS,* or *Really Simple Syndication,* is a data format that lets you add many Web sites to a tool called an *aggregator,* which allows for quick scanning through new posts. Adding a blog's RSS feed to an aggregator is known as *subscribing* to the blog. You can find out more about blogs and RSS by reading *Blogging For Dummies* by Brad Hill (Wiley Publishing, Inc.).

To make a successful blog, post new entries to your blog regularly. People visit more often if you regularly have something to say about

- ✔ Your game
- ✔ Your team
- ✔ Xbox 360

The Real World

The people around you might be gamers and you don't even know it! Here's how (and where) to break the ice and get them into your online community.

Work and school

The great thing about Xbox Live is that you can play games with people across the world. You can also play with the person who sits a few seats away.

Check your company or school intranet

Check your intranet for mailing lists and sites about gaming on Xbox Live.

If you can't find one, start one, if it's something you're allowed to do!

Wear an Xbox T-shirt

Advertising works! An Xbox T-shirt encourages other players to introduce themselves to you. Figure 17-5 shows a very fashionable T-shirt that any *Halo 2* player will recognize. It's a shirt from the *Red vs. Blue* video series, detailed at www.redvsblue.com.

Figure 17-5:
Wearing an
Xbox shirt
lets others
know you're
a player.

Make business cards with your gamertag and your favorite games, so people remember and look for you. For safety, consider leaving your personal information off the card.

Publicize your gamertag

If you want people to look for you on Xbox Live, publicize your gamertag

✔ On an Xbox T-shirt

Nothing says, "I'm a gamer" like a T-shirt with your Xbox Live gamertag!

✔ On your car

✔ On public discussion boards

Throw an Xbox 360 LAN party

If you've got enough friends who play Xbox 360, throw a LAN party and get some friends over. Tell your friends to bring their friends, and you'll meet others that way.

For information about throwing a LAN party, check out Chapter 12.

Gaming conventions

You can meet other gamers, including other Xbox Live players, at conventions.

Meeting players at gaming conventions is a lot like meeting players at school or work (except you know everyone is a gamer). You don't have to be at an Xbox-specific event to meet other Xbox Live gamers. When you go to a convention

✔ Wear a shirt that indicates you're an Xbox Live player.

✔ Have your gamertag printed on a card so you can give it out.

Gamer conventions happen around the world. Check out our updated list at www.xbox4dummies.com.

The following conventions are big events in major cities:

✔ United States
- **E3 Expo:** www.e3expo.com
- **International CES (Consumer Electronics Show):** www.cesweb.org
- **Penny Arcade Expo (PAX):** www.penny-arcade.com/pax
- **QuakeCon:** www.quakecon.org

✔ Europe
- **Leipzig GC:** www.gc-germany.de
- **Paris Electronic Sports World Cup:** www.esworldcup.com

✔ Japan
- **Tokyo Game Show:** http://tgs.cesa.or.jp/english

The World Cyber Games usually are scheduled in a different location each year: www.worldcybergames.com/main.asp.

Chapter 18

Ten Great Accessories

Many optional *peripherals* — hardware that isn't necessarily included in the product box — are available for your Xbox 360. Some peripherals are upgrades that improve gaming for all Xbox 360 users. Other peripherals are solutions for gamers who have other special needs or equipment. This chapter guides you through most peripherals for your Xbox 360.

In most countries (including the United States, Canada, the United Kingdom, Australia, and Singapore), the Xbox 360 comes in two distinct packages:

✔ **The loaded Xbox 360 System**

The Xbox 360 System includes many extras, such as a hard drive, a wireless controller, a headset, and a high-definition video cable.

Some of the peripherals we mention in this chapter are included with the loaded Xbox 360 System package. We point out which peripherals are included.

✔ **The Xbox 360 Core System**

The Xbox 360 Core System lets you start with minimum equipment and add pieces to fit your needs or your budget.

Memory Devices

Xbox 360 memory devices come in a couple of forms: hard drive and Memory Unit. Table 18-1 compares their capabilities.

Table 18-1	Xbox 360 Memory Device Capabilities	
Capability	*Hard Drive*	*Memory Unit*
Portability between consoles	Difficult	Easy
Save gamer profiles	Yes	Yes
Save games	Hundreds	A few
Play original Xbox games	Yes	No
Download Xbox Live content	Lots	A little
Download content from retail kiosks	No	Yes
Play Xbox Live Arcade games	Yes	Yes

You can use a hard drive and one or two Memory Units in the same Xbox 360 console.

Xbox 360 hard drive

If you purchase the Xbox 360 Core System, the Xbox 360 hard drive is the first peripheral you should get when you decide it's time to upgrade.

The hard drive is included with the loaded Xbox 360 System. If you need to install (or swap) a hard drive, Chapter 2 shows you how.

Figure 18-1 shows you what the hard drive on the Xbox 360 looks like.

Figure 18-1:
The Xbox 360 hard drive attaches to the outside of your Xbox 360.

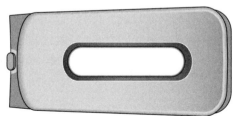

The Xbox 360 hard drive lets you

✔ Save your games.

✔ Download content from Xbox Live.

✔ Download Xbox Live Arcade games from Xbox Live Marketplace.

✔ Store music files you rip from your CD collection.

✔ Store digital pictures downloaded from your digital camera.

✔ Use hard drive–specific features in new Xbox 360 games. (Some developers may add them for games being released in the future.)

You can't copy information directly between Xbox 360 hard drives because you can't have two hard drives in the Xbox 360 console at the same time. The "Xbox 360 Memory Unit" section, later in this chapter, shows how to copy information from the Xbox 360 hard drive to a memory unit and then potentially to another Xbox 360 hard drive.

A hard drive by any other name works just fine

You can have more than one hard drive for your Xbox 360! Just give each hard drive a unique name.

Follow these steps to name the hard drive that's in your console:

1. **From the Xbox 360 dashboard, push the direction pad to the right to access the System blade.**

2. **At the System blade, scroll down and choose Memory.**

   You see your Storage Devices listed.

3. **Highlight the hard drive.**

   Because there's only one hard drive slot in your Xbox 360 console, you can name only the hard drive that's currently installed.

4. **Press the Y button to access the device options.**

5. **Select the Rename option to bring up the keyboard.**

6. **Use the keyboard to pick your own name for the hard drive.**

   The hard drive name can be up to 26 characters long.

7. **Press Start to complete the task.**

   Your hard drive is renamed.

Xbox 360 Memory Unit

Your Xbox 360 has two memory slots. You can place one memory unit in each of those slots if you want. The *Memory Unit* is a small card used to carry game-save data and backup information as well as to store Xbox Live downloadable content.

The memory unit is small — *really* small. You can pop one on a keychain, and you're ready to carry your Xbox Live information to a friend's house and join in a game on Xbox Live using your own credentials and statistics.

Figure 18-2 shows an Xbox 360 Memory Unit.

Figure 18-2: The Xbox 360 Memory Unit can store profile and game data.

The capacity of the Memory Unit is indicated on the front of the card. The larger the number, the more files and data you can hold on the card. At launch, a 64MB Memory Unit is available; that will easily hold

- ✔ Your Xbox Live profile data
- ✔ Several game save files

If you want to play games from the original Xbox, you need the Xbox 360 hard drive. The Memory Unit's function is similar, but it isn't exactly the same.

You can copy information between

- ✔ Two memory cards
- ✔ The hard drive and any memory card

This is all done from the System blade's Memory tab, which also lets you give the Memory Unit a unique name.

You can use a memory card for downloading content from special Xbox 360 kiosks you might find in retail stores and malls. Keep your Memory Unit with you, and you might be able to plug it in for extra goodies.

Wireless Gaming

Wires are one of the biggest problems when it comes to connecting interesting devices to your home entertainment system. The Xbox 360 has you covered with a couple of wireless devices for easy connection and play.

Wireless controller

After you get used to a wireless controller, it's hard to go back. The wireless controller gives you a lot of freedom, and it's easier to store than a wired controller.

The wireless controller is included with the loaded Xbox 360 System.

Convenient control

When you're done playing, there's no cord-wrapping; you just throw it on the shelf!

The benefits of a wireless controller include

- Your little sister won't trip on the cord.
- Your dog won't get tangled up in the cord.
- You won't get tangled in the cord and pull your Xbox 360 off the shelf.
- Your mom won't trip over the cord and get mad and take your Xbox 360 away!

Multiple players

You can use up to four wireless controllers with your Xbox 360 at a time. On any wired or wireless Xbox 360 controller, the lighted quarter of the Ring of Light in the center of the controller shows you which player you are on the console.

Table 18-2 lists players and their indicator lights.

Table 18-2	Player Indicators and Split Screen Areas	
Player Number	*Lighted Ring Section*	*Split-screen Area*
1	Upper left	Upper left
2	Upper right	Upper right
3	Lower left	Lower left
4	Lower right	Lower right

The power button on the Xbox 360 itself also reflects your player location in split screen games. If you add controllers, each controller is assigned a color that is displayed on both

✔ The lighted Guide button on the controller

✔ The power button on the console

That's much easier than tracing a tangle of cords back from the couch.

This location indicator is very handy if you're playing a split-screen game (such as *Perfect Dark Zero*) against up to three friends. The light on your controller corresponds to the part of the screen that you're controlling.

Batteries

The Xbox 360 Wireless Controller takes two AA batteries. You can try any disposable or rechargeable AA batteries in your Xbox 360 wireless controller, but a couple of special options are designed for maximum convenience and performance.

Xbox 360 Rechargeable Battery Pack

An Xbox 360 Rechargeable Battery Pack is probably a better option than any disposable batteries:

✔ You'll save money in the long run.

✔ Changing the battery pack is a little faster than swapping individual batteries.

After you charge up, the Rechargeable Battery Pack should let you play for about 25 hours.

Try not to play all 25 hours in a row.

If you never want to be without your trusty wireless controller, you need either

- Two Rechargeable Battery Packs, so you can charge one pack while you play
- A Play and Charge Kit, so you can, well, *play and charge* at the same time

Xbox 360 Play and Charge Kit

Maybe you're thinking, "I'm in the middle of an insane marathon gaming session, and my batteries are starting to run low. What can I do to keep playing without missing a beat?"

We're glad you asked. The Xbox 360 and its peripherals were obviously designed by real gamers because the Play and Charge Kit is something that only a gamer could come up with. The kit includes a wired adapter that plugs into your wireless Xbox 360 controller. That means you get to play and recharge the Rechargeable Battery Pack at the same time. (You can't charge regular AA batteries with the kit.)

When the battery is topped off, unplug and go back to gaming in all its wireless glory.

The Play and Charge Kit uses the USB connection from the Xbox 360 console to charge the controller, but it doesn't actually turn the wireless controller into a wired controller. You'll still be connected to your Xbox 360 wirelessly while you're tethered to the machine for charging.

Xbox 360 Universal Media Remote

The Xbox 360 is a lot more than a game system; it can be the center of your home entertainment experience, if you want it to be. (See Part III if that's the case.) But do you want to boss your entertainment hub with a game controller? The answer is likely a resounding, "No!" You want to use the coolest, funkiest controller around. You want a remote control that says, "I am the key to the control of your entertainment experience. Use me to unlock the door!"

There's no denying it: The Xbox 360 Universal Media Remote is big and impressive. When you get it, have your friends over to show them. It's absolutely amazing — all those buttons and all that control. It's enough to make a grown gamer cry.

Kids, if you want one of these remote controls, ask a parent first and show them a nice picture, like the one in Figure 18-3.

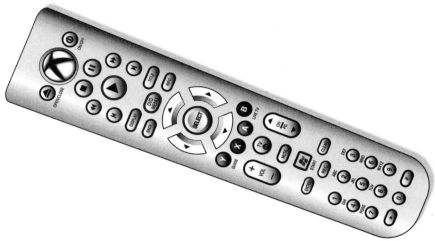

Figure 18-3: The Xbox 360 Universal Media Remote is resplendent with its many buttons.

What can you do with this remote control? You can

- **Control DVDs playing on your Xbox 360.**
- **Play music.**

  This includes MP3s and other music files from

  - A memory card
  - An MP3 player
  - A PC in your house
  - The Xbox 360 hard drive

  You can find out more about playing this type of content in Chapter 5.

- **Control your Windows Media Center PC through the Xbox 360.**

  This gives you access to the music, movies, TV programs, and even some games on your Windows Media Center PC — possibly the coolest thing you can do with your Xbox 360 remote.

  The Windows Media Center PC is described later in this chapter.

Wireless Networking Adapter

If you've got a wireless network in your home, then the Xbox 360 Wireless Networking Adapter is a must. This adapter is designed to attach snugly to the USB port on the back of your Xbox 360 and lets you get on your home network quickly and easily. Figure 18-4 shows the Xbox 360 Wireless Networking Adapter.

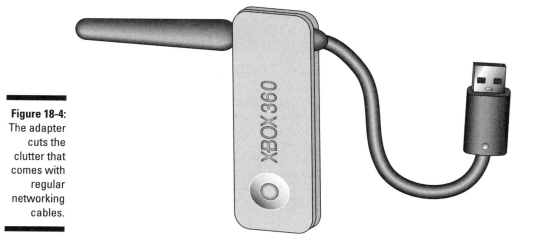

Figure 18-4: The adapter cuts the clutter that comes with regular networking cables.

The best part is that the adapter can use all the major WiFi protocols:

- ✔ 802.11a
- ✔ 802.11g
- ✔ 802.11b

Xbox 360 Headset

If you want to talk — actually speak — to other players on Xbox Live, you need an Xbox 360 headset. The Xbox 360 headset connects to the base of the Xbox 360 controller and features a noise-canceling microphone. This means that other players hear you clearly when you scream in pain.

The Xbox 360 headset is included with the loaded Xbox 360 System package.

There are a couple of ways to mute your headset microphone:

- ✔ **Use the Guide on the Xbox 360.** Just press the Guide button on the controller while you're playing and then mute the headset.
- ✔ **Press the switch on the piece of the headset that connects to the controller.** The mute switch is right above the volume control wheel.

Windows Media Center PC

The Windows Media Center PC was introduced in 2003 and has become an extremely popular option for PCs. The Windows Media Center PC features a version of Microsoft Windows that has special software for accessing music, pictures, video, and live TV on the PC.

The Xbox 360 is a Windows Media Center Extender right out of the box. This means that the Windows Media Center PC can stay under the desk in the office, and you can access the PC from the Xbox 360. Figure 18-5 shows what your TV screen looks like when you connect to your Windows Media Center PC through the Xbox 360 Media blade.

This Windows Media Center PC interface is called a *ten-foot UI* (user interface). The idea is that you can easily read everything on the screen from your couch, about ten feet away. You can also see some of the ten-foot UI thinking in the Xbox 360's interface design.

Figure 18-5:
The PC is connected directly to the Windows Media Center PC.

Of course, obtaining a Windows Media Center PC isn't quite like picking up a standard peripheral at the game store. PCs cost money; do a little research before you buy a new PC. If you're in the market for a new PC and own an Xbox 360, it just makes sense to consider buying a Windows Media Center PC. By doing so, you can make the PC a much more useful device.

Media Center PCs can have a range of features. You should know the PC's capabilities before buying it. Answer these questions before choosing:

- ✔ Do I want to record TV?
- ✔ Do I have enough network bandwidth to use the Xbox 360 as a Media Center Extender?

Recording TV

The ability to record a TV show isn't a requirement for Media Center PCs. Check out the specifications for the PC you're considering purchasing and find out whether the computer includes a TV capture card. If it doesn't and you want this capability, you need to buy a Windows Media Center–compatible TV capture card and add it later.

Assessing home network bandwidth

You need a very fast home network to use the Xbox 360 as a Media Center Extender. Movies and live TV take a large amount of bandwidth to play smoothly through the Xbox 360.

If you use an Xbox 360 console as an extender, you need a home network with one of the following connections:

- ✔ **A wireless network with either of these connections:**

  - • **802.11a wireless connection:** This type of wireless connection has a shorter range than the 802.11g connection, but throughput is nearly twice as high.

    802.11a is the recommended connection to use for a remote wireless Windows Media Center connection.

  - • **802.11g wireless connection:** This wireless speed is the minimum for streaming TV or video smoothly from the PC to the Xbox 360.

If your wireless network can't use WPA encryption, you can't use your Xbox 360 console as an Extender. (You don't have to use WPA encryption, but you need a network that's capable of using it.) That means you can't use an *802.11b* wireless network.

✔ **A wired Ethernet connection with 100 Mbps routers or network switches.**

 Older, 10 Mbps routers and network switches might be too slow to handle the bandwidth required to push the content between the Windows Media Center PC and the Xbox 360.

The Windows Media Center PC works through the Xbox 360 via the remote desktop protocol (RDP). This same technology can remotely control a PC running Windows XP Professional from another PC.

Video Connections

The video connections that you use determine how the Xbox 360 looks on your television, computer monitor, or any other display you happen to be using.

Component HD AV cable

The component HD AV cable is necessary if you want to play games in high definition.

The component HD AV cable is included with the loaded Xbox 360 System package in most countries (including the United States, Canada, Great Britain, Australia, and Singapore).

This cable has both component output for HDTV and a composite output for standard TV. This cable is a little engineering marvel that lets you

 ✔ Use both your HDTV and Xbox 360 to their fullest capacity when playing games.

 ✔ Switch quickly between the two anytime you want. Are you in the middle of a game when you realize the season premiere of *The OC* is about to start? No time to dawdle — switch over!

Figure 18-6 shows the component HD AV cable.

Figure 18-6: The component HD AV cable has plugs for component and composite output.

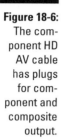

You need to flip a small switch at the base of the component HD AV cable to go between the component and composite cables. If you hook up the cable and you aren't getting video, check that first.

VGA HD cable

The VGA HD cable lets you play your Xbox 360 in high definition through that port on any monitor with a VGA input. You're in luck if you have VGA devices like these:

✔ **A really big, really nice computer monitor**

Most computer monitors have a VGA input.

✔ **A TV with a VGA input**

Check whether your HDTV has a VGA input. If it does, using the VGA input frees up your component inputs for such video devices as

- An HDTV cable box
- A component DVD player

VGA stands for Video Graphics Array. *VGA* is a computer video format that can display very high-resolution video; large (and even small) computer monitors can make great displays for an Xbox 360.

Figure 18-7 shows the VGA HD cable.

In some countries, the VGA HD Cable is the video cable that comes in the loaded Xbox 360 System.

Figure 18-7:
The VGA adapter lets you use the VGA port on your PC monitor or television.

Faceplates

Faceplates won't change the way that you play, but they're a lot of fun. You can attach a faceplate to your Xbox 360 and give it a completely different look. Faceplates can bring bling or make your components blend. Your Xbox 360 is white by default. A dark faceplate can make the Xbox 360 look more at home with the other components in your home entertainment system if they're dark. Of course, most people get a new faceplate for the cool designs and to add a bit of their own personality to the console. Maybe the faceplate in Figure 18-8 appeals to you!

Figure 18-8:
Faceplates let you personalize your Xbox 360.

Look for limited-edition faceplates in stores around the times that new games launch or when you can get to special events.

Original Xbox Games

*W*hen Xbox 360 went on sale, over 200 original Xbox games could be played on Xbox 360. But you need the right games, and the right Xbox 360 equipment.

Here's the story.

Hard Drives

With an Xbox 360, the hard drive is required for games designed for the original Xbox:

✔ If you bought the loaded Xbox 360 System, your console came with an installed hard drive.

✔ If you bought the Xbox 360 Core System, Chapter 2 shows how to install an optional hard drive.

There are a couple of reasons that the Xbox 360 console requires a hard drive for original Xbox games:

✔ The original Xbox console has a hard drive, so developers created games for the original Xbox with features that use hard-disk storage.

✔ Xbox 360 requires software downloaded from Xbox Live to make the original Xbox games run.

Software Downloads

There are three ways to get the necessary software from Xbox Live for original Xbox games.

Broadband Xbox 360 download

If you have a broadband Internet connection for your Xbox 360 console, you can download the software from Xbox Live. Follow these steps:

1. **Make sure your Xbox 360 is connected to Xbox Live.**
2. **Place your original Xbox game disc in the CD tray of the Xbox 360.**

   The backward compatibility patch will be applied automatically, as needed.

Computer access

If you don't have a broadband Internet connection for your Xbox 360, there are a couple of ways to get the software you need for original Xbox games on your Xbox 360:

✔ You can use any Internet-accessible computer to request a CD from www.xbox.com. You'll receive a CD in the mail with the software you need for the original Xbox games to work on your Xbox 360.

Microsoft charges a fee for mailing the CD.

✔ You can download the backward compatible files from www.xbox.com and create your own CD if you have both

   • A PC with a CD (or DVD) burner

   • Internet access (either dial-up or high-speed access)

For current instructions, go to

www.xbox.com/en-US/games/backwardscompatibility.htm

Outside the US, search Xbox.com for "backwards compatibility."

Compatible Xbox Games

This appendix lists all of the games certified to work on Xbox 360 when it went on sale to the public.

Some of these games are only certified to work in the United States and Canada. Those games are identified with two asterisks (**), which is the universal symbol for, "Not so fast, Rest of the World."

Microsoft has promised that eventually all original Xbox games will be made backward compatible. (Of course, with all those new next-generation Xbox 360 games, why would you want to go back to this line-up?)

Drop one of these old friends into your Xbox 360 and groove on a blast from the past!

AirForce Delta Storm

Alias

Aliens versus Predator Extinction

All-Star Baseball 2003

Amped®: Freestyle Snowboarding

Army Men®: Sarge's War

Atari® Anthology

ATV: Quad Power Racing 2

Baldur's Gate: Dark Alliance II

Barbarian

Barbie Horse Adventures Wild Horse Rescue

Batman Begins

Battle Engine Aquila

Battlestar Galactica

BMX XXX

Brute Force

Buffy the Vampire Slayer: Chaos Bleeds

Cabela's® Dangerous Hunts

Cabela's® Outdoor Adventures 06

Cabela's® Deer Hunt 2004 Season

Cabela's® Deer Hunt 2005 Season

Call of Cthulhu®: Dark Corners of the Earth

Call of Duty: Finest Hour

Casino

Chicago Enforcer

Circus Maximus

Close Combat: First to Fight

Colin McRae Rally 4

Combat Elite: WWII Paratroopers

Commandos 2: Men of Courage

Conflict: Desert Storm

Constantine

Crash Nitro Kart**

Crash Twinsanity

Crimson Skies®: High Road to Revenge

Crouching Tiger, Hidden Dragon

Dark Angel

Darkwatch

Dead or Alive® 3

Deathrow

Digimon® Rumble Arena®

Dinotopia**

Drake

Egg Mania: Eggstreme Madness

ESPN MLS ExtraTime 2002

Euro 2004

F1 2001

Fable®

Fable®: The Lost Chapters

Fairly Odd Parents: Breakin' da Rules

FIFA Soccer 2003

FIFA Soccer 2004

FIFA STREET

Fight Night 2004

Fight Night Round 2

Ford Mustang

Ford vs. Chevy

Forza Motorsport

Frogger Beyond

Futurama

Fuzion Frenzy®

Genma Onimusha

Goblin Commander: Unleash the Horde

Grand Theft Auto 3

Grand Theft Auto: San Andreas

Grand Theft Auto: Vice City

Gravity Games Bike: Street. Vert. Dirt.

Grooverider: Slot Car Thunder

Half-Life® *2*

Halo®

Halo® *2*

Halo® *2 Multiplayer Map Pack*

Harry Potter and the Goblet of Fire

Harry Potter and the Sorcerer's Stone

He-Man: Defender of Grayskull

Hitman: Contracts

House of the Dead 3

IHRA Drag Racing Sportsman Edition

IHRA Professional Drag Racing 2005

Jade Empire

James Bond 007: NightFire

Judge Dredd®*: Dredd vs. Death*

Jurassic Park: Operation Genesis

Kabuki Warriors

Kelly Slater's Pro Surfer

kill.switch

Lemony Snicket's A Series of Unfortunate Events

LOONS—The Fight for Fame

Manhunt

Mat Hoffman's Pro BMX 2

Max Payne

Max Payne® 2

Medal of Honor European Assault

Medal of Honor Frontline

Medal of Honor Rising Sun

Mega Man® Anniversary Collection

Metal Arms: Glitch in the System

MicroMachines

Mike Tyson Heavyweight Boxing

Monster Garage

Mortal Kombat®: Deception

MTV Music Generator 3

Murakumo: Renegade Mech Pursuit

MX World Tour: Featuring Jamie Little

Namco Museum

NBA LIVE 2004

Need For Speed Underground 2

NFL Blitz 2002

NFL Blitz 2003

NFL Blitz 2004

NHL Hitz 2003

NHL® 2004

Ninja Gaiden®

Ninja Gaiden® Black

Outlaw Golf 2

Outlaw Volleyball

Pariah

Phantom Crash

Pinball Hall of Fame

Pitfall®: The Lost Expedition

Predator Concrete Jungle

Prince of Persia: The Sands of Time

Pro Evolution Soccer 5

Pro Race Driver

Pump It Up: Exceed

Pure Pinball

*Puyo Pop Fever***

Quantum Redshift®

Rayman Arena

Raze's Hell

Red Dead Revolver

Red Faction® II

RedCard 2003

Robotech: Battlecry

Rocky Legends

Rogue Ops

Samurai Jack

Samurai Warriors

Scooby Doo! Night of 100 Frights

Scrapland

SEGA GT 2002

Shadow The Hedgehog

Shamu's Deep Sea Adventures

ShellShock: Nam '67

Sneakers

Sniper Elite

Soccer Slam

Sonic Heroes

Sonic Mega Collection Plus

Speed Kings

Sphinx and the Cursed Mummy

Splat Magazine Renegade Paintball

SpongeBob SquarePants: Battle for Bikini Bottom

SpyHunter® 2

Spyro A Hero's Tail

SSX 3

Stake

Star Trek: Shattered Universe

Star Wars: Starfighter Special Edition

Star Wars® Jedi Knight®: Jedi Academy

Star Wars® Knights of the Old Republic® II: The Sith Lords

Star Wars®: Episode III Revenge of the Sith

Star Wars®: Knights of the Old Republic

Street Racing Syndicate

Stubbs the Zombie in Rebel without a Pulse

Super Bubble Pop

Super Monkey Ball Deluxe

SX Superstar

Tecmo Classic Arcade

Teenage Mutant Ninja Turtles

Test Drive®: Eve of Destruction

Tetris Worlds

The Great Escape

The Hulk

The Incredible Hulk: Ultimate Destruction

The Incredibles: Rise of the Underminer

The Lord of the Rings: The Return of the King

The Simpsons Hit and Run

The Simpsons Road Rage

The Terminator Dawn of Fate

The Thing

Thief: Deadly Shadows

Tom Clancy's Ghost Recon

Tom Clancy's Rainbow Six® 3

Tony Hawk's American Wasteland

Tony Hawk's Pro Skater 4

Tony Hawk's Underground 2

Tork: Prehistoric Punk

Toxic Grind

Ty The Tasmanian Tiger

Ty the Tasmanian Tiger 2: Bush Rescue

Ty the Tasmanian Tiger 3: Night of the Quinkan

Urban Freestyle Soccer

Vexx

Volvo: Drive for Life

World Series® Baseball 2K3

Worms 4 Mayhem

Worms Forts: Under Siege

WWE Raw 2

XIII

Yourself!Fitness

Index

• Q •

• R •

• *X* •

• Z •

Game Shortcuts & Notes

Game Shortcuts & Notes

Game Shortcuts & Notes

Game Shortcuts & Notes

Game Shortcuts & Notes

Game Shortcuts & Notes

BUSINESS, CAREERS & PERSONAL FINANCE

Grant Writing FOR DUMMIES

0-7645-5307-0

Home Buying FOR DUMMIES

0-7645-5331-3 *†

Also available:

- Accounting For Dummies †
  0-7645-5314-3
- Business Plans Kit For Dummies †
  0-7645-5365-8
- Cover Letters For Dummies
  0-7645-5224-4
- Frugal Living For Dummies
  0-7645-5403-4
- Leadership For Dummies
  0-7645-5176-0
- Managing For Dummies
  0-7645-1771-6

- Marketing For Dummies
  0-7645-5600-2
- Personal Finance For Dummies *
  0-7645-2590-5
- Project Management For Dummies
  0-7645-5283-X
- Resumes For Dummies †
  0-7645-5471-9
- Selling For Dummies
  0-7645-5363-1
- Small Business Kit For Dummies *†
  0-7645-5093-4

HOME & BUSINESS COMPUTER BASICS

Windows XP FOR DUMMIES

0-7645-4074-2

Excel 2003 FOR DUMMIES

0-7645-3758-X

Also available:

- ACT! 6 For Dummies
  0-7645-2645-6
- iLife '04 All-in-One Desk Reference
  For Dummies
  0-7645-7347-0
- iPAQ For Dummies
  0-7645-6769-1
- Mac OS X Panther Timesaving
  Techniques For Dummies
  0-7645-5812-9
- Macs For Dummies
  0-7645-5656-8

- Microsoft Money 2004 For Dummies
  0-7645-4195-1
- Office 2003 All-in-One Desk Reference
  For Dummies
  0-7645-3883-7
- Outlook 2003 For Dummies
  0-7645-3759-8
- PCs For Dummies
  0-7645-4074-2
- TiVo For Dummies
  0-7645-6923-6
- Upgrading and Fixing PCs For Dummies
  0-7645-1665-5
- Windows XP Timesaving Techniques
  For Dummies
  0-7645-3748-2

FOOD, HOME, GARDEN, HOBBIES, MUSIC & PETS

Feng Shui FOR DUMMIES

0-7645-5295-3

Poker FOR DUMMIES

0-7645-5232-5

Also available:

- Bass Guitar For Dummies
  0-7645-2487-9
- Diabetes Cookbook For Dummies
  0-7645-5230-9
- Gardening For Dummies *
  0-7645-5130-2
- Guitar For Dummies
  0-7645-5106-X
- Holiday Decorating For Dummies
  0-7645-2570-0
- Home Improvement All-in-One
  For Dummies
  0-7645-5680-0

- Knitting For Dummies
  0-7645-5395-X
- Piano For Dummies
  0-7645-5105-1
- Puppies For Dummies
  0-7645-5255-4
- Scrapbooking For Dummies
  0-7645-7208-3
- Senior Dogs For Dummies
  0-7645-5818-8
- Singing For Dummies
  0-7645-2475-5
- 30-Minute Meals For Dummies
  0-7645-2589-1

INTERNET & DIGITAL MEDIA

Digital Photography FOR DUMMIES

0-7645-1664-7

Starting an eBay Business FOR DUMMIES

0-7645-6924-4

Also available:

- 2005 Online Shopping Directory
  For Dummies
  0-7645-7495-7
- CD & DVD Recording For Dummies
  0-7645-5956-7
- eBay For Dummies
  0-7645-5654-1
- Fighting Spam For Dummies
  0-7645-5965-6
- Genealogy Online For Dummies
  0-7645-5964-8
- Google For Dummies
  0-7645-4420-9

- Home Recording For Musicians
  For Dummies
  0-7645-1634-5
- The Internet For Dummies
  0-7645-4173-0
- iPod & iTunes For Dummies
  0-7645-7772-7
- Preventing Identity Theft For Dummies
  0-7645-7336-5
- Pro Tools All-in-One Desk Reference
  For Dummies
  0-7645-5714-9
- Roxio Easy Media Creator For Dummies
  0-7645-7131-1

* Separate Canadian edition also available
† Separate U.K. edition also available

Available wherever books are sold. For more information or to order direct: U.S. customers visit www.dummies.com or call 1-877-762-2974.
U.K. customers visit www.wileyeurope.com or call 0800 243407. Canadian customers visit www.wiley.ca or call 1-800-567-4797.

WILEY

SPORTS, FITNESS, PARENTING, RELIGION & SPIRITUALITY

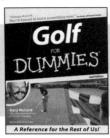

0-7645-5146-9

0-7645-5418-2

Also available:
- Adoption For Dummies
  0-7645-5488-3
- Basketball For Dummies
  0-7645-5248-1
- The Bible For Dummies
  0-7645-5296-1
- Buddhism For Dummies
  0-7645-5359-3
- Catholicism For Dummies
  0-7645-5391-7
- Hockey For Dummies
  0-7645-5228-7

- Judaism For Dummies
  0-7645-5299-6
- Martial Arts For Dummies
  0-7645-5358-5
- Pilates For Dummies
  0-7645-5397-6
- Religion For Dummies
  0-7645-5264-3
- Teaching Kids to Read For Dummies
  0-7645-4043-2
- Weight Training For Dummies
  0-7645-5168-X
- Yoga For Dummies
  0-7645-5117-5

TRAVEL

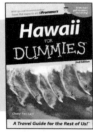

0-7645-5438-7

0-7645-5453-0

Also available:
- Alaska For Dummies
  0-7645-1761-9
- Arizona For Dummies
  0-7645-6938-4
- Cancún and the Yucatán For Dummies
  0-7645-2437-2
- Cruise Vacations For Dummies
  0-7645-6941-4
- Europe For Dummies
  0-7645-5456-5
- Ireland For Dummies
  0-7645-5455-7

- Las Vegas For Dummies
  0-7645-5448-4
- London For Dummies
  0-7645-4277-X
- New York City For Dummies
  0-7645-6945-7
- Paris For Dummies
  0-7645-5494-8
- RV Vacations For Dummies
  0-7645-5443-3
- Walt Disney World & Orlando For Dummies
  0-7645-6943-0

GRAPHICS, DESIGN & WEB DEVELOPMENT

0-7645-4345-8

0-7645-5589-8

Also available:
- Adobe Acrobat 6 PDF For Dummies
  0-7645-3760-1
- Building a Web Site For Dummies
  0-7645-7144-3
- Dreamweaver MX 2004 For Dummies
  0-7645-4342-3
- FrontPage 2003 For Dummies
  0-7645-3882-9
- HTML 4 For Dummies
  0-7645-1995-6
- Illustrator CS For Dummies
  0-7645-4084-X

- Macromedia Flash MX 2004 For Dummies
  0-7645-4358-X
- Photoshop 7 All-in-One Desk Reference For Dummies
  0-7645-1667-1
- Photoshop CS Timesaving Techniques For Dummies
  0-7645-6782-9
- PHP 5 For Dummies
  0-7645-4166-8
- PowerPoint 2003 For Dummies
  0-7645-3908-6
- QuarkXPress 6 For Dummies
  0-7645-2593-X

NETWORKING, SECURITY, PROGRAMMING & DATABASES

0-7645-6852-3

0-7645-5784-X

Also available:
- A+ Certification For Dummies
  0-7645-4187-0
- Access 2003 All-in-One Desk Reference For Dummies
  0-7645-3988-4
- Beginning Programming For Dummies
  0-7645-4997-9
- C For Dummies
  0-7645-7068-4
- Firewalls For Dummies
  0-7645-4048-3
- Home Networking For Dummies
  0-7645-42796

- Network Security For Dummies
  0-7645-1679-5
- Networking For Dummies
  0-7645-1677-9
- TCP/IP For Dummies
  0-7645-1760-0
- VBA For Dummies
  0-7645-3989-2
- Wireless All In-One Desk Reference For Dummies
  0-7645-7496-5
- Wireless Home Networking For Dummies
  0-7645-3910-8

HEALTH & SELF-HELP

0-7645-6820-5 *†

0-7645-2566-2

Also available:
- Alzheimer's For Dummies
  0-7645-3899-3
- Asthma For Dummies
  0-7645-4233-8
- Controlling Cholesterol For Dummies
  0-7645-5440-9
- Depression For Dummies
  0-7645-3900-0
- Dieting For Dummies
  0-7645-4149-8
- Fertility For Dummies
  0-7645-2549-2

- Fibromyalgia For Dummies
  0-7645-5441-7
- Improving Your Memory For Dummies
  0-7645-5435-2
- Pregnancy For Dummies †
  0-7645-4483-7
- Quitting Smoking For Dummies
  0-7645-2629-4
- Relationships For Dummies
  0-7645-5384-4
- Thyroid For Dummies
  0-7645-5385-2

EDUCATION, HISTORY, REFERENCE & TEST PREPARATION

0-7645-5194-9

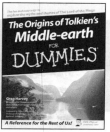

0-7645-4186-2

Also available:
- Algebra For Dummies
  0-7645-5325-9
- British History For Dummies
  0-7645-7021-8
- Calculus For Dummies
  0-7645-2498-4
- English Grammar For Dummies
  0-7645-5322-4
- Forensics For Dummies
  0-7645-5580-4
- The GMAT For Dummies
  0-7645-5251-1
- Inglés Para Dummies
  0-7645-5427-1

- Italian For Dummies
  0-7645-5196-5
- Latin For Dummies
  0-7645-5431-X
- Lewis & Clark For Dummies
  0-7645-2545-X
- Research Papers For Dummies
  0-7645-5426-3
- The SAT I For Dummies
  0-7645-7193-1
- Science Fair Projects For Dummies
  0-7645-5460-3
- U.S. History For Dummies
  0-7645-5249-X

Get smart @ dummies.com®

- **Find a full list of Dummies titles**
- **Look into loads of FREE on-site articles**
- **Sign up for FREE eTips e-mailed to you weekly**
- **See what other products carry the Dummies name**
- **Shop directly from the Dummies bookstore**
- **Enter to win new prizes every month!**

* **Separate Canadian edition also available**
† **Separate U.K. edition also available**

Available wherever books are sold. For more information or to order direct: U.S. customers visit www.dummies.com or call 1-877-762-2974. U.K. customers visit www.wileyeurope.com or call 0800 243407. Canadian customers visit www.wiley.ca or call 1-800-567-4797.